AMERICAN REBELS

Also by Jack Newfield

A Prophetic Minority

A Populist Manifesto (with Jeff Greenfield)

Bread and Roses, Too

Cruel and Unusual Justice

The Permanent Government (with Paul DuBrul)

City for Sale (with Wayne Barrett)

Only in America: The Life and Crimes of Don King

*Somebody's Gotta Tell It: The Upbeat Memoirs of
 a Working-Class Journalist*

The Full Rudy: The Man, the Myth, the Mania

RFK: A Memoir

AMERICAN

⋆ ⋆ REBELS

EDITED BY JACK NEWFIELD

NATION BOOKS
NEW YORK

AMERICAN REBELS

Compilation Copyright © 2003 Jack Newfield
Introduction 2003 Jack Newfield

Published by
Nation Books
An Imprint of Avalon Publishing Group
245 West 17th St, 11th Floor
New York, NY 10011

Nation Books is a co-publishing venture of the Nation Institute and
Avalon Publishing Group Incorporated.

A longer version of "Rachel Carson" by Terry Tempest Williams
appears as "One Patriot" in *Patriotism and the American Land*, published by The Orion Society.

Library of Congress Cataloging-in-Publication Data is available.

ISBN 1-56025-543-9

9 8 7 6 5 4 3 2 1

Book design by Simon M. Sullivan
Printed in the United States of America
Distributed by Publishers Group West

An Editor's Note

This is not meant to be a rigorously prioritized certification of the top forty rebels in American history. It is intended to be an unsentimental celebration—with the emphasis on the under-appreciated, and the lesser known, especially in the arts.

America's most famous and written-about rebels are intentionally not included here because they are just too familiar. This group includes Martin Luther King, Tom Paine, Eleanor Roosevelt, Muhammad Ali, Jackie Robinson, Herman Melville, Louis Armstrong and Eugene Debs.

There are only seven living people because this is conceived from a historical perspective. In some cases, writers did not deliver on their promises. I regret the absence from these pages of Lenny Bruce, Gene Kelly, Roberto Clemente, Billie Jean King, Orson Welles, Marlon Brando and Walter Reuther. I feel their omission more sharply than the Reader will. They are all particular favorites of mine.

The original seed of an idea for this book came from a lunch with Ham Fish, the president of the Nation Institute. And this volume could not have been assembled without the editorial judgement and craftsmanship of Carl Bromley and Ruth Baldwin of Nation Books, and the editing assistance of Hillary Frey.

—Jack Newfield, September, 2003

Table of Contents

INTRODUCTION

DURING MUCH OF the 1960s I kept an antiwar poster on my wall. It featured this quotation from Albert Camus: "I should like to be able to love my country, and still love justice too."

This desire—this calibrated emotion—is the foundation of this book. This anthology of specially commissioned essays attempts to reconcile authentic patriotism with original artistic creation, unpopular opinion, and real moral principles that don't change with the winds.

This collection attempts to locate and define a coherent American tradition consistent with Camus's words. It includes rebels in politics, education, journalism, religion, literature, film, sports, music, law, popular culture, and social struggle. These are real rebels against conformity, commercialism, racism, oligarchy, the bogus, conventional wisdom, stacked decks, and sacred cows.

The Americans celebrated in these pages can variously be described as rebels, visionaries, revolutionaries, radicals, liberals, nonconformists, outsiders, insurgents, prophets, and pathfinders. They don't all fit under any one ideology or party. Most were too much free spirits to be categorized. They are part of a continuum of conviction and creation in our tangled national history. But they were all distinctively American.

Some, like Walt Whitman, Bob Dylan, John Garfield, and Frank Sinatra, are iconic. Others are less well-known but have earned a much broader appreciation; among them are Samuel Fuller, Fannie Lou Hamer, Paul O'Dwyer, Robert Frank, and Michael Harrington. Still others are comparatively obscure—almost cult figures—revered by a small, intense following. In this category are Edward Abbey, Benjamin Mays, Father Mychal Judge, and I. F. Stone. Others, like Margaret Sanger and John Steinbeck, have faded from memory and deserve a new shaft of sunlight.

Most of them did not lead perfect lives—few humans do. They all did heroic things, even if they didn't always lead heroic lives. Some had lousy second or third acts in their lives. A few, however, are close to sainthood, including Father Judge, Dorothy Day, and Bob Moses. Others, like Miles Davis and Hank Williams, certainly had their dark side demons.

At its most revered peaks, this is a native tradition that stretches from Jefferson and Tom Paine, through Lincoln, Whitman, Thoreau, to the founders of the labor unions, to Eugene Debs, the early blues singers, to Woody Guthrie and John Steinbeck, to Eleanor Roosevelt and Martin Luther King.

This is the tradition of populist patriotism that I have felt a kinship with since the early 1960s. It is an attitude, and a value system, more than it is a party or a platform. It is an alloy of individualism, antiauthoritarianism, talent, egalitarianism, underdogism, multiculturalism, artistic freedom, fearless independence, and affinity for the common man.

Some of my own defining experiences took place on those occasions where I felt most free to love justice and my country at the same time—when I planted myself in this rebel tradition.

I still remember singing "We Shall Overcome" in Brown's Chapel in Selma, Alabama, in February of 1965. Martin Luther King was in the pulpit, his arms linked with Andrew Young and John Lewis. The rally was for the right to vote, which was soon to be secured by the Voting Rights Act of 1965, after thousands had gone to jail for nonviolent civil disobedience.

I remember riding in an open car with Robert Kennedy as he campaigned for president through Watts and East L.A. At each stop in the Mexican-American neighborhoods, a mariachi band greeted him with a Mexican-styled "This Land Is Your Land," which was his campaign theme song.

From the vantage point of the trunk of his car, I could see, with piercing clarity, the hope shining in the eyes of all these blacks and Latinos, who would give him 90 percent of their votes on the day he was assassinated.

Even during the pits of the 1960s, when I felt the most depressed and alienated by America's racism and military interventionism, I was still able to find aspects of America where I felt at home. Baseball, and later basketball, became my nationalism. I healed from the assassinations of King and RFK by listening to The Band, Carole King, Van Morrison, and Aretha Franklin during the summer of 1968.

There was always an alternative America I could pledge

allegiance to—the America of the Bill of Rights, sports, blues, jazz, art, unions, writers, and social protest. This identification with part of our history and part of our culture, kept me sane; I never became anti-American.

I loved my country because it had produced Walt Whitman, Jackie Robinson, Muhammad Ali, Norman Mailer, RFK, Miles Davis, George McGovern, Willie Mays, Herman Melville, Bessie Smith, Sandy Koufax, Cesar Chavez, Janis Joplin, Larry Bird, Lenny Bruce, Sam Cooke, Fiorello LaGuardia, Walter Reuther, Roberto Clemente, Murray Kempton, and above all Dr. King.

I was able to convince myself that they represented an alternative conception of this country, that they were just as legitimate and American as the burglars of the flag whom I loathed: Nixon, Kissinger, George Wallace, Senator Bilbo, Henry Ford, John D. and Nelson Rockfeller, Henry Frick, General Custer, Richard Helms, Antonin Scalia, Jimmy Swaggert, Jerry Falwell, J. Edgar Hoover, Joe McCarthy, and Spiro Agnew.

My America is Jimi Hendrix playing his solo, electric guitar version of the National Anthem, to close the music festival at Woodstock.

My America is Dr. King's "I Have a Dream" speech on that hot August afternoon in 1963, when he seemed to be secretly channeling Scripture, the Constitution, and Abraham Lincoln. And he was preceded to the podium that day by Bob Dylan, Joan Baez, and Mahalia Jackson, a Whitmanesque trifecta of table setters.

America is Bruce Springsteen singing "Youngstown" and "Philadelphia" with their echoes of Woody and Steinbeck. It is Dylan singing of answers blowing in the wind, and "Blind Willie McTell," and "Every Grain of Sand," and sounding a little like the ghost of Son House. It is Hank Williams singing (and writing) "I Saw the Light," and "Alone and Foresaken." And it is Robert Johnson singing (and writing) "Terraplane Blues," and "Love in Vain."

Whenever I hear Dylan, Bruce, Johnson, and Hank, I can hear America singing.

America is Studs Terkel talking about Chicago, Pete Hamill writing about New York, Faulkner writing about Mississippi, Ellison and Baldwin writing about Harlem. It is Jacob Riis and Walker Evans photographing the destitute, and Ansel Adams shooting the natural beauty of the American West.

America is books by Rachel Carson, Jane Jacobs, Ralph Nader, and Michael Harrington—all published between 1961 and 1965—that changed the national consciousness and consensus about the environment, cities, automobiles, and poverty. We are a democracy that can be changed for the better by books and the free flow of information.

This book, at bottom, is a celebration of history, standards, individualism, and an alternative America.

It is a Hymn to the bravery of rebels past, present, and hopefully future.

Jack Newfield
New York

NORMAN MAILER

PETE HAMILL

OVER THE PAST half-century, one American writer has imposed himself with great power on the collective consciousness from New York to Tokyo. He was not the greatest writer of his time, a distinction that in the end is temporal, subjective, and worthless. But there is simply no way to look back across the decades without acknowledging the size of his ambition, while respecting his art, his audacity, his intelligence, and his stirring recklessness. We can't understand the time of his time, and ours, without consulting his life and work. The miracle is that he's still with us. The writer is Norman Mailer.

Born in Long Branch, New Jersey in 1923, shaped by Brooklyn and Harvard and the army, he burst on the scene in 1948 with *The Naked and the Dead*, the first big American novel about the Second World War. Across all the years that followed he has remained, in crucial ways, a war novelist.

In *Barbary Shore*, *The Deer Park*, *An American Dream* and *Why Are We in Vietnam?* (among other fictions), the battlegrounds were domestic, the essential combat a struggle between the forces of personal liberation and those right-wing legions he saw correctly as imprisoning and potentially totalitarian. He clearly identified the McCarthyite menace, the surging faceless power of the growing American super-state, and tried to find ways to describe them that broke out of the certainties of left and right. Mailer's fictional master-piece is almost certainly *Harlot's Ghost*, his great, imperfect 1991 novel about the Cold War and what it did to all of us, including those who fought it in the shadows.

But he came to the so-called real world as a war novelist, too. We can't understand the culture wars that erupted in the 1960s without reading deeply into Mailer's work in the second half of the 1950s and then through the most tumul-tuous decade of the American twentieth century. His declara-tion of personal independence was *Advertisements for Myself* (1959), and in its pages he declares war on the prevailing postwar culture, its cult of caution and restrictions, on his nov-elistic contemporaries, on bourgeois safety, on fear itself. The book is rude, narcissistic, brilliant, and totally original. Mailer makes clear that he will not be a writer in a gray flannel suit. He will not kick rocks like Faulkner and say that he's only a farm boy. He will be Norman Mailer, without false modesty, with fully declared vaunting ambition and belief in his own powers, as different as Muhammad Ali would be later, when he made clear that he wasn't Joe Louis. No matter what else life might hold, Mailer says, he will not be a Nice Jewish Boy from Brooklyn. Life, he tells us, is combat.

In 1960, he began to back up his declarations with his first extraordinary work in journalism. In October that year, his piece on the 1960 Democratic National Convention appeared in *Esquire,* an article he called "Superman Comes to the Supermarket." Great journalists from H. L. Mencken to Murray Kempton had gone to conventions before, of course, and wrote about them in marvelous ways. But Mailer came as a war novelist, his eye trained to find details that revealed character, or larger truths, all placed against a wider sense of drama (which is to say, conflict). He saw Jack Kennedy in a new way, as a player in an existential drama, his arrival on the world stage suffused with myth, his vivid presence a political advertisement for the self.

In addition, Mailer had spent much time in the 1950s immersed in modern jazz, absorbed by the style and music of Miles Davis (among others) and he brought to his journalism one of the key lessons of the beboppers: a sense of disruptive surprise. Miles, Charlie Parker, Max Roach (like Mailer, a graduate of Boys' High), Thelonious Monk had shown what could be done with the most banal, familiar Tin Pan Alley melodies. They took those melodies apart, the way Picasso and Braque took apart the visible world to invent cubism, and infused the blues with deeper, more alienated, more urban emotions. In all the journalism that followed, Mailer maintained that sense of surprise.

The best of his journalism (and every writer should be judged by his best works) usually went beyond anything written by more conventional writers, and that is why it has such enduring value. In *The Armies of the Night* (1968), *Miami and the Siege of Chicago* (1969), *The Prisoner of Sex* (1971), *The Fight* (1975), *The Executioner's Song* (1979), Mailer was looking for facts, the way every journalist must, but he was also absorbed by context. Mythic context, social context, political context. Along with personal context, the way these stories fit into his own life.

His own life was, by his own admission, often a mess. In the 1950s, the large, drunken weekend party was virtually an institution in many parts of New York, from the Village to the Upper West Side, from Brooklyn to the Bronx, a kind of hangover from Prohibition. The possibility of violence was general (I know, I was there, too). Mailer was evolving his own romantic theories about the outlaw style, the existential superiority of the street hoodlum who lived beyond the law. His extraordinary essay, "The White Negro," is the best example of that romanticism. In columns and other scattered pieces, he proclaimed the need for orgiastic sexual liberation, for the primacy of the self, for freedom from all conventions. Madness was better than boredom.

Mailer wasn't alone, of course, in the dangerous grip of alcoholic delusions of grandeur. Sober, he was brilliant, often thoughtful, capable of doubt and uncertainty. Drunk or high, he drifted into various guises: the Texas sheriff, the English don, the glittery-eyed street thug: the many voices of Mr. Hyde. Those who loved him were often alarmed by the sudden personality shifts, and feared his descent into madness.

On November 19, 1960, a little more than a month after the publication of his brilliant "Superman" essay in

Esquire (which he believed, possibly correctly, had tipped the tight election to Kennedy), Mailer stabbed his wife Adele at a huge, drunken party in their apartment on Broadway and 94th Street. She narrowly avoided death. The fears of Mailer's friends seemed now to be justified. Mailer spent seventeen days at Bellevue and did no jail time (Adele refused to press charges), but that night would stain most of the rest of his public life.

That public life was driven by the need for reputation, which was more important to Mailer than it is to most writers. He wanted to be known, to have his generation's equivalent of the immense reputation of Ernest Hemingway (whom he described to me once as *Life* magazine's version of the "the cavalry of American literature"). Writers from Lord Byron to André Malraux had merged literary accomplishments with towering nonliterary public fame. But among Americans of Mailer's generation Hemingway was the great star, eclipsing (in a time of mass communications) such earlier celebrities as Mark Twain and Jack London. Mailer wanted the celebrity, but instead got notoriety. For obvious reasons. On the day after he stabbed his wife, he went off to sit for an interview with Mike Wallace.

And yet the notoriety did not end his career. If anything, in the midst of personal storms, his talent flourished while his notoriety did in fact become celebrity, because of the power of his work. His combative style was perfect for television and for public debates. His conflicts with William F. Buckley (verbal) and Gore Vidal (eventually physical) were covered by tabloids and the *New York Times*. His parties remained large and dangerous. His drinking went on for a long time. But then he would retreat monastically into the work, as if bleeding for each word, and the work continued to be brilliant and disturbing.

His 1969 campaign for the New York mayoralty (with writer Jimmy Breslin as his running mate for President of the City Council) was a heady mixture of scandal, irreverence, and innovative ideas, and added to his celebrity. He was not Hemingway (whose 1961 suicide had shaken him badly). But he was Mailer. When he spoke, attention must be paid.

Along the way, he went through more marriages (that gave him more children), and finally attained a version of peace after marrying the painter Norris Church in the fall of 1980. She was his sixth wife. His ideas kept evolving into an original mixture of left and right. He brooded in print about cancer, plastic, architecture, birth control, God and the Devil, and as always, on the power of the state, meditations that irritated some of his readers and made others think. He flirted with moviemaking. He acted in *Ragtime*. The drinking tailed off. He began spending more time on his fiction and less time on television. By the mid-1980s, he seemed to settle into a patriarchal sense of himself, the scarred, battered survivor of all the century's wars, foreign and domestic.

That's the way I think of him now. The old foot soldier is now engaged in a long work of fiction under the skies of Provincetown but in the summer of 2003 he still found time to write about George W. Bush and his nasty little war (in the *New York Review of Books*), without taking his ideas off the rack. Some critics have lately been either patronizing or dismissive of his accomplishments, but he might yet astonish even them. Meanwhile, it has been a privilege to be alive while he was working the room, even on those occasions when he was brave enough to play the fool.

WOODY GUTHRIE

STEVE EARLE

WHEN BOB DYLAN took the stage at the 1965 Newport Folk Festival, all leather and Ray-Bans and Beatle boots, and declared emphatically and (heaven forbid) electrically that he wasn't "gonna work on Maggie's farm no more," the folk-music faithful took it personally. They had come to see the scruffy kid with the dusty suede jacket pictured on the covers of *Bob Dylan* and *Freewheelin'.* They wanted to hear topical songs. Political songs. Songs like "The Lonesome Death of Hattie Carroll," "Masters of War," and "Blowin' in the Wind." They wanted the heir apparent. The Dauphin. They wanted Woody Guthrie.

Dylan wasn't goin' for it. He struggled through two electric numbers before he and the Paul Butterfield Blues Band retreated backstage. After a few minutes, he returned alone and, armed with only an acoustic guitar, delivered a scathing "It's All Over Now, Baby Blue" and walked.

Woody Guthrie himself had long since been silenced by Huntington's chorea, a hereditary brain-wasting disease, leaving a hole in the heart of American music that would never be filled, and Dylan may have been the only person present at Newport that day with sense enough to know it.

One does not become Woody Guthrie by design. Dylan knew that because he had tried. We all tried, every one of us who came along later and tried to follow in his footsteps only to find that no amount of study, no apprenticeship, no regimen of self-induced hard travelin' will ever produce another Woody. Not in a million years.

Woody Guthrie was what folks who don't believe in anything would call an anomaly. Admittedly, the intersection of space and time at the corner of July 14, 1912, and Okemah, Oklahoma, was a long shot to produce anything like a national treasure.

Woody was born in one of the most desolate places in America, just in time to come of age in the worst period in our history. Then again, the Dust Bowl itself was no accident, either.

After the Civil War, the United States government and the railroads, mistakenly believing that the Great Plains would make swell farmland, killed off all the buffalo, effectively neutralizing the indigenous population, and opened up vast expanses of prairie to homesteading. Problem was that the head-high buffalo grass that thrived in the thin topsoil had slowly adapted to its deceptively hostile environment over several thousand years. It took less than seventy years for nonnative water- and mineral-greedy crops to wring every last nutrient from the traumatized earth, creating a vast man-made desert and setting in motion a mass migration of folks from Texas, Arkansas and Oklahoma out west to California, where they hoped against hope for a better life.

Most found only bigotry and exploitation at the hands of wealthy fruit and vegetable growers. Woody found an audience. He sang in the migrant camps and on the picket lines up and down the lush interior valleys. A few well-meaning outsiders were sympathetic to the plight of the migrants, but they were college boys who used a lot of big words like "proletariat" and "bourgeoisie" and unintentionally made the Okies feel small. But Woody was one of their own. He spoke their language and he sang their songs, and every once in a while he'd slip in one of those big words in between a tall tale and an outlaw ballad. As he became more outraged, he became more radical, but his songs and his patter always maintained a sense of humor and hope. He said, "I ain't a Communist necessarily, but I been in the red all my life."

Woody arrived at his social conscience organically, over a period of years. Socialism made a lot of sense in the Great Depression. Capitalism had, after all, essentially collapsed and wasn't showing any significant signs of reviving in Pampa, Texas, where Woody spent his late adolescence. The ultimate hillbilly autodidact, he divided his time between teaching himself to play several musical instruments only tolerably well and frequent marathon sessions in the public library, where he educated himself clandestinely. He followed his own haphazard curriculum, one book leading him to another in an endless scavenger hunt for answers that invariably posed even deeper questions. An acute interest in psychology segued into medieval mysticism and from there he stumbled into Eastern philosophy and spiritualism. He went through a poetry period, a Shakespeare period, even a law book period. When, a few years later, he began to travel around the Southwest by thumb and freight train, his mind was wide open when he encountered crusty old radicals who handed out copies of *The Little Red Song Book* and preached the Gospel of Union. It was only natural that when he began to make up his own songs, he drew on the despair and pain he had witnessed all his life and the lofty ideas that ricocheted around in his head for inspiration. He became the living embodiment of everything a people's revolution is supposed to be about: that working people have dignity, intelligence and value above and beyond the market's demand for their labor.

Not that Woody was a rank-and-file worker. In fact, he managed to avoid manual labor more strenuous than sign-painting his entire life. He was, however, born into the working class and managed to distinguish himself not by "pulling himself up by his bootstraps" and toeing the line, but rather by trusting his own talent and vision.

He was no angel, either. Those closest to him sometimes found him hard to love. His family (he had two) sometimes suffered for his convictions, as he constantly sabotaged himself, especially when things were going well financially. In the long run, his political integrity was unassailable, because money and its trappings made him genuinely nervous. By the time the 1950s blacklists got around to folksingers, Woody wasn't affected, as he was already succumbing to the disease that had institutionalized and eventually killed his mother, and he was slowly slipping away. Ramblin' Jack Elliott got there in time to hang out with him out in Coney Island. By the early 1960s, Woody was hospital-bound, but he spent weekends at the home of longtime fan Bob Gleason. Bob Dylan and other up-and-coming folkies made the pilgrimage and sang for him there. When Woody finally died, on October 3, 1967, at the age of fifty-five, he was eulogized in the *New York Times* and *Rolling Stone*. He left behind an army of imitators and a catalog of songs that people will be dusting off and singing for as long as they make guitars.

For me personally, Woody is my hero of heroes and the only person on earth that I will go to my grave regretting that I never met. When I invoked his name in "Christmas in Washington," I meant it. Clinton was being reelected in a landslide and I had voted for him and I wasn't sure why and I needed something to hang on to, someone to say something. I needed, well . . . a hero.

Does all this mean that the world would be a different place if Woody had dodged the genetic bullet and lived? You bet your progressive ass! Just imagine what we missed! Woody publishing his second and third books! Woody on the picket lines with César Chavez and the farmworkers singin' "Deportee"! I could go on forever. I have imagined hundreds of similar scenarios, but then at some point it always dawns on me how selfish I am.

Let him go. He did his bit. Besides, as much as we need him right now, I wouldn't wish this post-9/11 world on

Woody. He hated Irving Berlin's "God Bless America" more than any other song in the world. He believed that it was jingoistic and exclusive, so he wrote a song of his own:

> This land is your land, this land is my land,
> From California, to the New York Island
> From the redwood forest, to the gulf stream waters
> This land was made for you and me.

BOB MOSES

Tom Hayden

Late one night in October 1961, I flew from Atlanta to Jackson, Mississippi, with Bob Moses. We didn't sit together during the silent one-hour flight, nor did we make eye contact at the empty airport. Not that it wasn't legal. You simply wouldn't take the chance.

The next day, with my late friend Paul Potter of the National Student Association, I rented a car and drove two hours south from Jackson to McComb, a fiercely segregated town of 12,000. We had arranged to meet Moses by pulling up to a gas-station parking lot with our lights out, changing cars, lying low in the back seats and finally being smuggled into a basement room with blankets covering all the windows. There we discussed the voter-registration drive and freedom school opening in town.

This was shortly after the Freedom Rides had shaken Mississippi and the Deep South, exposing the violence that awaited any who challenged the segregated status quo. Today, when early civil rights workers are widely honored, it is well to remember the national mood in those days. At the time, Attorney General Robert Kennedy, who eventually converted to the cause, wondered aloud if the Freedom Riders "have the best interest of the country at heart," since they were providing "good propaganda for America's enemies." In an Oval Office transcript, President John F. Kennedy, who finally welcomed the 1963 March on Washington after inital reservations, referred to John Lewis, now a U.S. Congressman, and the Student Nonviolent Coordinating Committee, as a "sons of bitches." The *New York Times* editorialized that "nonviolence that deliberately provokes violence is a logical contradiction." A Gallup poll that summer had revealed that 63 percent of Americans opposed the Freedom Rides.

Of course, patience was in the eye of the beholder. It had been 100 years since the beginning of the Civil War, eighty years since the imposition of Jim Crow laws and thirteen years since Democratic Party liberals like Hubert Humphrey had adopted a civil rights platform. And still people were being killed for registering to vote. As recently as a month before our trip, a farmer named Herbert Lee had been shot in broad daylight by a white Mississippi elected official. Louis Allen, a witness to Lee's murder, became a marked man; he was killed two years later.

Bob Moses took Herbert Lee's death personally. Lee had drawn venomous racist attention by driving Bob around the back roads looking for volunteers. Bob himself had been badly beaten on the head and face by the son-in-law of the man who shot Herbert Lee. Beatings of other civil rights workers became routine.

The institutions of liberalism seemed powerless to act. Officials of Robert Kennedy's Justice Department, on Moses' invitation, visited Mississippi sharecroppers clandestinely to see for themselves. They urged Moses to leave Mississippi because they couldn't,—or wouldn't,—protect the voter-registration effort. Institutions like the black churches and the NAACP lacked the independent strength for such campaigns. To organize for the most elementary rights to live, one had to learn the solitude of expecting to die.

People like Bob learned about organizing inside what they called "the iceberg." Bob was raised in the North, attended Hamilton College and Harvard graduate school in the 1950s, visited Zen centers in Japan, and was teaching at Horace Mann, a prep school in New York, when the sit-ins and Freedom Rides began in 1960. After a volunteer stint at Martin Luther King, Jr.'s New York office, he traveled south to join a three-member civil rights office in Atlanta. Then he took an exploratory bus trip through the Black Belt, finally being drawn to rural Mississippi.

Among the stalwart black sharecroppers he met, Bob began to evolve a new model of how things work. In the orthodox model, institutions are supposed to represent and defend organized constituencies. But along the way they became frozen in the iceberg themselves. The people they were supposed to represent were frozen, too, by fear of white violence. Frozen by feelings that they didn't count in the big picture of things, and above all by feelings that they were unqualified to participate in government. Democracy was meaningless when so many people were frozen psychologically.

So Bob listened. When people asked him what to do, he asked what they thought. At mass meetings, he usually sat in back. In group discussions, he mostly spoke last. He slept on floors, wore sharecroppers' overalls, shared the risks, took the blows, went to jail, dug in deeply. Gradually the ice melted; the rock of hope was revealed. People were empowered for the first time.

Radicals of that era advocated a strategy they called "political realignment," which meant the fashioning of a liberal Democratic Party by breaking the connection with the party's racist Dixiecrat wing. The notion had seeped into Bob's thinking, too, with the difference that he really meant to make it happen. Not through the endlessness of gradualism, but by boiling the iceberg. Not because it was some ideological dream, but because black people needed leverage against the structure of fear.

So Bob continued trying to educate the Justice Department to the necessity of breaking the link with segregation. But the results never led to a breakthrough. For example, the Kennedys were persuaded to encourage foundation funding for voter-registration drives as an alternative to radical direct action, but they wouldn't replace segregationist judges or protect civil rights workers on the front lines. Louis Allen was found murdered in Amite County while the Student Nonviolent Coordinating Committee (SNCC) was holding a strategy meeting on what to do next. It was plain that the movement couldn't protect those it encouraged to stand up. Bob knew that getting the Justice Department on the phone, or bringing national figures like Harry Belafonte,

Dick Gregory, and Bob Dylan to Mississippi, was at least partial protection against the reign of terror. His budding idea was to force the nation, at least north of the Mason-Dixon line, to share the terror and finally take a stand on Mississippi. The same June night that President Kennedy made a personal civil rights appeal on national television, a sniper killed NAACP Mississippi field secretary Medgar Evers in front of his family in Jackson.

Not long after, JFK himself was killed, and the whole country suddenly felt more like Mississippi. But in the same month as the Kennedy assassination, 90,000 Mississippi blacks shed their fears to cast a "freedom vote," mocking their exclusion. They set up their own voting booths outside the frozen walls. It was an underground vote, like an underground railroad, demonstrating that some freedom was in the air. The project Bob built was becoming an alternative structure, exposing and chipping away at the iceberg. In the spring and summer of 1964 came the Mississippi Freedom Democratic Party and Mississippi Summer. The new party would challenge the credentials of the state's official delegation at the Democratic National Convention, while hundreds of Northern, mostly white volunteers would enter Mississippi to work in "freedom schools" and registration projects.

While the 1964 Summer Project participants were training in nonviolence before leaving for Mississippi, word came on June 21 that three civil rights workers had "disappeared" in Neshoba County: James Chaney, Andrew Goodman, and Michael Schwerner. Bob had the burden of breaking the news. No one backed down. FBI Director J. Edgar Hoover told President Johnson that the missing activists might have staged their disappearance to inflame the situation, or perhaps that "these three may have gotten rather fresh" with the locals.

In Mississippi that summer, there were thirty bombings, thirty-five church burnings, thirty-five people shot, and eighty beaten up. But the Freedom Democrats continued moving toward the goal of sending an alternative, legal, racially open delegation to challenge the official Dixiecrats at the convention. It was the most significant model of participatory democracy built in the 1960s. The project was the brightest alternative to the war, violence, and repression that were building just beyond our knowledge. If the cause of the Freedom Democrats had been taken up by the Democratic Party, the rhetoric of political realignment would have turned into reality, and the War on Poverty would have become the priority instead of war in Vietnam.

It was not to be.

On August 2, the U.S. government fabricated an incident in the Gulf of Tonkin ("a very delicate subject," said Pentagon chief Robert McNamara), thus starting the Vietnam War. While LBJ prepared the subsequent congressional war resolution on August 4, the FBI found three brutalized bodies in a Neshoba County dam site. During an August 9 memorial service at the burned-out Mount Zion Church, Bob Moses questioned how the United States could fight for freedom in Vietnam, but not in Mississippi. On August 20, LBJ declared an official War on Poverty with a $947 million appropriation while also signing a military augmentation fifty times greater.

While the Freedom Democratic Party buses headed for Atlantic City, where the convention was held along a garish boardwalk, LBJ plotted to employ the party's leading liberals to undermine the FDP challenge. Hubert Humphrey, the hero of the 1948 civil rights debate, was dispatched to stop these Mississippi black people from taking the promise too seriously. The Humphrey plan encountered trouble as rank-and-file Democratic delegates from Northern states were moved by eloquent testimony from sharecroppers like Fannie Lou Hamer. Humphrey lectured the arriving Freedom delegation that LBJ "will not allow that illiterate woman to speak from the floor of the convention." Walter Reuther, leader of the United Auto Workers, was flown by private jet to help quell the Freedom challenge. He did so in the hope that Johnson would nominate Humphrey as Vice President. "We can reduce the opposition to this to a microscopic fraction so they'll be completely unimportant," he pledged.

The Humphrey compromise failed to meet the test of either participatory democracy or political realignment. It boiled down to offering two delegate-at-large seats to the Freedom Democrats while seating the official segregationist party and promising to reform the process four years later. "We didn't come all this way for no two seats," said Hamer. We came to bring our morality to politics, not politics to our morality, said Bob. Humphrey, "having used all the heart-strings I had" (as he forlornly explained to the President), broke down and cried. At one point LBJ stole off to bed in the afternoon and privately threatened for twenty-four hours to quit the presidency. Only days after the convention, LBJ's National Security Adviser, McGeorge Bundy, said the President would have to send "substantial armed forces" to Vietnam, yet Johnson had already pledged "no wider war."

The possibility of transformation was gone. In hindsight, if Johnson had conceded a meaningful voice to the

Freedom Democrats, he still would have defeated Barry Goldwater that November. Dixiecrats like John Stennis, chairman of the Senate Armed Services Committee, would have lost their leverage on Vietnam. But Johnson heeded the pleas of politicians like Representative Carl Vinson, who told the President, "We just cannot take any more civil rights advocates now."

How consciously we may never know, but Johnson was heading for the war that would prove disastrous for himself, the Democratic Party and the country. One year later, when Johnson signed the Voting Rights Act after the bloodshed at the Selma bridge, it was already too late. The fires that began in Watts the summer after Freedom Summer would blaze through hundreds of Northern ghettos in the next three years.

Bob was deeply wounded by the betrayal. He had, after all, followed the rules, registered voters, built a local and state party organization, made a thorough legal case to the credentials committee, all the while putting lives at risk. It was a remarkable organizational achievement, turning "the stones the builders rejected" into polished gems of community leadership. Beyond anyone's expectation, he outorganized Lyndon Johnson, who, conceding that the convention delegates would support the Freedom Democrats, simply made sure no floor vote happened.

But the battle was lost. Bob told me it might take fifty years before it could happen again. After a while, he dropped his burdensome last name, becoming Bob Parris. He took part in the earliest anti–Vietnam War demonstration in Washington, traveled to Africa, escaped a draft order, taught school under asylum in Tanzania.

Bob ultimately returned to the Harvard area with a MacArthur Fellowship. In the 1980s he began the Algebra Project, modeled on the early freedom schools, using participatory techniques to help black youth avoid disfranchisement in the computer age, as their parents had experienced in the industrial age. The last time I saw him was in the 1990s, on another flight to Mississippi, for a reunion of the 1964 volunteers, where I was deeply moved to sit on the floor and listen to so many of the movement's grown-up children, including Bob's, take part in freedom-circle discussions of their own.

Bob would deny credit for these 1960s organizing achievements, and rightly so, since they depended on thousands of self-determined community people and organizers. But Bob was the catalyst and the example. He helped the country to look in the mirror and confront itself. If the country sought to escape what it saw, there was nothing Bob felt he could do. His 1964 prediction—that the country would unravel if it failed to heed the Freedom Democrats' challenge—was accurate: Voting rights without political power would accelerate the displacement of Southern blacks to Northern cities, where they would join the growing class of the new unemployables, form gangs, and initiate a cycle of violence.

Some say Bob was more a mystic than an organizer. If so, he was the most practical mystic I ever met. He was an organizer of organizers who organized people to free themselves of organizers. The legacy of Freedom Summer led directly to the Berkeley Free Speech Movement through the leadership of Mario Savio, who was a SNCC volunteer in McComb. It continued in the draft resistance, the 1967

Vietnam Summer, echoing all the way to labor's still-ongoing Solidarity Summers.

Others say Bob's style was too decentralized, too anarchistic, that he and SNCC should have built lasting institutions. But the hard truth is that even well-meaning institutions wear out the spirit and become accommodated to the status quo. Of course, we need them, but no institution ever aroused the degraded poor through a membership application. Only a prophetic organizer can do such work, as seen in the base communities of liberation theology, the underground efforts of antisweatshop organizers, the dangerous struggles of women against fundamentalism and the brave souls slowing rain-forest destruction today. "Maybe you did come only to boil and bubble and burst out of sight and sound," Bob himself once said. That seems enough for one life.

HANK WILLIAMS

MARK JACOBSON

IT IS ONE of those myth moments people from America, a land too new to have a pantheon of Olympian gods or a Yahweh to call its own, are so adept at manufacturing: Hank Williams, the greatest country singer of all time, dead at twenty-nine in the back of a powder blue Cadillac outside the don't-blink-or-you'll-miss-it town of Oak Hill, West Virginia. On New Year's Eve, to boot. First they said it was a heart attack, but the fans knew better, back in 1953 and today, too. They know Hank died not only from the drinking and the ingestion of pills prescribed by bogus doctors throughout the South. He succumbed to a surfeit of myth/art, and a special knowledge of the highest American form of that particular expression, which is the blues.

A man with a instinctive grasp of the American myth-scape and his place within it (he formed "Hank Williams and His Drifting Cowboys" at age thirteen while growing up in Montgomery, Alabama, a place not exactly known for its cattle drives), Hank sang the blues like no one else, fusing Jimmie Rodgers' high-register hillbilly yodel with the low-moan syncopation of black sharecropper bards like his street-singing mentor, Rufus (Tee Top) Payne and the great Charley Patton. What came of it was a music without which there could have been no Elvis, and probably no Chuck Berry, which would mean no rock and roll, at least in its earliest, wildest, most miscegenated form. As Berry, who thought of himself as a bluesman and loved white hillbilly music pushed the envelope, Hank Williams pressured from the opposite end. He was a self-designated "peckerwood," growing up in the highly segregated environs of Montgomery, Alabama (where, at age fourteen he won $15 for singing "WPA Blues" and came to be called "The Hillbilly Shakespeare"). Yet, like Eminem and thousands more, he readily boasted that he learned how to sing on the "other" side of town, i.e., the black side.

Williams did present some rather conventional complaints/tropes of bluesiana. Troubled by a congenital spina bifida condition, his back always hurt him, which made him drink. His wife, the well-lampooned Audrey Mae, whom he married at a filling station in Andalusia, Alabama, ran around and gave him grief, which made him drink more. But there is always something about a Hank Williams record which goes deeper, beyond rationality and

the exhaustive scholarship accorded early and mid-twen-
tieth-century American music. Probably the greatest folk-
based American songwriter outside of Bob Dylan (who has
always rated Hank "my favorite"), a singer whose falsetto
whine imbues the sort of heartbreak to rival Al Green,
Sam Cooke and Billie Holiday, Williams transcended the
twelve-bar blues form and the particular limits of his Deep
South cracker roots. It is no great stretch to say that when
considering the uppermost range of blues-based artists,
people like Patton, Robert Johnson, Sonny Boy
Williamson, and even

Louis Armstrong, Hank Williams more than holds his
own, which sets up the certain-to-be-contentious argument
that the greatest American bluesman might actually be a
white man. Except that, as anyone who ever heard tunes
like "I'll Never Get Out of This World Alive," "Cold, Cold
Heart", or the nonpareil "I'm So Lonesome I Could Cry"
understands, his was an artistry that, for a blessed moment,
made race irrelevant.

A good number of mid-century of iconic American
artists died young (Charlie Parker, James Dean, and Jimi
Hendrix among them), and to be sure there is a built-in
romance in the early exit, the glorious, short-lived
Achilles comet snuffed out in mid-streak. Possibly because
he talked with a drawl and wore the kind of goofy
embroidered suits which disqualified him from liberal
Woody Guthrie–style art-hero status in the minds of
knee-jerk Peter, Paul, and Mary–loving civil rightists,
Hank Williams is rarely included in the pop gallery of
eternally frozen youth. Cynics might contend that it was
just as well that Hank didn't live long enough to see his

loudmouth, modestly talented, yet huge-selling son, Hank Williams Jr. (nicknamed by his father "Little Bocephus" after a popular Grand Olde Opry ventriloquist dummy) scream "are you ready for some football?" on a thousand *Monday Night Football* broadcasts. But with Hank, we don't think of time stolen, and the hundreds of great songs he might have written if he lived to be eighty-nine like Roy Acuff, his publisher and keeper, who was still paying Williams $50 a month against royalties well into his hit-making days. In retrospect, Hank never seemed young, singing to the young, even on those scratchy 1941 demos when he billed himself as "The Singing Kid." He was always too knowing, too much in touch with hurting side of life both personal and spiritual, too much the bluesman. By the time he joined the Louisiana Hayride in his middle twenties, his voice already had taken on the ring of eternal authority.

It was as if Williams lived his life on fast-forward, his body and soul pitched at such a speed that it was outfitted for only a twenty-nine-year stretch. Remarkably prolific considering his infirmities and general dissoluteness, he managed to record thirty-nine Top Ten country singles in less than six years—better than six a year, which beats out even the Beatles. The range of these tunes, from jocularities like "Window Shopping", "Setting the Woods on Fire," "Jambalaya," and "Hey, Good Lookin' (whatcha got cookin'?)" to the desolate soul-wrench of stuff like "My Son Calls Another Man Daddy" and "The Angel of Death" is likewise amazing, considering the uniform excellence of the work. Among the ninety-odd songs in the "Original Singles Collection," there is not one tune, however elemental-seeming in composition, that doesn't have *something* interesting about it.

Yet, despite all the success and subsequent lionization, there remains an outsideness to Hank Williams, as if the testimonials to his consummate artistry and down-home soul parroted endlessly by the corporate types at Country Music Association award shows signify nothing more than lip service to an unruly ghost everyone would just as soon stay dead and buried. It figures that when the insurgent non-Nashville "alt. country" movement, noting the more than passing coincidences between Hank's story and the life later played out by Kurt Cobain, has adopted Williams as its patron, harrowed saint. The mainstream world has never known what to do with Hank Williams. The Hollywood dementos got George Hamilton to play him in *Your Cheating Heart—The Hank Williams Story* for chrissakes! It is a grievous cinematic mistake that, outside of the odd Rip Torn Hank-like portrayal in the long-forgotten *Payday*, has not yet been corrected.

Dead half a century—it was fifty years to the moment last New Year's Eve—Hank still sells, but he has yet to be packaged in the manner of, say, Jim Morrison, one more American music icon who died young. While Morrison remains forever sexy in his callow way, still at home on the cover of *Rolling Stone*, the picture of Hank Williams which stands out is the hair-raising shot taken of him in 1952, as he left jail, where he had landed on a drunk-and-disorderedly charge. By far the biggest star in the history of a form which was already on its way to reconfiguring itself from raucous "hillbilly" to the often sterile Nashville "hat" music of the 1990s and today, Williams had been banned from the Grand Ole Opry and many other high-paying venues for showing up drunk or not at all. Hugely famous but flat broke, he landed back in Montgomery, living in the boardinghouse run by his mother, the formidable Lily, the erstwhile organ player at the Mount Olive Church, who bought Hank his first guitar at Sears for $3.50 back when he was ten. Taken 19 weeks before his death, greatest of honky-tonk heroes appears in the jailhouse photo shirtless, his rib cage visible in the manner of a concentration-camp survivor, skin pulled tight across the angular features of his face. His eyes are tormented dots, his mouth, through which passed some of America's most sublime self-knowledge, including the chill of "I'll Never Get Out of This Life Alive," is a sickened, horrified gash. It is as if he has seen some awful apocalyptic vision and cannot free himself from it. Then again, maybe he sees another kind of Paradise, like the one described in "I Saw the Light": "No more darkness, no more night," Williams sings "Now I'm so happy, no sorrow in sight." Perhaps that's the reason for the look of horror on Hank's face: in a world without pain, what would he write?

BOB DYLAN

GENE SANTORO

EVERYONE KNOWS WHAT happened when Bob Dylan fronted an electric band at the 1965 Newport Folk Festival. That's why August 3, 2001 saw 100 reporters merge into a crowd of 10,000 in the resort's narrow streets. Following Aaron Copland's "Fanfare for the Common Man," the short guy in the silver shirt, black suit, fake beard, wig, and tall white Stetson bounded onstage with four black-clad bandmates and into a punchy string-band version of "Roving Gambler," a folk blues. At sixty-one, Dylan returned to the scene of the crime.

Or maybe he hadn't, and not just because of Heraclitus,

with whom he would surely agree about feet and the same river twice. For the assembled multitude who came to the rock where the prophet stood, it was an Event. For the enigmatic bard, his Cassandra streak and razor wit evident after years of trying to banish or submerge them, his restless decades-long quest for something to believe in an implacable universe transformed by his art into an uneven but awesome legacy (40-plus albums, 500-plus songs, 200-days-a-year of roadburn), gunning his rapid-fire way through revamped classics, smiling like Mona Lisa with the highway blues, it's impossible to say. For the shaman onstage, is this just another turn in the maze he runs outside the Gates of Eden, looking for love, jubilation, transcendence, apocalypse, hope, death—an answer, an exit? How can you tell the dancer from the dance?

"I'm mortified to be onstage," Dylan has said, "but then again, it's the only place I'm happy."

Myth can be more fun and sharper-sighted than history and, even, as Dylan the mythmaker knows, truer. The years have surfaced variant accounts of 1965 Newport, but the legend reports the booing was loud, spontaneous, and universal, as folk fans rejected Dylan's contemptuous noise. Whatever. After three electric and three acoustic tunes, he quit.

But as he moved over from protest singer to surrealistic prophet, from born-again Christian to born-again Jew, Dylan's life and music registered, however elliptically, his times. This is one reason people have translated him into hero, antihero, sellout, savior, asshole, religious zealot, burnout, political radical, and artist. Unless it was useful, Dylan resented being reduced in rank from prophet (he has always credited divine inspiration for his work, and his imagery rages with Blake and the Bible) to mere mirror-holder, and he has managed to translate himself anew—the protean artist. That is his genius, the soul linking his tangled life to his web of art—and his art to his audience.

Like the decade he's a symbol of, Dylan is many things: an aging rock star who loves the road; a multimillionaire who has an un-American lack of interest in personal hygiene; a double-talking celebrity with a ferocious sense of privacy who spends his life with his ears full of the transcendent sounds in his head alongside the roar of the star machinery and its need for lubrication. Such is the dilemma of any commercial artist. But few—if any—other pop songwriters have been considered for the Nobel Prize in Literature.

The nineteen-year-old came to 1961 Greenwich Village with a Woody Guthrie playbook on his knee, but he loved Buddy Holly's Stratocaster and Elvis's Sun sessions and knew he wanted to be a star. He shifted to folk music when it supplanted rock and roll as the sound of rebellion; for young Bobby Zimmerman, rebellion was propulsion.

He cast himself as a shadow observer hoboing through life, with his BO and irresistible charm and coldhearted focus and genius. He lives in introverted, near-constant turbulence, buffeted by external winds and his creativity, which produce constant alienation. The chorus for his life is extensive: Minnesota folkie madonnas, Village political sophisticates, endless lovers who sing his praises and want to protect him; ex-acolytes and musicians and business associates wailing the I-been-abused blues; core loyalists and friends; and fawners, often from the same pool as the abused. They agree he is an unbelievably private, often surprisingly inarticulate man with unshakable drive and talent. In book after book, Dylan flickers like a strobed and ultimately elusive image through their crosscut glimpses.

The Village folkies, leftish, middle-class, longing for cultural authenticity and artistic purity, loathed the world of commercial showbiz—everything Albert Grossman, Dylan's manager, represented. But pop culture is where their hero dove headlong. Even before the 1965 Newport Festival, Dylan drew electric guitars and drums—the evil talismans of showbiz—from his toy chest, where they'd been waiting alongside Harry Smith's *Anthology of American Folk Music*, Hank Williams, Little Richard, and Elvis.

By 1965 he had rerouted American pop culture. So many circuits were wired into him that his only rivals as musical transformers are Louis Armstrong, Miles Davis, Ray Charles, and Elvis—and, like them, he got recurrent abuse about betraying his "pure" talent. But for Dylan, purity is a pointless abstraction; like St. Paul, he believes virtue is manifest only in being tested. "To live outside the law," warns one of his ruthless lines, "you must be honest." And so he absorbed the *Great American Songbook*, Johnny Mercer and Muddy Waters, and the totemic anthology. A deadly mimic, he learned to phrase from blues and soul, though his voice was ridiculed. His creative outbursts, the nonstop writing, tumbled all he heard and read and did into his high-torque personalized songs; tapped by the shades of Blake and Rimbaud, he'd become a seer or shaman who quavered to America's deep rhythmic structures.

The Beatles and Stones survived past the British Invasion because they jumped on Dylan's millennial bandwagon, adapting his Jeremiah's cry, his truthteller's story forms, his sly ironies and probing sarcasm and haunted paradoxical loves; his far-reaching grasp of forms, his impossible phrasing, his poet's fecund sense of language in play. They gave him back American rock; he gave them art. The British Invasion upended the record industry by demonstrating that "the kids" wanted something else; Dylan altered what "the kids" wanted. He realized Woody Guthrie's dream—a true popular art.

My first Dylan albums were *Bringing It All Back Home*, *Highway 61 Revisited*, and *Blonde on Blonde*, so for me, Dylan's value was never narrowly political: He's got everything he needs, he's an artist, he don't look back.

In *Dont Look Back*, D. A. Pennebaker doesn't try to make Dylan a poster boy for the folk revival; he grasps the protean artist behind the duplicity. Dylan acts the manipulative creep; the defensive master of the counterlunge; the insular and sometimes inarticulate star; the smartass provocateur; the hyperintense performer; the chainsmoking, coffee-drinking, spasmic-twitching composer sitting endlessly at typewriters and pianos. And yeah, the nice guy. It's a portrait of the artist as Zelig.

"Like a Rolling Stone" hit number two in August 1965. In July 1966, Dylan's motorcycle accident pulled him out of the public eye and augmented his Garboesque mystery. At Big Pink with The Band, he played old songs and scrambled up new ones. *John Wesley Harding*, released then but recorded earlier, returned to roots: a

Polaroid cover and unaffected songs dashed with surreal humor and mysticism. Then *Nashville Skyline* disappointed fans—the newly lightened voice, the genial love songs, recalled why critics always found Milton's Satan more fascinating than his God. Then came the muddy electrifying basement tapes of Dylan and the Band rooting around America's history.

In the 1970s and 1980s Dylan seemed preoccupied: a dedicated family man waging legal battles with Grossman, evading stalkers who ransacked his garbage. There were musical spots of light on *New Morning*, "Tangled Up in Blue" on *Planet Waves* ranks high, and *Blood on the Tracks* was a masterpiece. In 1979 he was born again and his art atrophied. He drifted through drug abuse, exploding relationships, financial crashes—all culminating in the late 1980s, when he tried to join the Grateful Dead. The band sidestepped him, but *Dylan & The Dead* marked his turnaround. He began choosing his sidemen and sets more carefully. His bands became jamming roadhouse warriors. He'd become the touring rock troubadour he'd imagined himself as a kid.

In 1994, on MTV's *Unplugged*, Dylan sang some of his most wondrous and paranoid and surreal creations: "Tombstone Blues," "All Along the Watchtower," "Rainy Day Women #12 and 35," "Desolation Row," "Like a Rolling Stone," "With God on Our Side," and "The Times They Are A-Changin'." Then he licensed "Times" for ads by the Bank of Montreal and Coopers & Lybrand.

He was resurrected, though hardly the same, and his near-death in 1997 refocused him further. *Time Out of*

Mind and *Love and Death* drew on Delta and Chicago blues, rockabilly and jazz ballads; his lyrics had bite and power, barbed humor about loss and hope and entropy and pain and faith and death in an indifferent world—topics for grown-up rockers. "Not Dark Yet" and "Trying to Get to Heaven" and "Highlands," about going into that good night, were delivered in a weary, scuffed-leather croak whose phrasing danced. One jazz musician told me, "The closest thing to what he does with his voice is Sonny Rollins's sax."

So Dylan was the only real bluesman born of the 1960s. Where once he sang defiantly, "When you got nothing, you got nothing to lose," now he observed, "When you think that you've lost everything, you find out you can always lose a little more."

MICHAEL HARRINGTON

MAURICE ISSERMAN

IN THE EARLY 1960s, Mike Harrington became famous as "the man who discovered poverty." He announced his discovery in *The Other America,* a slender volume published in 1962 for which he had the most modest of expectations; if it sold 2,500 copies, he told a friend the year before it appeared, he would be well satisfied.

As it turned out, *The Other America* did considerably better. It caught the eye of liberal policymakers in Washington with its analysis of a "culture of poverty" that confined millions of Americans to the economic margins of a less-than-universally affluent society, and led to an invitation to Mike in early 1964 to take part in the early deliberations of the federal task force that drew up the program for Lyndon Johnson's "war on poverty."

For Mike, the desire to end poverty was not simply a matter doing good on behalf of the less fortunate. Rather, as he argued in *The Other America*, affluent Americans should be angry and ashamed to live in a society that, having the resources to provide everyone a decent standard of living, instead allowed itself to be divided into two nations. "The fate of the poor," he wrote in his conclusion, "hangs upon the decision of the better-off. If this anger and shame are not forthcoming, someone can write a book about the other America a generation from now and it will be the same or worse." The war on poverty, "oversold and underfinanced" as Mike would often say of it in later years, enjoyed partial successes in the 1960s but never came close to accomplishing its stated goal of bringing economic opportunity within the grasp of all Americans. *The Other America*, on the other hand, was an unqualified success. Since its publication, it has gone on to sell well over a million copies; in an end-of-the-millennium survey, *Time* magazine listed the book as one of the ten most influential works of nonfiction of the twentieth century.

Mike's friends in the 1960s were pleased with his new prominence, but could scarcely conceal their astonishment at his abrupt rise from obscurity. "Three years ago," Jack Newfield mused in a profile of Mike for the *Village Voice* in the fall of 1964, "Michael Harrington's reputation as a socialist preacher with the eloquence of Debs and a debater with the logic of a Talmudic scholar was confined to one faction of the Young People's Socialist League and the back room of the White Horse Tavern."

Little in Mike's early life suggested he would grow up to become the man who discovered poverty. Born to comfortable circumstances in St. Louis in 1928, and educated at Holy Cross, Yale Law School, and the University of Chicago, he stepped off the conventional path to success in his early twenties. He dedicated his early adulthood instead to a strenuous pursuit of the cultural and political margins of American life, in the better drinking circles of Greenwich Village and, after a stint as a Catholic Worker, as chief organizer of a succession of fiercely sectarian socialist youth groups whose combined national membership would not have sold out a showing of *The Battleship Potemkin* at the 250-seat Bleecker Street Cinema.

But even in his obscure days, Mike had the quality of transcending his surroundings. People came to hear him speak in seedy little halls, where the dust lay deep on unsold copies of yellowing radical newspapers, and somehow came away thinking about the future revival of the left, not its current unpromising circumstances.

Judith Malina, co-founder of the Living Theater, was one of those who encountered Mike in those years in the backroom of the White Horse Tavern. (The White Horse, located on the corner of Hudson and West 11th streets in the West Village, was in those days a hangout for a variety of grizzled longshoremen, accomplished writers, Irish folksingers, and would-be revolutionaries. It is surprising that no one ever wrote a folk song about the White Horse, it seemed such a perfect embodiment of its cultural moment and a certain kind of bravely isolated adversarial stance.) Briefly romantically smitten with Mike, though too much of an anarchist to be won to his socialist politics, Malina described one evening's encounter with him in a 1954 entry in her journal. It was shrewd appreciation of a good performance by a fellow actor. "At the White Horse," she wrote, "Mike Harrington and his friends talk; most of it is chatter, but it's never the solemn defeatism of the [San] Remo" [a rival drinking establishment a few blocks to the east]. Mike was good-looking, and that was certainly part of his appeal to the audience gathered around his table. He "doesn't rave in extravagant adjectives about what he likes, but smiles acceptingly, and his approbation is highly valued . . . ." He had another gift, noted by Malina. "Mike is heroic . . . That is, he takes in the environment and its people and includes them in a generalization of which he is the center. Thus the hero is in control without needing to be in command."

A good example of what Malina meant by Mike's ability to offer a "heroic generalization" is found in an article he wrote for the liberal Catholic weekly *Commonweal* in 1959, titled, interestingly, "The Other America" (the first time he used those words in print):

The 1950s had been grim years for American radicals; in the first half of the decade Mike and his comrades liked to compare themselves to the doomed supporters of "an annihilated legion," a phrase attributed to Leon Trotsky's widow Natalya. But as the decade came to a close, Mike saw signs of great and hopeful changes in the making. Unrest in the Soviet bloc swept away the notion, popularized in the dystopian writings of George Orwell and Hannah Arendt, that totalitarianism was the wave of the future. Mike argued that it was time for American intellectuals to discard the equally mistaken notion that the spread of "mass culture" had destroyed the possibility of a resurgent radicalism in the United States.

Drawing on his travels across the country as an itinerant agitator, Mike had come to believe that an "other America," that is, an alternative America—a nation of generous democratic values and artistic and social creativity, a nation not "dominated by gadgets and mass media"—lay preserved beneath the surface of a homogenized, profit-driven mass culture. In Seattle, for instance, where he had recently visited:

The people live in the presence of Mount Rainier. . . . Driving in the city, one never knows when the turning of a corner will reveal the aspect of beauty. On a clear day, each hour, each period, is given a special definition by the mountain. And this geography enters into a culture. It is, of course, intermingled with the history of the region: logging, the IWW, the Seattle General Strike of 1919 . . . the weatherbeaten and brawling tradition of a port. Thus the coffee cups in many restaurants in Washington are bigger than they are in the East. Their shape developed out of an outdoor, working world and they are part of the texture of life in the area. At the trucker's stop in the Cascade Mountains where breakfast is ten strips of bacon, four eggs, and a pile of home fries, these coffee cups are one of the forms defining a history and a way of living. They are related to the towering fact of the mountain.

As an apprentice revolutionary, Mike had prided himself on his mastery of a rigorously scientific socialism. But no stretch of dialectical materialism could get him from Mount Rainer, to oversized coffee cups, to Wobblies. There was instead a kind of unabashed lyricism in the passage, reflective of a boyhood ambition to grow up and become a poet. Long after abandoning his laureate aspirations, Mike retained the habit of viewing his options and surroundings through a literary lens, a sometimes-romantic projection of what a world in which he might play a role commensurate to his talents and attuned to his values could be and should be like. His weatherbeaten Seattle truckers were literary brothers to the "husky boilermaker from Frisco" who, in John Dos Passos's 1936 novel, *The Big Money,* hopped a freight car to come east and join the protest against the execution of Sacco and Vanzetti (an event which led Dos Passos famously to declare, "all right we are two nations. . . .").

Although he would come to criticize the more extravagant claims made on behalf of the revolutionary potential of the "youth culture" of the 1960s, Mike's own radicalism on the eve of the new decade contained within it a distinct countercultural strain. He saw no contradiction between the personal impulses that had led him to the jumbled streets of lower Manhattan and the larger social transformation to which he was politically committed.

If there was a teleological element to Mike's socialism, it was no longer (if it had ever really been) based on his acceptance of some iron law about the falling rate of profit or the like. It was instead closely related to the outsider's stance he had chosen for his own cultural orientation. His youthful bohemianism was not primarily shaped by a desire to stand apart and in doing so shock or deride his elders. Rather, he assumed that what most people wanted in life was something that could not be delivered in the consumer market, a sense of self-worth and personal autonomy sustained by respect earned within a community of self-defining equals, Greenwich Village writ large. He had faith in the socialist future, but it was value-driven rather than economically-determinist.

Michael's radicalism had evolved from the pinched sectarianism of his earliest days in the movement; like the fabled coffee cups of Seattle, his vision of politics had grown generous and expansive. Although steeped in European intellectual theory (both Catholic and Marxist), his cultural impulses reflected a distinctly indigenous tradition of radical individualism. On the eve of the 1960s he had come to believe that if the "other Americas"—the *alternative* America of intellectuals and students and artists and his Greenwich Village neighbors, and the *excluded* America of the poverty-stricken and the dispossessed—could united in coalition with a democratic labor movement, they would represent a powerful redemptive force for social justice. And if over the next several decades things didn't turn out to be as simple and straightforward as Mike's heroic generalization would have had them, there may still be something to be learned from his parable of the bigger coffee cup.

EDWARD ABBEY

TERRY BISSON

Edward Abbey (1927-1989) was the quintessential American: the Easterner who headed West, pulling up stakes and lighting out for the Territories, looking back over his shoulder only to make sure no one was following.

He was also the quintessential American writer: the maverick by design as well as temperament, scorning the establishment, courting fame while pretending to flee from it, hiding rather than flaunting his education and literary sophistication.

Abbey wrote some twenty books, most of them collections of occasional essays, two of them immortal gems, but all with the same theme: the awesome beauty and ongoing rape of the last great American wilderness, the high desert of the Colorado Plateau. His greatest (if not his favorite), *Desert Solitaire*, is about nature's power to save us from ourselves; and his most popular (if not his best), *The Monkey Wrench Gang*, is about our power to save it from ourselves, or at least slow its desecration, provided we are willing to act the outlaw.

Abbey loved the desert as only a kid from the green-robed East can love the naked Earth unclothed. His father, a part-time Appalachian trapper and logger, read him Whitman ("resist much; obey little") and bragged of once shaking Big Bill Haywood's hand. The poet and the Wobbly fit together perfectly in Ed. It was while riding the rails as a young man that he first encountered the wide open spaces of the West, where the cliché fit the reality like a key in a lock.

Arizona opened all his doors, and they stayed open. After a brief stint in the military (he left boot camp on V-J Day) Abbey took his G.I. Bill to the University of New Mexico, in Albuquerque. He had already started writing, a discipline he honored faithfully until the day he died. He looked up novelist William Eastlake, and wedged himself into Wallace Stegner's writing program, where he and Wendell Berry were classmates. There was never any question about his orientation: rebellion. He wore dark clothes and drank jug wine. Rexroth and Patchen were his beacons. He scrapped his first attempt at a novel, *Down the Road*, when Kerouac's was published in 1956.

But Beat was only a temporary pose for Abbey. He had a higher ambition than to be part of a school, even the most successful one since Bloomsbury. He wanted to be the head-master, the teacher, the student and the dropout all in one.

Like Gary Snyder, another of the Beats whose accomplishments transcended even their overweening ambition, Abbey went to work as a Park Ranger. It was seasonal, solitary work that suited him perfectly. "Lazy scheming loafers," he was later to call himself and his colleagues. "Put them to work."

Abbey's fame and influence rests on two singular works. The first of these, *Desert Solitaire*, a memoir of his time as a ranger at Arches Park, in southern Utah, immediately established him as a poetic and precise nature writer (a term he grew to hate); "the Thoreau of the West," Larry McMurtry was to call him. Published in 1968, it alternated haunting evocations of the slickrock desert with sardonic reflections on man's place in the universe: "I'm a humanist; I'd rather kill a man than a snake." It put Edward Abbey on the map as an articulate rebel with a profane and profound sense of humor; and 1968, you will recall, was a good year for rebels.

Even this contemplative work was a call to action, decrying the National Park Service's thralldom to corporate interest and exhorting readers to pick up a rock and "throw it at something big and glassy." This was a theme Abbey was to develop in all his works, becoming more radical and more explicit as he went along.

By the time *Desert Solitaire* came out, Abbey had already written several novels, among them *The Brave Cowboy*, made into a film which Kirk Douglas considered his best. *Lonely are the Brave* ("Pompous is the Title," Abbey once quipped), about a maverick cowboy who refused to join the modern world, was Abbey's last and only homage to the conventional hat-and-boot iconography of the Old West.

The Brave Cowboy was a success, but it was Abbey's third novel, *The Monkey Wrench Gang*, that made him famous. Published in 1975, it was inspired (as the saying goes) "by real events," and it inspired and is still inspiring many more. Monkey-wrenching is sabotage. Adopted by radical environmentalists (primarily Earth First, which calls Abbey its patron saint) it was and is enormously effective, both in practical and PR terms. It's a David-and-Goliath thing.

In the novel, a small group of dedicated misfits (a macho ex–Green Beret, a Mormon rancher, a droll M.D. fond of classical music and dynamite and, of course, a pretty girl) drive bulldozers off cliffs, pull up survey stakes, cut power lines, trash billboards, and generally act in an exemplary manner to preserve the West from those who would "develop" it. It's a how-to book: how to place charges, where to get explosives, which goo to pour into carburetors (Karo Syrup is good); it's an environmentalist's manual of arms, detailing security measures and secret signals, tools and procedures for a guerrilla war against corporate greed and arrogance. People have tried it, and it works. This is the kind of reader response that Abbey sought and treasured.

In one of the innumerable Web sites dedicated to Abbey, an unnamed comrade tells how the writer was too "technologically challenged" in real life to hot-wire a bulldozer. No matter. His fictional hero, George Washington Hayduke, is the hot-wirer from Hell. Abbey was always quick to admit that he lacked the skill and courage of his heroes. He even once claimed it was all made up for laughs.

The claim itself brought laughs.

The Monkey Wrench Gang is dedicated to Ned Ludd, but Abbey had bigger targets in mind than mere machines. The fictional (and real) target of this exemplary novel is the Glen Canyon Dam, which turned one of the world's wonders into a playground for JetSkis and a power source for the lights of Las Vegas. The ultimate aim of the Monkey Wrench Gang and, indeed, of the book itself, is to bring down the dam. Abbey's hatred for this monumental environmental crime was very personal. He was among the last to make the trip first made by John Wesley Powell in the 1870s.

Hayduke, the hard drinking ecoterrorist, is Abbey's second-greatest fictional creation; the first was himself. He cultivated the image of the hard-drinking literary redneck. He had a network of like-minded friends, a resentful circle of ex-wives, and a legion of enemies among the mining corporations, the cattle companies, the developers and despoilers of the West. Professional environmentalists hated him, too; he called the Sierra Club the Sahara Club and never forgave their role in making possible the inundation of Glen Canyon.

Enemies suited Abbey. He loved a fight, which meant he could stay in the wilderness for only so long. The notoriety brought by *The Monkey Wrench Gang*, together with the literary respectability of *Desert Solitaire*, combined to provide him a bully pulpit, which he used to spout off on feminism (bad), mountain lions (good), immigration (give 'em a rifle and send 'em home), cowboys (peasants on horseback), and the National Parks (rip out the roads). He was politically correct only about his one big issue, but that was enough.

And always his reputation grew, like a weed. Abbey was successful as only a handful of American writers have been, winning the admiration of his peers, the love and respect of his readers, and the grudging recognition of the establishment. He was as leery of that as a coyote eyeing a trap. Offered a prize by the American Academy of Arts and Letters, he turned it down, claiming he had a river to run. "At least I won't have to gloss anymore," he said, when told he was dying. He was barely in his sixties. He wanted to croak in the desert under the stars, but dying is as hard as living, and his friends finally hauled him back indoors where he died under the black peasant's sabot on his wall. Then they buried him in a still-undisclosed location, where his friends are said to gather for a few beers every year on his birthday. His name still sends a shudder through all those who would build a new ski resort, poison a coyote, or carve a road into a canyon wilderness.

Do a Web search and tell me Edward Paul Abbey is no longer around. Hell, there's even an Ed Abbey refrigerator magnet, available online. He would have liked that. The refrigerator was one of the few machines he genuinely admired, because it kept his beer cold.

Was he serious? Did he really mean that those who loved the wilderness should break the law to save it? Did he really believe that the laws of nature are more sacred than the laws of man?

Yes.

Edward Abbey was for pulling up stakes, literally and explicitly: "Always remove and destroy survey stakes, flagging, advertising signboards . . . and other such artifacts of industrialism."

The legacy of Edward Abbey is the triumph of literature. He stole the title of one of his last books from his own
readers' graffiti. Hayduke Lives is more than a threat,
more than a warning. It's a promise that sooner or later, the
dam will come down.

MURRAY KEMPTON

JACK NEWFIELD

MURRAY KEMPTON ONCE made me cry on the subway. It was in September of 1958, and I was reading his *New York Post* column, datelined from Sumner, Mississippi, on the trial of the men who lynched and mutilated fourteen-year-old Emmett Till. I was riding on the G train from my home in Bed-Stuy to my classes at Hunter College in the Bronx, when his deadline literature touched my romantic twenty-year-old heart.

This column described an uneducated sixty-four-year-old black sharecropper named Mose Wright, as he risked his life in rural, white supremacist Mississippi, to point out

Till's killers to an all-white jury that would deliver an acquittal in one hour.

Murray Kempton had the moral authority that comes only from special talent married to personal honor and grace. Presidents, mobsters, and the working people who read his column, all accepted his judgments as impartial and incorruptible. As a reporter, he was as much in a class by himself as Shakespeare or Sugar Ray Robinson were at their chosen crafts.

And his book on the 1930s, *Part of Our Time*, published in 1955, is as original and enduring as any nonfiction work of the last fifty years.

This book was written before Dr. King's victorious Montgomery bus boycott, and by a man still in his thirties. Still, one of the most visionary sentences in this book reads: "We have seen in the past few years, I think, the beginning of a revolution in the position or the Negro in America. It has been carried out by Negroes whose first decisive act was their rejection of the revolutionary myth."

But for all his premature maturity, Kempton never made much money in the newspaper business; he was in hock to the IRS for years. His books were out of print for years. He never compromised his dignity enough to become of those shouting heads on television. He once said, with typical, self-deprecating humility, "I can't remember many things I've ever done for the poor, beyond, of course, enduring a lifetime conscription in their ranks."

He never became much of a celebrity, except to his younger peers in the newspaper business. We watched him at trials, funerals, and political conventions the way rookie ballplayers once studied Ted Williams taking batting practice. Admirers talk about Kempton's intricate ironic prose style, but tend to forget how steely his moral judgment was on every big issue he covered. His commitment to honest reporting, his acute sense of history, and his indifference to fashion kept him ahead of the pack on McCarthyism; civil liberties; civil rights and racism; the Vietnam War and foreign interventionism; labor corruption; police abuses and prosecutorial excesses; human rights and democratic values.

His right/wrong batting average was much higher than his more celebrated contemporaries like Walter Lippmann, James Reston, and his own muse and fellow Baltimore native, H. L. Mencken. Part of Murray's strength was that, in his own head, he was composing his columns to inform his readers, not to appeal to our rulers. He was painfully aware of human weakness, so his opinions were usually tempered with forgiveness, proportion, and the possibility of redemption.

Murray once advised me to abstain from writing about public figures that I had strong emotions against, and confided that he had stopped writing about Albert Shanker and Rudy Giuliani because he was uneasy about how strident he sounded to himself, writing about them.

The range of Murray's learning was astonishing. He often quoted from the obscure (at least to me) seventeenth-century British historian, the Earl of Clarendon. He had studied William Tyndale's version of the Bible. He could quote from memory relevant passages from Henry James, Henry Adams, Yeats, Proust, and Bessie Smith. He knew the batting records of Willie Mays and the sidemen on all of Frank Sinatra's records. He even once won a Grammy for his liner notes on a Sinatra album. He could tell the excellent from the bogus in any genre.

When Murray died in May of 1997, the obituaries stressed his sympathies for rascals. But even where his actual views where more complex and changeable. He did enjoy the company of some gangsters like Fat Tony Salerno, who was sort of the Tip O'Neill of the underworld. But he had no time for the rest of the mob's predatory punks—at least, if they weren't being hunted by a prosecutor at the moment.

He was widely thought to approve of Jimmy Hoffa, but he told me, shortly before his death, in a taped interview, that Hoffa "was one of the worst guys I ever met."

He also helped tutor the young Kennedy brothers during the late 1950s about how to investigate some of the mob-ruled paper locals of the Teamsters. He saw labor corruption from the perspective of the rank-and-file truck drivers and retirees who lost their pensions. He was like a radical worker/priest in his approach to labor racketeering.

Murray did appreciate Sonny Liston, the ex-con, mob-owned heavyweight champion of the early 1960s. He saw Liston as a lower-class punching bag for snobbish moralists; And he wrote a wonderful columns about him on October 3, 1962, at a time when respectable society was trying to ban Liston. He wrote:

"We have at last a heavyweight champion on the moral level of the men who own him. Floyd Patterson sounded like a Freedom Rider. We return to reality with Liston. Liston has already helped us grow as a country, because he's the first morally inferior Negro I can think of to be given equal opportunity."

Murray's unique sensibility included what he described as "my losing-side consciousness." He attributed this to his family's roots in Southern aristocracy and their "Confederate view of everything." His great-grandfather wrote the Fugitive Slave Act of 1850.

He loved the tragic dignity of the doomed cause—the Loyalists in Spain, the Democratic Socialists of the 1930s, Adlai Stevenson in 1952, and Mose Wright taking the witness chair in Sumner, Mississippi. His affection for life's losers and underdogs helped shape his view of power, which seemed to be that almost anyone who captured political or corporate power had connived or cheated to get it. And so their authority was tainted. He felt that all winners were suspect, all governments abuse power.

Murray's politics were to oppose the king, regardless of what party the king was enrolled in. He had started out as a union organizer for the ILGWU, and as a labor reporter, and his basic kinship was always with working people, even more so after unions began to lose membership, and PATCO was broken by Ronald Reagan in 1981. Other columnists, who tracked trends and had a need to on the winning side of life, began to demean unions. But the striker on the picket remained central to Murray's "losing-side consciousness," as they had been when he wrote his labor-centered masterpiece, *Part of Our Time*. (The book's heroes are A. Philip Randolph and Walter Reuther.)

One scoundrel Murray wholly detested was J. Edgar Hoover, partly because Hoover reminded him of Allan Pinkerton, the nineteenth-century detective agency founder who used goons to break strikes for the railroad and steel trusts. Hoover called Murray "a snake" and "a rat," and assigned agents to follow Kempton and develop a file on this gentle patriot.

In conversation, Murray was a mordant spontaneous

wit. On the night of the Nixon-Humphrey election in 1968, I was with him. At 3:00 A.M., before the winner was clear, he announced he was going home to bed. I asked how he could leave before the outcome was known.

"I know Mayor Daley," he explained, "and he's not the sort of man who would steal the presidency from the same man twice." He said this in front of Kennedy in-law Steve Smith, who knew something of what happened in Chicago in 1960. Once I slipped into the seat next to him during the murder trial of Jean Harris. I asked what he thought of the proceedings so far. "I must say I was with her till the third shot," he said. "And, as you know, there were five!"

One year, the day before the St. Patrick's Day parade, Murray asked journalist Jim Dwyer if he was planning to march with his countrymen. "I don't think so," Dwyer responded. "I'm tired of seeing suburban kids throw up on the steps of the Metropolitan Museum."

"If they puked on the steps of the Whitney, I'm sure they would exhibit it," Murray, the traditionalist, replied, not missing a beat.

Murray Kempton was more fun to hang with than the Earl of Clarendon. Or even Dorothy Parker, the famous jukebox of wisecracks. At bottom, Murray Kempton was a dedicated reporter. He walked up all the tenement steps. He went to Sumner, Mississippi. Into his seventies he moved around the city on his bicycle, dressed like a gentleman, the earphones from his portable CD player draped around his neck, looking for truth and paradox.

He wrote better that the rest of us, and thought deeper than the rest of us. But the essence of what he did was to go, observe, and ask the impertinent question with impeccable manners. He much preferred to be called a reporter than the higher-status journalist, or columnist.

He won the Pulitzer Prize and two George Polk Awards, and quipped he was prouder of the Polk because it was "named for a reporter not a publisher."

Murray once interviewed the great comic performer Bert Lahr and shrewdly asked the actor how he kept his edge, and raised himself for the 512th performance of a role he was weary of. Lahr replied, "You can't ever be sure when someone who knows might come in to get out of the rain, and you wouldn't want him to catch you out."

Kempton took this to heart and then expanded on it in a speech he gave to a convention of reporters in 1978, telling the Lahr anecdote to set up his credo of professionalism. "You are never secure from the accidental attention of somebody who might, know," Kempton told us that night.

"The only final importance of newspapers may very well be that people leave them on subways. And on the lonely, morose grumble of the Rockaway Line, some Richard Wright, some James T. Farrell, some Norman Mailer, some Grace Paley—in the guise of an adolescent with his time to come—may pick you up, and, by heaven, you have a duty to be ready for cross-examination."

And I remembered myself, at twenty reading Murray's column on the subway, and being moved to tears, by the courage of Mose Wright, and the thought of a dead boy.

ROBERT FRANK

ADAM SHATZ

IN 1947, A twenty-two-year-old Swiss photographer named Robert Frank wrote his parents from New York. "This country is really a free country," he marveled. "Nobody asks to see your identification papers."

Flash-forward eight years. It's November 7, 1955, and Frank is driving with his wife, Mary, and their two young children, Andrea and Pablo, in Little Rock, Arkansas, when they are pulled to the side of the road by a police officer, Lieutenant R. E. Brown, who notices their New York license plates. Papers, please. In his report, Brown noted that "the individual later identified as Robert Frank of

New York" was in need of "a haircut and a shave," that he spoke with "a strong foreign accent," and that he had a lot of photographic equipment in the back of his car, not to mention a pile of maps, some of whose directions were marked in red. He had a Jewish name and a Jewish employer, and you know how those Jews like to stir up racial tension. This wasn't enough to indict him, even in the Jim Crow South, but it suggested to Lieutenant Brown that the man he'd stopped was guilty of something, so he took him in for questioning. For the next several hours, Frank was grilled by a counterespionage specialist who wanted to make sure that he wasn't working on behalf of a "foreign or hostile power of Communist persuasion."

Three days later, Frank was released without charge. And yet the Arkansas policeman wasn't entirely wrong in suspecting him. For the man they arrested *was* a subversive, just not the kind they were looking for. Traveling across the country with his Leica in a beat-up Ford on a fellowship from the Guggenheim Foundation, Frank was compiling what he called "a visual study of a civilization" that laid siege to the self-congratulatory clichés of Eisenhower's America. *The Americans*, the book of eighty-three photographs that emerged from Frank's road trip, is perhaps the most influential work of postwar American photography. Today, Frank's America is discernible not only in the photography of Gary Winogrand and Lee Friedlander, but in the documentaries of D. A. Pennebaker and Albert Maysles, in the films of John Cassavetes, Bob Rafelson and Jim Jarmusch, and in the music of Bob Dylan and Tom Waits.

What made *The Americans* so unsettling (and so unnerving to would-be witch-hunters) is that it wasn't explicitly a work of social protest whose "message" could be identified, digested, and neutralized. Frank wasn't a rebel in the traditional sense of speaking truth to power; he had no desire to address power in the first place. His revolt cut far deeper than the usual left-wing critiques. As alert as he was to racial oppression and social exclusion—themes at the center of *The Americans*—he was even more interested in the spiritual poverty of this most God-fearing of lands. Although much in America has changed since 1958—not enough, but much—one thing remains as true today as it was then: It's one thing to question the justice of American society and quite another to question The Dream. To be sure, a nation wouldn't be a nation without a healthy supply of illusions. Still, it's hard to imagine a country that believes more fervently that it is a happy—no, the happiest—place to live. In *The Americans,* Frank explored a different America; sad, desperate, and not altogether sure of itself; an America that, to many viewers, looked like another country.

Robert Frank was born in 1924 to Jewish parents in Zurich. His mother was Swiss; his father, a prosperous interior designer who painted in his spare time, was a German citizen who had emigrated to Switzerland after World War I. On November 25, 1941, the family suddenly became stateless when Hitler denied citizenship to German Jews. Four years later, Robert Frank acquired Swiss citizenship, but his childhood was racked by insecurity. "Being Jewish and living with the threat of Hitler," he once suggested, "must have been a big part of my understanding of people that were put down or held back." As a teenager, he apprenticed in the studio of

Michael Wolgensinger, a graduate of the Bauhaus who believed photography's mission was to "convey essence, form and atmosphere"—a mission Frank assumed as his own, although his sense of "essence, form and atmosphere" would be distinctly less classical than his mentor's. In his early twenties, he read Sartre's existential trilogy, *The Roads to Freedom*, and discovered the work of Paul Senn and Werner Bischof, whose unsentimental photographs of war-ravaged Europe strengthened his conviction that peaceful, complacent Switzerland was "too closed, too small for me," and that it was time to see the world for what it was. In February 1947 he boarded the Liberty ship, freighter S.S. *James Bennett Moore* en route to New York. There he presented a book of forty photographs to Alexey Brodovitch, the distinguished art director for *Harper's Bazaar*, who hired him on the spot. He worked for Brodovitch until the following year, when *Harper's Bazaar* shut down its in-house photography studio. Not one to stick around for long in any one place, Frank traveled throughout South America and Europe. He came back to New York in 1953 with a trove of haunting images: coal-smudged Welsh miners and London bankers stiffly attired in black hats, Spanish parades and Parisian streets, peasant celebrations in Peru and desolate roads in Bolivia. On his travels, Frank came to view picture taking as a kind of visual diary, transforming objective facts into personal ruminations, refining an astonishingly lyrical understanding of the play of light and shadow, and juxtaposing images in a manner that infused them with meanings more intense than they might have possessed alone. The photojournalist made himself into an artist without

ever ceasing to be a reporter of fact, as if art were simply
a heightened form of documentary observation.

Two years after returning to New York, Frank submitted
a proposal to the Guggenheim Foundation:

> What I have in mind is observation and record of what one nat-
> uralized American finds to see in the United States that signi-
> fies the kind of civilization born here and spreading elsewhere
> . . . . I speak of the things that are there, anywhere and every-
> where—easily found, not easily selected and interpreted. A
> small catalog comes to the mind's eye: a town at night, a
> parking lot, a supermarket, a highway, the man who owns three
> cars and the man who owns none, the farmer and his children,
> a new house and a warped clapboard house, the dictation of
> taste, the dream of grandeur, advertising, neon lights, the faces
> of the leaders and the faces of the followers, gas tanks and
> post offices and backyards.

The proposal is telling for a number of reasons. Notice,
first of all, that Frank emphasizes that his view represents
the subjective, therefore limited, findings of "one naturalized American." This was to be, as he put it, a "spontaneous
record of a man seeing this country for the first time"—the
perspective of a man who was then in the process of
applying for citizenship, for whom traveling across the
country was a way of becoming a part of it. Also note the
phrase "finds to see," which, awkward though it is, under-
scores Frank's interest in things that one might not otherwise see (or find worthy of photographing). And what are
these things that one has to "find" in order to "see" them?
They are, paradoxically, the most apparently obvious things

of all, the things that are "there, anywhere and everywhere," the things right in front of our noses. And it is these things, he suggests, not the Lincoln Memorial or Mount Rushmore, not the Grand Canyon or the Empire State Building, that comprise America's civilization.

Frank received the grant, in part thanks to letters on his behalf from his American mentor Walker Evans (whose 1938 *American Photographs* served as a model for *The Americans*), Brodovitch, Meyer Schapiro, and Edward Steichen. From 1955 to 1956, he crossed the United States in the Ford that Peggy Guggenheim had given him, often in the company of his family. He went everywhere, guided by an insatiable desire to see the many faces of America: rich and poor, black and white, urban and rural, sacred and profane. According to his friend Jack Kerouac, Frank prowled like a cat when he worked, moving quickly, hungrily, and, more often than not, furtively around his subjects. He seldom spoke to people, most of whom weren't aware that they were being photographed. He often kept his Leica hidden under a coat or jacket, revealing it only when he was ready to shoot, and sometimes took his pictures from the hip or chest. He used whatever light there was, as a result of which some of his pictures are underlit, others overexposed; they aren't masterpieces of composition, and they're not meant to be. To say that they lack a clear subject, that they're off-balance or out-of-focus is true, but it's about as insightful as saying that Thelonious Monk's playing seems choppy. That he took all of his pictures in black and white was no accident. "Black and white is the vision of hope and despair," he explained. "This is what I want in my photographs." By the time his trip was over, he'd shot some 687 rolls of film—about 20,000 photographs. Of these he selected eighty-three, making *The Americans* a triumph not only of vision, but of editing and montage.

What do we "find to see," as Frank might have said, in those eighty-three images? A country frankly observed, stripped bare of patriotic sloganeering. A country where the flag serves less as a symbol of pride than as a kind of veil, shielding Americans from an honest assessment of themselves, their lives, their mythologies. A country divided by race, class, and religion, where white babies are groomed to lord over the black women who raise them, where preachers sell salvation as if it were lemonade. A country so vast and sprawling and diverse it hardly seems accurate to call it a nation. A country where the hopes are large and the pleasures small. Which isn't to mock the hopes, the sincerity of which he understood, or slight the pleasures, which Frank evoked as well as anyone. As Kerouac observed in his shrewd, beautiful introduction to *The Americans*, "That crazy feeling in America when the sun is hot on the streets and the music comes out of the jukebox or from a nearby funeral, that's what Robert Frank has captured."

Photography is among the most invasive, indeed aggressive of arts; its fundamental drive is to capture—or, in a more belligerent metaphor, to "shoot"—things in its field of vision, especially things it hasn't seen before. (Writers do the same thing, but they betray their subjects at a distance.) That the camera has flourished in America is to be expected. What artistic tool better embodies the pioneering spirit? On the road, Frank made his share of visual conquests: black motorcyclists, Puerto Rican drag queens, Hasidim overlooking the East River, a gaunt, wrinkled

Jehovah's witness selling *Awake!* And yet there is hardly a trace of exoticism or of the freak show (as in Diane Arbus), no hint of the collector's pride. Frank isn't unveiling a world for our delectation or amusement. Still less is he appealing for our moral sympathy or political solidarity, in the manner of engagé photographers from Riis to Salgado. Insofar as these photographs contain a "message," it is, in Kerouac's apt summary, "This is the way we are in real life and if you don't like it I don't know anything about it 'cause I'm living my own way." Frank's drag queens look flirtatious and inviting rather than tragic, as comfortable in their world as "we" are in ours.

Other subjects make it clear they'd rather not be disturbed, protesting his unexpected intrusion into their lives. Frank is said to be especially fond of the photograph of a black man and woman lounging on a hill in San Francisco. Suddenly aware of his presence, they stare back at him, as if to counter his attempt to shoot them. Is the look on their faces one of anger or defiance or fear? What is their relation, and what were they talking about before they were interrupted? Frank leaves the enigma intact, so much so that it nearly becomes the true subject of the frame. "When people look at my pictures I want them to feel the way they do when they read a line of a poem twice," he said. His "obsession," he also said, is "to reveal and to hide the truth." Then again, "maybe nothing is really true. Except what's out there. And what's out there is always changing." Drag queens aside, very few of the photographs in *The Americans* were of people or places that Americans hadn't seen before. (Whether they'd acknowledged them is another matter.) Frank photographed bars, lunch counters, cars, trolleys, funerals, barbershops, cocktail parties, casinos, parades, political ralleys, newsstands, factories, men's rooms, banks, department stores, university commencements, roads, rivers, casinos, and drive-ins. It wasn't what Frank photographed so much as how he did so that proved so disconcerting. After all, there's nothing more startling than a familiar thing seen in a different light. As the curator and critic John Szarkowski observed, the emblems of Americana, the most public features of American life, "looked different in Frank's pictures: shabbier, and somehow suddenly hopeless." He suggested—with cool detachment, not handwringing—the pathos underneath the pageantry, the loneliness of all those crowds. And if there is one theme that resonates more powerfully than any in Frank's images, it is solitude, an experience with which most of his Americans seemed to be bitterly acquainted. Look, for example, at the politician in the photograph entitled "Political Rally—Chicago." There is no audience to be seen, just the speaker, a little man speechifying from a ledge with his mouth wide open, his arms outstretched, one of which is reflected in the window behind him. To the extent that he's having a dialogue, it would appear to be with himself. Frank wasn't blind to the freedoms of American life. The road appears in his photographs as a promise of mobility and adventure, the "hope" offsetting the "despair" of the settled existence. And yet one has the sense, looking at the Americans' faces, of a people adrift, wandering in search of a salvation that never arrives; a people whose sorrow is directly proportional to their belief in the Dream.

No publisher in New York wanted to publish *The*

Americans, which was first published in 1958 in France by Robert Delpire under the title *Les Américains,* with a selection of anti-American essays that might have landed a conviction in Little Rock. When Grove Press published it the following year, with the introduction by Kerouac, recently made famous by the publication of *On the Road,* the reviews were, in a classic case of reaction formation, almost uniformly hostile. "Chicago has more valid facets to its personality than haranguing politicians," James M. Zanutto complained in *Popular Photography,* "New York more than candy stores and homosexuals."

Several critics harped on its alleged stylistic deficiencies, much as jazz critics suggested that Ornette Coleman avoided chords because he didn't know how to play changes. Today one can have only pity for them; they were fully in step with the times, only the times they were a-changing. This was just a few years after Allen Ginsberg read "Howl" to a Beatnik soiree in San Francisco, and a year before Cassavetes's *Shadows* and Coleman's *The Shape of Jazz to Come.* As much as Coleman's free associations on his plastic saxophone, Ginsberg's hallucinatory ode to drug experimentation and ass fucking, and Cassavetes's jump cutting, Frank's grainy, improvisatory approach ("spontaneous glance—accident truth" was how Ginsberg described it) defined the new sensibility. None of these works was avowedly political; none identified problems in need of remedy (why fret over the problem when you already know the solution—FREEDOM!); none had a movement to fall back on. They were profoundly individual acts of rebellion, staged by people who couldn't help themselves. And yet all suggested, and encouraged, shifts in consciousness that were occurring in the minds of thousands of young Americans, shifts that would assume dramatic, and collective, political form during the upheavals of the 1960s.

After *The Americans,* Frank all but abandoned still photography until the early 1970s. He made *Pull My Daisy,* a film with Alfred Leslie and the Beats, and *Cocksucker Blues,* an exceedingly unflattering documentary about the Rolling Stones, which the Stones fought to have banned. (Frank's photographs provided the cover of the band's dissolute masterpiece of Americana, *Exile on Main Street,* a worthy companion piece to *The Americans.*) With its narrative juxtapositions and intricate use of motifs (flags, crosses, the Road, the jukebox), *The Americans* implied a shift toward moving pictures, but Frank was never as masterly a filmmaker as he was a photographer.

When he returned to photography in the early 1970s, he was living in Nova Scotia with a new wife, the painter June Leaf, and he was interested in a different, and no less troubled region of the mind, that of family intimacy—his own. In 1974 his daughter Andrea perished in a plane crash over Guatemala; his son Pablo began to show signs of mental illness. Like Dylan after the motorcycle accident, like Godard after his faith in Maoism collapsed, Frank turned inward, taking color Polaroids of his family, of the house they shared, of rooms left uninhabited by the dead, of the water and skies of Nova Scotia. He set his pictures up in rough, poetic sequences and jotted painfully confessional notes on them—cries, pleas—as if, like one of his Americans, he were hoping for some kind of illumination. Only, unlike them, he knows it isn't coming. Photographing in color,

Frank caught more of the despair than the hope. These are photographs of "desperation and endurance," qualities Frank said he admired in New Yorkers. For all their beauty—and Frank has become a painter of gesture, working mainly from his home rather than the road—his late photographs offer no promise of redemption. Artistry is their only consolation, and one suspects that, for Frank, that's no consolation at all.

Visceral though it is, Frank's family album is strangely less communicative than *The Americans*, a work of "journalism" that has the intimate power of fiction. And its meaning, like that of the best fiction, has evolved with time. The kinetic force that Kerouac responded to has mellowed, giving way to the somberness of an elegy. More important, the photographs no longer strike us as the work of a "naturalized American." Frank, who got his passport five years after the publication of *The Americans*, has spent the last three decades in Canada, and still speaks (when he speaks, which isn't often) with a German accent. And yet, like Tocqueville's writings on American democracy and the great films noirs of émigré directors like Fritz Lang, Billy Wilder, and Max Ophuls, his vision of this country, by turns loving and alienated, incisive and mystified, has become naturalized. America hasn't looked the same since.

PAUL O'DWYER

JIM CALLAGHAN

PAUL O'DWYER has J. Edgar Hoover, of all people, to thank for the summing up of his life's work: "He is an agin'er," Hoover noted in O'Dwyer's FBI file. And so he was. Civil libertarian. Lifelong friend of underdogs. Antiwar protester. Indefatigable foe of tyrants everywhere. Almost from the day he landed on a New York dock in 1925 with $25 in his pocket, he did justice to the memory of his hero Tom Paine, the pamphleteer who inspired the American Revolution with *Common Sense*.

I met O'Dwyer in the summer of 1968 when he was running for a New York U.S. Senate seat on an antiwar platform.

I was twenty-one and he was sixty-one, but he was a hero to my generation. I had heard some stories about his defense of those who the Irish patriot Wolfe Tone called "the men of no property." In that chaotic summer, he was with the young protestors, leading a candlelight march in the streets of Chicago against the President of the United States, Lyndon Johnson, and Mayor Richard Daley's Gestapo.

Later, in 1974, O'Dwyer hired me to be one of his special assistants at City Hall. He became my mentor and could be, sometimes during the course of one day, funny, demanding, winsome, tough, angry—but always supportive; there wasn't a trace of morbid Irish sentimentality about him. I met friends of his who had fought in the Spanish Civil War and had served in the Irish Republican Army in 1916, as well as people like Isabel Allende and Cesar Chavez. Still, not all of his clients or friends were famous. I heard about the Puerto Rican woman he had represented for free when she sued New York's Board of Elections. She—and hundreds of thousands of others—had been forced to take a literacy test in English and O'Dwyer had taken her case all the way to the U.S. Supreme Court—and won. I discovered that he had worked his way through law school as a longshoreman on the city's piers. And his talk about the rights of workers wasn't just idle chatter. In 1968, after he won the Democratic primary for the U.S. Senate seat, he was offered free national television exposure for an interview show. Upon his arrival at the studio, union strikers greeted him. When a producer suggested he sneak in through a side door, O'Dwyer was livid. "I walk in picket lines," he said, grabbing a placard. "I don't cross them."

Until I met him, I never realized the depth of his involvement in the movement for social change, starting in the 1930s and ending in the 1990s. I never knew he was a gun-runner for Israel, or that he spent $16,000 of his own money in 1963 to defend Kentucky coal miners—abandoned by the corrupt leaders of the United Mine Workers—or that his political career suffered because of his stalwart defense of civil rights and civil liberties. His City Hall staffers were called "O'Dwyer's radical kids" by the constables on patrol at City Hall; he was teaching us an important lesson about life: Things aren't always as simple as they appear to be. He told the writers Jimmy Breslin and Pete Hamill to make sure they went to see the "other side" when visiting the north of Ireland in the '70s, where a war of liberation was raging. By that he meant the hard-line paramilitary Unionists—supporters of the British—who he thought held the key to any peace settlement. In fact, O'Dwyer had become friends with Unionists, who were some of the most hated men in the Irish-nationalist ghettoes of Belfast and Derry. He told me that his sense of justice was based on watching the marauding British troops terrorize his country during the Irish War of Independence that started in 1916. "I thought that to come to America and to treat others the way the Irish were treated would be a betrayal of my heritage," he said. "It was all about fair play."

Indeed, O'Dwyer had a genetic disdain for bullies, which led him to the cause of young dreamers trying to establish a new nation called Israel in 1947. While world philosophers endlessly debated the issue and his left-wing friends castigated him, O'Dwyer raised hundreds of thousands of dollars to buy bazookas and other arms for the freedom fighters to defend themselves against the British as they tried to snuff out the country before it was born. O'Dwyer became the stakeholder for the Hagannah and was trusted enough to handle the cash that was used to buy weapons for the fledgling army of resistance. Here he was—a lawyer whose brother was New York's mayor, risking not only arrest but disbarment for committing a felony that would have led to the loss of his right to practice his profession.

O'Dwyer felt that a lawyer's obligation was to defend those getting a raw shake. He fervently believed in the "right to counsel," and didn't much care what anyone thought of his clients. His sixty years as a lawyer included many pro bono cases where he kicked in his own money to save the day. One of those cases was in 1971 in Harrisburg, Pennsylvania, when he helped Daniel Berrigan escape a jail sentence ("I think he was disappointed," O'Dwyer laughed later) with his devastating cross-examination of Hoover's star witness, the paid informant Boyd Douglas. O'Dwyer believed that any year where you just "made money" as a lawyer was a wasted one. He ran six times for elected office, and won only twice. He was too liberal for the Irish, too Irish for the liberals, and not enough of a Cold Warrior for the Social Democrats. The highest office he held was City Council President, first in line of succession to the mayoralty, during New York's hard fiscal times in the mid-1970s. It was then that New York Governor Hugh Carey discovered just how much of an agin'er O'Dwyer, then in his late '60s, really was. When Carey and his coterie of rich businessmen were plotting ways to remove New York's Mayor Abe Beame from office for alleged malfeasance, misfeasance, and nonfeasance, it suddenly occurred to Carey that O'Dwyer was next in line to be mayor. "He's too damn fucking radical," Carey said. "We can't let that happen." This led to an inside joke between Beame and O'Dwyer. "Don't worry Abe, for as long as I'm around, I'm your insurance," O'Dwyer would say ruefully. Carey was angry because O'Dwyer's pro-worker sensibilities led him to suggest that the city file for bankruptcy and postpone paying the interest on billions of dollars of city bonds, something which countries around the world have since done. For O'Dwyer, it was an easy decision: He thought it was madness to pay millionaire bankers first while laying off 30,000 workers, including teachers, cops, and firefighters. When David Rockefeller and others charged the city high interest rates in its moment of need, O'Dwyer seethed. He stood alone among city officials in calling it "highway robbery."

O'Dwyer earned his first entry in his FBI file in 1941 for battling prosecutors in FDR's Justice Department when they tried to deport Harold Obermaier of the hotel trades union for being a "subversive," Paul's favorite type of person. Indeed, the more powerful the foe, the more of a challenge it was to O'Dwyer. Long before anyone ever heard of Jackie Robinson, O'Dwyer and others formed a committee during World War II called "End Jim Crow in Baseball." They regularly picketed the three New York baseball stadiums, demanding that the owners hire blacks. Their efforts led the mayor to appoint a sports committee to study ways to desegregate baseball. The political pressure ultimately led to the signing of Robinson in 1945. The familial love he felt for his brother Bill, New York's progressive mayor from 1946 to 1950, didn't stop him from taking on the city administration, either. The brothers sometimes would go for months without talking to each other, mainly because of positions that Paul took that were at odds with Bill's positions. Two years before Joe McCarthy arrived on the national stage, O'Dwyer was redbaited by Bill when he ran for Congress in 1948. He accused his younger brother Paul of associating with too many Communists in the American Labor Party. "I couldn't argue with him on the facts," Paul told me years later. "But I just wish he would have picked a more appropriate time to say it."

The following year, he took on his brother's appointees on the city's Board of Education when it voted to ban a book about Paine. He sued his brother's administration and the Metropolitan Life Insurance Company when they received city tax abatements to build a sprawling housing project in Manhattan that openly banned blacks. O'Dwyer identified easily with the struggle for civil rights; he connected it to the pain of Belfast and Derry, and his native country's long suffering. "I first met Paul in 1947 on a picket line to protest the whites-only Levittown housing development in Long Island," said Percy Sutton, a prominent black politician, at O'Dwyer's funeral in 1998 (he was 91). "Housing which would keep us out, African-Americans, veterans, including some of us who wore the uniforms of our unit, the Tuskegee Airmen. When he joined us that day and later spoke out in support of our cause, we saw in him an eloquent and ferocious warrior in that which we knew even then would be a long struggle to remove the barricades of indignities, injustices, and inequities injuring our lives." Sutton and New York Congressman Charles Rangel always talk about O'Dwyer being with them in the Deep South, representing young blacks arrested for trying to register voters in the early 1960s—an action that earned him the sobriquet of "nigger-lover" among his fellow Irish. (That is what I heard when I was campaigning for him door-to-door in my working-class Irish neighborhood in 1968.) He was also one of the attorneys for Fannie Lou Hamer and the black members of the Mississippi Freedom Democratic Party when they challenged Lyndon Johnson at the Democratic National Convention in 1964.

But it wasn't just about being a lawyer. In the summer of 1966, he put his own life at risk by marching with James Meredith, after his shooting, to complete the freedom march from Jackson, Mississippi, to Selma, Alabama. O'Dwyer's FBI file, which ended in 1976, is a road map to his radicalism. It is clear that his phones were tapped and that Hoover had agents following him to meetings. Hoover declared him a national security risk and a threat to the president. (The biggest "threat" to the president came when O'Dwyer lent his Wall Street law offices to the "Dump Johnson" movement in 1966. It was there he and his co-conspirators planned strategies to end the Vietnam War.)

Like Paine, who died in obscurity, O'Dwyer faded from the radar of popular political culture after his defeat for re-election as City Council President in 1977, but he continued to play a role in the city's politics and the Irish civil rights struggle, still unsettled nearly seventy years after he arrived in his adopted city. He helped elect his friend David Dinkins as the city's first black mayor in 1989. He told me it was one of the happiest days of his life even though "it took too long." He served as the city's ambassador to the United Nations. In 1992, he convinced Bill Clinton to stay in the presidential race, telling him he was the only person who could bring peace to Ireland. And he never relented in his defense of those who were getting pushed around. One of his last public acts, at the age of eighty-six, was to fight again with his fellow Irish in 1993 when the St. Patrick's Day parade committee vented their homophobia in public by denying the Irish Lesbian and Gay Organization the right to march with their banner. He spoke on their behalf and advised them to apply for their own permit to march. For O'Dwyer, it was just another day at the office—the sense of fair play that he learned from his parents in his native heath was again being assaulted. As Percy Sutton said in his eulogy: "Please be assured that in no time at all, Paul will protest some injustice that he will find in his place of final abode. Paul will protest because it is in his nature to protest."

CÉSAR CHAVEZ

PETER EDELMAN

ROBERT KENNEDY ALWAYS said one person could make a difference. When he met someone who was making a difference he connected. Sometimes the result was a friendship that lasted until one of them died.

So it was with César Chavez. Sometime in early 1966 (I was working for Robert Kennedy in his Senate office), I received a call from Jack Conway, the head of the Industrial Union Department of the AFL-CIO and a top lieutenant to Walter Reuther of the United Auto Workers. He asked if I could get Kennedy to go to California to participate in some Senate subcommittee hearings on the grape strike going on out there. (There was actually a Senate Subcommittee on Migratory Labor. Those were the days.) Conway said he and Reuther would appreciate it if Kennedy would attend. His presence would assure national attention for the hearings and the union's organizing campaign.

Conway said there was a young Mexican-American labor leader named César Chavez whose United Farm Workers were an AFL-CIO union, and he wanted to get them on the national map. I had read a favorable article about Chavez in the *New Republic* that was written by my friend, Andy Kopkind, so Conway's call resonated.

There had never been a successful effort to organize farmworkers in the United States, and there hadn't even been a serious attempt for years. Their wages were horribly low, working conditions terrible, housing awful, and coverage by the laws protecting other workers nonexistent. The growers often reneged on promised wages, and typically provided no toilet facilities in the hot sun of the fields. If the workers complained, they were fired. A steady supply of legal immigrants was available to replace them, courtesy of federal government policy.

I walked into Kennedy's office and said something not much more complicated than, "Jack Conway called and said . . ." and then—quickly—grape strike, Walter Reuther, César Chavez, Andy Kopkind. He said fine, he'd be glad to go.

I said to myself, what does he mean, fine. Doesn't he want to know more? But this was a man who operated in shorthand, so I thought okay, fine means fine. A few weeks later we got on the plane to go to the hearings, and right after the plane had taken off Kennedy turned to me and said, "Why the hell am I dragging my ass all the way to California?" Probably stammering a little, I said again what I had said in his office, and he seemed satisfied. At least, he didn't press the matter.

The main focus of the hearings was the campaign by the United Farm Workers to organize some vineyards owned by the Schenley Corporation. The UFW figured that Schenley, as a major national corporation, wouldn't want the embarrassment of resisting an organizing effort and would cave fairly easily, laying the groundwork for actions against other growers.

The hearings were already under way when we arrived in Delano, California, the headquarters of Chavez's union. It was almost time for lunch when we walked into the high school auditorium where the hearings were taking place. The county sheriff was testifying. He was explaining that he had ordered the arrest of the pickets, who had all been on the highway and not on private property, because he was concerned about their safety and wanted to protect them. Kennedy listened for a few minutes, until it was his turn to question. He pressed the sheriff on why deputies had taken pictures of the pickets, and then elicited the fact that people were being arrested even though they had not violated the law. He asked, "How can you go arrest somebody if they haven't violated the law?"

"They're ready to violate the law," the sheriff replied.

It now being time for lunch, Kennedy said, "Can I suggest in the interim period of time . . . that the sheriff and the district attorney read the Constitution of the United

States?" The auditorium, packed with farmworkers and their supporters, erupted in applause.

In the parking lot Kennedy and Chavez met. It was a riveting scene. They bonded immediately. Chavez, himself a child of poor farmworkers, had a mystical quality. He was a very quiet man, short in stature, with a face that was as purely kind in its appearance as that of any human being I have ever seen. The two of them stood talking, eye to eye, in a low conversational tone that was barely audible even to the first ring of people around them. A crowd gathered, two deep, then four deep, and finally ten or fifteen people deep. It went on for maybe five minutes, maybe even ten. I don't know what they said to each other. I do know that when it was over they were friends for life.

Chavez's commitment to the cause of justice for farmworkers was formed out of bitter personal experience. Until he was eleven, his parents had a farm and some small businesses, in southwestern Arizona right near the Mexican border. They were forced into the migrant labor stream when they lost the farm to foreclosure in 1938. Maybe Chavez understood the injustice and the exploitation of the migrant life more pointedly because he had experienced something better.

After serving in the U.S. Navy during World War II, Chavez went to work organizing in the Mexican-American community to get people to register and vote, and in 1962 he turned to the hard challenge of trying to start a farmworkers union. All the while he had been reading and thinking about how to organize a union where the employers have an unlimited supply of immigrant labor to replace people who go out on strike. He had stopped his formal schooling in the eighth grade, but his voracious reading had steeped him in the tactics of Gandhian nonviolence, which served as the template for his organizing.

By the time Chavez and Kennedy met, Chavez's nonviolence had become a spiritual mandate as well as an unflagging tactic. Kennedy's support, following on that of Walter Reuther, brought wide public attention, and wider and wider circles of public support, especially in the religious community. Immediately in the wake of Kennedy's visit Chavez undertook a 245-mile walk to the state capital in Sacramento, by the end of which his feet were blistered and he needed a cane to walk, but he garnered several new contracts, including Schenley.

Chavez and Kennedy stayed in close touch. Kennedy was the farmworkers' best friend in Washington. The national attention attracted by Chavez's organizing helped get the minimum wage extended to farmworkers—thirty years after the national minimum wage had been enacted for most other workers. There were more hearings, and Kennedy showed up to ask grower witnesses a simple question: "Why won't you let these workers vote on whether they want a union?" When they squirmed, he pressed. His prosecutorial skills, infamous in the view of some of his detractors, were being put to a new and quite different use.

In 1968, as Kennedy was vacillating about whether to run for President, Chavez undertook a public fast to dramatize what was now an effort to effectuate a national boycott of all California grapes. He sent word to Kennedy that he would break the fast only if Kennedy would join him as he did so. The union's staff were deeply worried about the damage the fast was doing to Chavez's health, and they said so with more urgency in each succeeding telephone call. Kennedy was worried, too. He finally found a time when he could go, on the day following a political speech in Des Moines, when he was already halfway across the country. By then the fast had gone on for twenty-five days.

The subtext was plain throughout the series of conversations —the boycott would get far more public attention if Kennedy were linked to it. Yet no one mentioned this point, and everyone was truly more concerned about the effect the fast was having on Chavez. I always thought Chavez knew that endangering himself would help get Kennedy there. But Chavez was getting him there for the cause, *para la causa*. And Kennedy must have known that, too.

On March 10, 1968, as Kennedy flew to Delano to be with Chavez, he told me and John Seigenthaler and Ed Guthman, who had been his closest aides in the Justice Department, that he had decided to run for President. The New Hampshire primary took place two days later, and Kennedy announced his candidacy four days after that. Did Chavez's jeopardizing his health for his cause set an example that influenced Kennedy as he wrestled with his own course? No one knows, but we do know that his fervent support of Chavez paid off politically. Chavez organized Mexican-Americans to register and vote in the presidential primary in California, and contributed substantially to Kennedy's win there.

Chavez became world famous, and the target of virulent opposition. Frustrated growers fomented break-ins at the union's offices, the Teamsters Union tried to muscle in on the contracts the union had won, growers brought well-financed lawsuits for damages allegedly caused by the union's boycotts, and Chavez was the object of at least two assassination plots. On the other hand, Governor Jerry Brown was a strong supporter, and in 1975 convinced the California legislature to pass a state Agricultural Labor Relations Act, which gave California farmworkers the legal right to organize that eludes them nationally to this day. Chavez kept up the fight against all the continuing resistance, and finally passed away in 1993 at a relatively young sixty-six years of age, his health broken by the repeated fasts he had undertaken.

What Kennedy saw that day in March 1966 was the real thing. Chavez was a quiet (and very determined) man and a devout Catholic. He never owned a house or a car, and never made more than $6,000 in a year. He didn't think of himself as a union organizer but as the steward of a movement for social justice for Mexican-Americans generally. César Chavez was a man who made a difference.

JOE LOUIS

BUDD SCHULBERG

RALPH ELLISON'S *Invisible Man* was an apt title for the entire black race in America in the 1930s. In the eyes of white people, they simply did not exist. The *New York Times'* boast that it printed "all the news that's fit to print," should have added, "for white people." When young Joe Louis was winning amateur boxing titles in the early '30s, the outstanding black men in our country were ignored. W.E.B. Du Bois and A. Phillip Randolph were nonpersons to every white newspaper. Even famous entertainers like Louis Armstrong, Paul Robeson, and Bill "Bojangles" Robinson were barely mentioned. For a black baseball player to play in the big leagues was unthinkable. The National Football League was no better, and as for the colleges, when a Southern college objected to playing Columbia with its one Negro player, New York's great liberal arts college obligingly dropped him from the line-up.

It's only against that backdrop of know-nothing racial prejudice that the impact of Joe Louis can be understood. The heart of the Joe Louis story is his historic break through the race barrier. Almost a hundred years ago, there was another great black heavyweight, Jack Johnson, but there was no way he could challenge for the heavyweight title in America. He had to chase the champion all over the world before finally catching up with him in Australia. There he beat on the hapless white Tommy Burns so fiercely that the police finally intervened at the end of the fourteenth round.

The myopic racism of the day was nakedly expressed by Jack London, at ringside to cover the fight for the *New York Herald*. "He is a white man and so am I," wrote this avowed socialist who preached international understanding (apparently for whites only). "Naturally I want the white man to win." And when Johnson's hand was raised, London called on the undefeated ex-champion, Jim Jeffries, to come out of retirement to put this overweening black boy in his place. "But one thing remains," London begged in his postmortem for the *Herald*, "Jeffries must emerge from his alfalfa farms and remove that smile from Johnson's face. Jeff, it's up to you."

"The Fight Between the White Champion and the Black Champion," as it was billed in Reno in 1910, was less a boxing match than a primitive tableaux in bitter race relations. In Jeffries's corner were all the previous champions, the impassioned Caucasians John L. Sullivan, Bob Fitzsimmons, and "Gentleman" Jim Corbett, who mouthed racist epithets at Johnson through the fight. When the hopelessly overmatched old champion finally went down for the count, a deathly silence fell over the crowd. As our bereft Jack London typed out his lead, "Once again has Johnson sent down to defeat the chosen representative of the white race," race riots were breaking out all over the country.

As a resented black champion in a rabid white world, Johnson did nothing to endear himself. In a time of uptight segregation, Johnson not only consorted with white women but flaunted them, lording it around Chicago in a chauffeur-driven open phaeton with two white women all over him. The entrance to his notorious nightclub, Cafe de Champion, displayed a blow-up photo of him liplocking with his white wife. Her suicide, partly due to his having so many other white lovers, including a scandalous affair with his 18-year-old white secretary, provoked a lynch atmosphere, with Johnson being railroaded to jail, jumping bond to escape to Europe, leaving behind the unwritten law of boxing: no more black heavyweight champions.

It may have been unwritten in the 1910s and '20s, but it was adhered to as faithfully as if it had been engraved in stone. After the gifted troublemaker Johnson held up his black middle finger to white America, there would be eight successive flour-faced champions through the 1920s and into the late '30s. The most frustrating example of a heavyweight contender being denied his deserved title shot because of the wrong pigmentation was Harry Wills.

When Wills knocked out a brace of white contenders and clearly outclassed "The Wild Bull of the Pampas," Louis Firpo, famous for his fight with Jack Dempsey, the New York State Athletic Commission finally made Wills its Number One contender, ruling that Dempsey could not defend his title until he met Wills. Dempsey's promoter, the same old foxy Tex Rickard from Johnson-Jeffries days, finessed that one by taking his champion to Philadelphia to face Gene Tunney. The white race was saved again.

As a young fight fan growing up in Los Angeles, I knew an impressive heavyweight by the name of George Godfrey. When I asked him about fighting in Madison Square Garden, in those days the pot of gold at the end of every boxer's rainbow, he shook his head. "Only if I lost, son. My color can't win in the Garden." That was the hard truth when teenaged Joe Louis was coming out of the Bottoms, a ghetto within the ghetto in hard-times Detroit. When Joe's discoverer, John Roxborough, the soft-spoken community-minded numbers man from Detroit, and the hard-nosed numbers boss Julian Black in Chicago, brought their young amateur champ to the veteran trainer Jack Blackburn, Blackburn turned them down. A bitter ex-fighter still smoldering at the way the race barrier had prevented him from earning a decent living at the trade he had mastered, Blackburn told them, "I don't care how good he is. He's the wrong color. Bring me a white boy so I c'n make some money." It was only when Black promised the meanspirited trainer $35 a week and expenses, sweet money in '34, that Blackburn lucked into the job that would become his legacy.

He was a master teacher, and the twenty-year-old

prodigy was a master pupil. From mid-1934 to mid-1935, the Louis-Blackman team won twenty-two straight victories, almost all knockouts, including two over the highly rated Lee Ramage. Roxborough and Black felt their boy was ready for New York. "Yes, but is New York ready for Joe?" asked the old cynic Blackburn. Roxborough put in a call to Jimmy Johnston, "The Boy Bandit," who ran boxing for the Garden. Roxborough told Johnston he had a fighter so good he should be fighting in the Garden.

"Yeah, I hear he's pretty good, but if he comes in here, he's got to lose a few."

"He's undefeated, and we want him to stay that way."

"Look, I don't care if he knocks out Ramage. He's still colored. Don't you have any white boys out there?"

Roxborough hung up. Johnston had made a $10 million mistake. Nobody had told him Roxborough was black. Blackburn said, "I told you so." But he hadn't figured on a most unlikely do-gooder, "Uncle" Mike Jacobs, "Machiavelli on Eighth Avenue." A ticket scalper from the age of twelve, he had a genius for squeezing that extra dollar from the box office. He didn't care whom he was touting, Enrico Caruso, the Barrymores, the suffragette Emmeline Parkhurst, World War I. He made a million dollars from his concessions at military posts. He had no pretensions as a social thinker, but Jacobs's sixth sense of what the public would and would not buy gave him an insight into society that was color-blind. He knew his New York, and he knew fight fans were tired of the mediocre white heavyweights after Tunney, with their fixed fights and foul tactics. And maybe the times had something to do with it. Roosevelt and his New Deal promised social change if not revolution.

Jacobs might still call African-Americans "schwarzes" but his favorite color was green, and he smelled money in bringing to New York the devastating puncher who had captured the imagination of the Midwest.

This was a social experiment, and his managers were taking no chances. Determined to make Joe the un-Johnson, Roxborough let the press know his seven commandments:

1. He would never have his picture taken with a white woman.
2. He would never go into a nightclub alone.
3. There would be no soft fights.
4. And no fixed fights.
5. He would never gloat over a fallen opponent.
6. He would keep a "deadpan" in front of the cameras.
7. He would live and fight clean.

Condescending rules, perhaps, but after the Johnson debacle, the twenty-one-year-old was clearly on trial in the court of public opinion.

One often gets the feeling in history that the right man has a way of coming along at the right moment. Abe Lincoln in the Civil War. FDR in the Depression. Aside from his blistering talent in the ring, the man-child Joe Louis had exactly the right personality for the role he was thrust into—as an ambassador from the Negro race (as it was called then) to the white ruling class. Joe didn't have to feign modesty or behaving himself in public. He was naturally shy, especially as an uneducated youth from the Bottoms, suddenly thrust into the limelight in Eastern society. It wasn't his nature to lord himself over inferior opponents.

His mother had raised him well. He was a mother's boy. The first thing he did with that big advance from Jacobs was buy her a nice house and drive her there to show it off to her, completely furnished.

At the same time, he was never the Uncle Tom the white press was hoping for. He didn't have to be programmed to act with dignity. It came as naturally to him as his punching power. Hyping his New York debut against the Italian giant, Primo Carnera, a tabloid photographer brought him a watermelon as a prop and asked him to pose with it. "Sorry, I don't like watermelon," Joe said. Polite but firm. His handlers smiled. They knew Joe loved watermelon. They also knew he could spot a black stereotype as quickly as a telegraphed right hand.

Overnight this totally unprepared man-child was thrust into a tense international conflict he knew nothing about. The fascist dictator Mussolini was ready to invade the East African black nation of Ethiopia. There were fascist sympathizers and "Save Ethiopia" placards at the press conferences. It wasn't the first time that a prizefight had been suffused with nationalistic fervor. All the way back in the early nineteenth century, when the former slave from Virginia, Tom Molineaux, challenged the bare-knuckle champion Tom Cribb, even the august London *Times* had sounded the alarm: "The honor of the English nation is at stake."

Young Joe had to deal with a hostile American press, with two of its most famous columnists, Arthur Brisbane and Westbrook Pegler, both devoted racists, warning of the riots that would erupt if "an American colored man" is allowed to face "the Italian military reservist." The canny Mike Jacobs actually played up the racial tension to fill

Yankee Stadium that long-ago summer evening. The announcer, Harry Balogh, felt obliged to beg the over-wrought audience not to satisfy the doomsday warning of Brisbane and Pegler: "Ladies and gentlemen, before pro-ceeding with this most important heavyweight contest I wish to take the liberty of calling upon you in the name of American sportsmanship, a spirit so fine it has made you, the American sporting public, world-famous. I therefore ask that the thought in your mind and the feeling in your heart be that, regardless of race, creed, or color, let us all say, may the better man emerge victorious. Thank you."

When Louis destroyed his Goliath in less than six rounds, the multitude of Italian Americans and an official cheering section from Benito himself quietly folded their Il Duce banners and stole away. Next-morning newspapers across the country signaled the breakthrough: the first time the name of a black man hit their front pages. Years later Joe would remember that night as the best he ever had. "If you was ever a raggedy kid and you came to some-thing like that night . . ."

Louis' sudden fame may have been a milestone on the road to racial equality, but the press was still not ready to accept him for what he was: an exceptional young athlete, not yet articulate but basically intelligent and increasingly aware of the awesome responsibilities being thrust upon him. Sportswriters still saw him as a Caliban, a savage, a subhuman force. In describing Joe's victory, a writer for International News Services set the tone: "Something sly and sinister and perhaps not quite human came out of the African jungle last night . . ." The celebrated sportswriter, Grantland Rice, seconded the motion, describing Joe as a

"jungle killer" and the eminent sports columnist, Paul
Gallico, weighed in with, "He lives like an animal, fights
like an animal, has all the cruelty and ferocity of a wild
thing."

Against this wall of prejudice, the real Joe Louis kept
breaking through. There was a quiet decency about the
young man that belied all the heavy-breathing "ferocious
black panther" metaphors. He was a world-beater, but he
wasn't a man eater. If black pastors were building their
sermons around their new Messiah, they weren't alone. A
Time magazine cover hailed him as the Black Moses. And
in the most publicized fight since Dempsey-Tunney, Louis
against the quixotic ex-champion Max Baer, even when
announcer Harry Balogh introduced Joe with his back-
handed "Although colored, he stands out in the same class
with Jack Johnson and Sam Langford . . ." the fans in
Yankee Stadium gave Louis a welcome at least the equal of
Baer's. That had never happened in America before. And
when Louis hit Baer so hard in the fourth round that the
fallen fighter decided to hoist the white (some said yellow)
flag, he surrendered with a characteristic quip; "When I
get executed people are going to have to pay more than
twenty-five dollars to watch it."

The political symbolism of the great heavyweight
championships was never more applicable than in the
Louis-Schmeling series. Another ex-champion, Max
Schmeling was considered over the hill when Mike Jacobs
dug him up to meet Louis, already hailed as "the
uncrowned" heavyweight champion. Adolf Hitler and
Josef Göebbels were so upset at the prospect of a member
of the "master race" being humiliated by an American [of

the "mongrel race"] that they tried to short-circuit Schmeling's challenge. They also urged him to give up his Jewish New York manager, Joe Jacobs (no relation to Mike). But Schmeling stood up to his Führer. He was a professional, and Jacobs had made a lot of money for him in America. When he landed in New York on the S.S. Bremen there were Jewish pickets to greet him, and when Louis went into training there were German-American Bundists with swastikas. There was also a country-club atmosphere at his training headquarters. The hard-nosed Jack Blackburn was disgusted. Celebrities from both coasts overran the place. And beautiful women. The columnist /TV host, Ed Sullivan, introduced Joe to golf, and Joe spent hours chasing little white balls. He had his white fans with him that night back in Yankee Stadium, but for the first time, he was less than perfect. After jabbing, he kept dropping his left hand, exposing his chin to Schmeling's straight rights. Fighting with courage but in a losing cause, young Joe was down and out for the first time in his life.

In seclusion with the shades drawn in his Chicago apartment a few days later, he had lost everything except his sense of humor. Without saying much, he had a way with one-liners. Asked if he'd like to see movies of the match, he said, "No, I saw the fight."

But Hitler and Göebbels were singing "Deutschland Über Alles." They sent the Hindenberg for Schmeling and he flew home to a hero's welcome. Göebbels greeted him at the airport with *Heil Hitler!* and the Führer gave a gala reception for him where they watched a film of the fight. Hitler ordered Göebbels to dress it up as a feature documentary, and it played to enthusiastic audiences all over

Nazi Germany. It was the best PR for Der Führer since Leni Riefenstahl's *Triumph of the Will.*

How Louis, rather than Schmeling, got the title shot against the aging and vulnerable champion Jim Braddock, is a story of wheels within wheels, most of them spun by that master spinner, Mike Jacobs. Göebbels and Hitler worked like big-time fight promoters to bring the Braddock-Schmeling fight to Berlin. Braddock's manager, Joe Gould, told me of a phone call he had from Schmeling, who put Göebbels himself on the phone. The Reichsmeister for Propaganda told Gould he was prepared to give him whatever he asked to deliver Braddock in Berlin. Joe said he wanted $500,000 in cash in a New York bank. "No problem," said Göebbels. And eight first-class tickets to Germany, suites in the Hotel Adlon, and training expenses. No problem. And one American referee and one British referee. No problem. Anything else? "Yes" Gould told me he told Göebbels, "And I want you to let all the Jews out of the concentration camps." "Göebbels hung up," Gould said. Like all those Jacobs' Beach managers, Gould knew the hustle. He knew he had Jacobs and Louis over a barrel. All he wanted, to pass up the Schmeling fight already signed and announced in New York, was 10 percent of Louis for the next ten years. Done deal. Just one of those nasty little things that would contribute to Joe's woes in the postwar years.

When Joe knocked out Braddock, the old champion who had nothing left but pride, the ghost of Jack Johnson was finally laid to rest. While there were cheers for Braddock's courage, the 20,000 blacks in the nosebleed seats and the even larger white audience spreading from ringside gave

Louis a color-blind ovation for the greatest heavyweight fighter they had ever seen. New champions usually like to rest on their laurels for a while, but the first time someone called Joe "champ" that night, he said, "I don't want nobody to call me champ till I beat that Schmelin'." So the stage was set for the most politically charged heavyweight championship fight in the history of the ring.

Between Louis-Schmeling I in 1936 and the rematch two years later, the skies had darkened. Germany had swallowed Austria, there was a Berlin-Rome-Tokyo Axis, little Czechoslovakia was threatened, the vilification of Jews intensified. The democratic world had come to realize that Hitler meant every apocalyptic word he had written in *Mein Kampf*. So Louis-Schmeling II was seen as nothing less than the war to come. Democracy vs. Fascism. Good vs. Evil. If Schmeling won, Hitler's fervid theories of a master race would be reaffirmed. A victory for Louis would recharge the hopes of everyone who yearned for an order of decency and an end to man's inhumanity to man.

That may sound like hyperbole, but in those almost-hysterical prewar days, both sides of the Atlantic looked on Louis and Schmeling as the flag-bearers of their respective countries and political systems. It was the first (and surely the last) time in history that the heads of both nations summoned their fighters to impress upon them the magnitude of the coming conflict. Hitler lay his hand on Max's shoulder and reminded him of his responsibility to prove the superiority of the master race by knocking out the black savage again. FDR took time out from his pressing day to invite Louis to the Oval Office, feel his muscles and say, "Joe, these are the muscles we need to beat Germany."

The kid from the Bottoms, who had earned just $59 in his first fight only four years before, literally had the whole world on his shoulders. As if he needed any further motivation, in his training camp his backers would read quotes allegedly from Schmeling expressing his confidence that a white man could always beat the inferior "nigger." Actually these were Göebbels-inspired, and later the basically decent Schmeling would deny to Joe that he ever made such statements. But at the time Joe admitted that while he had never felt any animosity for any of his opponents, this time he not only had revenge in his heart but a fire in him to defeat a mortal enemy.

When Louis destroyed Schmeling in the first two minutes of the first round, his biggest victory may have been the cheers that rose from the crowd when he entered the ring. And 70 million fans glued to their radios across the country were rooting for him, too. Never again would the color line be drawn on the most celebrated of boxing titles. Joe Louis had opened the door through which would pour the thousands of world-class athletes who have become household names, from Jackie Robinson and Willie Mays to Muhammed Ali to Jim Brown and Michael Jordan. As he did so often, Heywood Broun, in the *New York-World Telegram*, summed it up best: "One hundred years from now some historian may theorize, in a footnote at least, that the decline of Nazi prestige began with a left hook delivered by a former unskilled automotive worker who had never studied the policies of Neville Chamberlain and had no opinion whatever in regard to the situation in Czechoslovakia.. . . but. . . he exploded the Nordic myth with a boxing glove."

Already an icon in our contemporary culture, Joe actually polished his image when his reaction to Pearl Harbor was to enlist in the Army. Sportswriters no longer described him as black or subhuman. Now he was a great American patriot and with the possible exception of FDR, the most famous man in the country, if not the world. He donated his entire purse from two title defenses—against tough opponents Buddy Baer and Abe Simon— to Army and Navy Relief, giving them more than $110,000, for which the government expressed its gratitude by taxing him on the income as if he had put it in his own pocket. That twisted judgment, with compound interest over the years, would contribute to his postwar calamities. But in the immediate aftermath of Pearl Harbor, Joe's stature continued to grow. At the Boxing Writers Association dinner, former [city] Mayor Jimmy Walker praised Joe for risking his title for service charities: "You laid a rose on the grave of Abraham Lincoln." At a Navy Relief dinner in Madison Square Garden, when presidential candidate Wendell Wilkie said we would win because God is on our side, Pvt. Joe Louis went him one better: "I've only done what any red-blooded American would do . . . we will win because we are on God's side."

President Roosevelt sent him a telegram to congratulate him on his choice of words, and that slogan over Joe's picture became a favorite recruiting poster, while "Joe Louis Named The War" became a popular poem featured on the front page of the multimillion circulation *Saturday Evening Post*. In later years, he would be put down by Ali and others more militant for being an Uncle Tom, but in his own quiet way, Louis stood up to racism in the Army.

He refused to give boxing exhibitions for his fellow GIs unless the audience was desegregated. When he heard from Jackie Robinson that he and other college graduates had been denied access to Officers Training School, Joe went over the head of his commanding officer to get them admitted. Never part of the civil rights movement, he might be considered its one-man forerunner.

When Branch Rickey, emulating Mike Jacobs, finally gave Jackie Robinson a chance to play with the Brooklyn Dodgers, almost the first thing Jackie said was that he wouldn't have been there without Joe Louis. "He's been an inspiration to all of us. He made it easy for me and all the other fellows in baseball." He went on to say that Rickey must have been thinking of Joe Louis when he decided to let him play big-league baseball.

Jackie Robinson was on his way up to the Hall of Fame. But for his mentor, Joe Louis, after that resounding crescendo at the end of World War II, it was all downhill.

After having earned millions in the ring, and more than $600,000 for the second Billy Conn fight alone, Louis came out of the war not only dead broke, but with that IRS monkey on his back. With the clock running on the interest, it built up to a million dollars and counting. It wasn't all the IRS's fault. There were costly divorces, easy-come-easy-go generosities, self-indulgence, 50 percent to his managers, Mike Jacobs' share and that under-the-table 10 percent to Jim Braddock. You could make a case that every time he fought, he was giving away 110 percent of himself. Even so, for America's favorite son in the war years, it was a bitter pill. He had to begin wrestling for a living, and at one match, an IRS agent grabbed his $500 check at the box office. When his mother died and left him $600, the IRS took that, too. F. Scott Fitzgerald could have had Joe in mind when he wrote, "Show me a hero and I'll show you a tragedy."

Addicted to drugs, reduced to shilling for Caesars Palace, and hounded by the merciless IRS almost to the end of his life, Joe Louis became practically a forgotten man to the civil rights generation and the throng of cocky young baseball, football, basketball, and boxing millionaires today. But for all their exploits, Emmett Smith, Tiger Woods, and Barry Bonds aren't going to be buried at Arlington. And there's a very good reason why Joe Louis is there. He taught white America a lesson they would never forget. He taught black America, so long denied its sense of dignity, that hope was on its way.

The night Joe Louis knocked out Max Schmeling on the eve of World War II, there were spontaneous parades all over America. A democratic carnival. Placards held high in parades proclaimed, "Joe knocks out Hitler!" An interracial celebration. The old radical slogan: "Black and white/ unite and fight" had suddenly become social reality.

"Joe Louis came from the black race to represent the human race," said the Reverend Jesse Jackson at his funeral. So on his birthday, April 20, let us all make the pilgrimage to Joe's resting place at Arlington, at least in spirit, place a rose on his coffin, and pledge ourselves to the complete achievement of social democracy in America, still a work in progress.

ARETHA FRANKLIN

GERRI HERSHEY

AS A SHY girl in postwar Detroit, Aretha Franklin roller-skated through the crucible of civil rights history. She was raised amid heroes, esctatics, martyrs, and saints. Imagine what she heard as they thundered through her father's New Bethel Baptist Church, and put their feet under the Reverend C. L. Franklin's bountiful table. The titans preached and marched with him: Martin Luther King, Jr., Ralph Abernathy, Benjamin Hooks, Andrew Young. The stunning, otherworldly Sam Cooke, singing gospel then with the Soul Stirrers, knocked the sisters down like dominoes when he cried, "Whoa, Lord!" in "Pilgrim of

Sorrow." But most beloved to C. L.'s girl (whose own mother died when she was ten) were those divas of Baptist devotion.

"How I loved my gospel ladies," Aretha once told me, adding that we could not understand her art—even those unholy "sock-it-to-mes"—without crediting the women who nourished and schooled her: Miss Clara Ward and her mighty stalwarts Frances Steadman and Marion Williams, all substantial, extravagantly wigged ladies who defied gravity by leaping *straight up* off the high-octave bridge in "This Little Light of Mine." And the queen herself: Mahalia Jackson. "Mahalia would come in and she'd head right for the kitchen," Aretha said. "She'd put up a pot of greens. We'd sit around and talk. Then maybe we'd sing. They were so strong, those ladies. And always there for me."

Towering above this well-corseted pantheon was her father, whom Aretha loved like no other. His influence, she says, was engulfing. In Clarence LaVaughn Franklin's church and home, passion was a staple, sweet and abundant as the ladies' Sunday homemade ice cream. Aretha ate so much of that it made her head hurt. Appetites were huge after three-hour services that took the faithful to another galaxy and dropped them, faint, back on Hastings Street. Reverend Franklin was a pinstriped supernova on the gospel circuit, commanding up to $4,000 an appearance in the 1950s, taking his daughters Carolyn, Erma, and Aretha barnstorming on the Southern gospel circuit in a silver '57 Eldorado. Chess Records pressed over sixty albums worth of his rolling-thunder sermons. Bobby Blue Bland has fessed up to lifting his eerie signature squall from Franklin's most famous sermon, "The Eagle Stirreth Her Nest." Franklin was what Harry Belafonte called a "super whooper," the "Man with the Million-Dollar Voice," whose incantatory, bust-a-phrase-and-repeat-it cadence drove the preacher's own mother to perilous bouts of jubilation. Big Mama, as she was known to all, would charge the pulpit, upending floral arrangements like a bee-stung heifer in the petunias, tussling furiously with the ushers who struggled to subdue her—and got their Sunday shoes scuffed for the trouble. As they led her away, Big Mama shot back a defiant amen to her boy: "You're mighty right!"

Wide-eyed Aretha got the message: *Good* news. Even in the worst of times, the African-American church was about good news: Faith! Redemption! As the song put it, A Change Is Gonna Come. It was good news, even if it rose from the vilest suffering and lay a distant lifetime away. It was this incandescent optimism that guided the civil rights movement—and often acted as flame retardant against a justifiable, but dangerous anger in the streets. And it was this same radiance that would grant us the miracle of Aretha Franklin, Queen of Soul.

She had the fire as a child. She always knew she would sing, she told me. But she became certain of her destiny in a crackling gospel moment: It was at a funeral, when Clara Ward was singing a relative home. Miss Ward was getting *happy*, singing outside and above the grief. She crouched, took off her hat and flung it, discus-style, at the coffin. "That *did* it," Aretha said. She was a teenaged mother of two when the men from Chess Records set up their equipment at New Bethel and, with C. L.'s beaming approval, she sailed into a solo of her favorite Clara Ward song, "The Day Is Past and Gone." The interpretation matches Ward's, almost note by note. But listening to it almost half a century later, you can hear the gathering strength of the diva ascendant. Aretha may not be old enough to drive Daddy's Eldorado but she is in full command when she asks the congregation, "Can I moan a little here?"

Over a decade later, in March of 1967, she didn't ask permission of her pop audience. She just let fly. *You're a no-good heartbreaker . . . You're a liar and you're a thief . . .* That moan came roaring out of the radio, blasting past the burble of the Turtles' "Happy Together," and the Rascals' mellow "Groovin'." Aretha's first solid hit, "I Never Loved a Man (The Way That I Love You)" was the first time anyone had heard such audacious female sounds on AM radio. By then Diana Ross and the Supremes were in full, fussy Copa mode, cutting supper-show stuff like "The Happening." Messy, bluesy Janis Joplin was more an FM chick. James Brown, who had sung his way out of the county jail with sweet gospel, was grunting and squealing plenty on *It's a Man's Man's Man's World.* But until Aretha, no lady ever heaved and groaned between the Dr Pepper ads. Coming back soon after with "Natural Woman," "Respect," and "Dr. Feelgood," Lady Soul covered the full curriculum of any women's studies course in about nine minutes flat. (Question to the ladies here: Which of us *didn't* crank up Miss 'Ree to gird for the tussles of date night, punching out the chorus of "Think" with a Maybelline wand?)

Despite the wild efficiencies of those singles, Aretha's secular success hardly happened overnight. Like Bessie Smith, she was discovered and signed by that spelunker of hidden genius, John Hammond. For his label, Columbia, she cut jazz, blues, and pop standards, but nothing seemed to fit. Recalling one harrowing record-company convention in Puerto Rico, Aretha said she hid in her hotel room and watched another oddball Hammond protégé wander the beach alone. In the few words she did speak to Bob Dylan back then she sensed a mutual discomfort: "Neither of us knew where we were headed then," Aretha remembered. " 'Cause neither of us was what you call—ah—mainstream."

Dylan went electric and amped up his social and romantic urgencies. And how was it Aretha finally found her new groove? "We took her back to church," explained producer Jerry Wexler, who was put in charge when she switched to soul powerhouse Atlantic Records. Wexler had the good sense to haul the lady far away from the studio mainstream to tiny Muscle Shoals, Alabama and sit her down at the piano lining out arrangements learned from gospel genius Reverend James Cleveland. Wexler encouraged her to write, sometimes with her sister Carolyn. He surrounded her with a funky house band of rednecks and soul men. Of those days she declares: "This new Aretha music was raw and real and so much more myself. *I loved it!*"

Her second album heralded the triumph: *Aretha Arrives*. These were a young artist's days of heaven. Her new sound was immediate. Right there. And it would play perfectly in the restless 1960s Temple of Now. Between May and December of 1967, Aretha had six consecutive Top Ten hits. Wexler, an enthusiastic if ad hoc archivist, showed me Aretha's handwritten notes from some of their sessions. They are covered with scrawled happy faces and smiles. Her first marriage was going bad, but she had the music and a mission, appearing often with Dr. Martin Luther King, singing to raise money for the movement. Within a year, she would return to "Aretha Franklin Day," in Detroit, presented with the Southern Christian Leadership Award by Dr. King.

Aretha's good news sound landed amid bad, confusing times, when a nation was wrestling with its most ancient and tenacious demons: racism, imperialism, sexism. (Read: civil rights, Vietnam, the nascent women's movement.) So it was Aretha's fate to be an anthem singer in an American time so singular—and so divided—that her music was borne with equal fervor to dance clubs and to the barricades. There was a secular optimism afoot for those under-thirties; a change had to come. Everybody could find a reason to live in Aretha's delivery, and a tailor-made message in her lyrics. And that really is the genius of a great popular artist: that so many very different people can read so many legit meanings into their work.

This has also been Aretha Franklin's burden. If Kate Smith's wartime "God Bless America" bound everyone, snugly, safely in the red, white, and blue, (she sang it in 1943 in the Irving Berlin film, *This Is the Army*) Aretha Franklin's "Respect," released in June of 1967, was one obliging, multitasking *Marseillaise*. As first recorded by Otis Redding, the song was a domestic statement of intent ("respect when I come home"). But Aretha's lambent version—peppered with those sock-it-to-mes she whipped up with Carolyn—was triple threat. It dealt with sexual politics, freedom, and human dignity. It functioned as a clarion call to enlightened dissent. Thus "Respect" played in the Marlboro-and-patchouli scented dorm rooms cluttered with copies of *The*

Second Sex and *The Feminine Mystique*. It boomed from civil rights headquarters in the hot, explosive summer some dubbed the season of "Retha, Rap and Revolt," holding at number one for eleven weeks—as real bullets began to fly. While "Respect" ruled the charts, race riots erupted at Jackson State, in Newark. In Aretha's hometown, forty-three people died as federal troops sought to contain disturbances there. "Respect" went to Vietnam in the rucksacks of mortally terrified grunts. By then, nearly half a million U.S. troops had been sent there, among them Aretha's brother Vaughn.

When I asked Aretha about accompanying so many boys into the valley of death, her soft speaking voice got lower still: "I'm sure all those guys were in a lot of pain, something you or I can't ever imagine. But if they found pain in my music, it has to be their personal interpretation. What they hear and what I feel when I sing it can be very, very different. Sometimes I wish I could make them understand that."

How much we demanded from this Lady Liberty. Although the lyrics of "Respect" invite the listener to "find out what it means to me," Aretha has stiff-armed inquiring minds, choosing to let the music speak for itself: "What I feel singing, and where it comes from, is something I keep to myself." Still, it's clear, even in the diva-stilted prose of her 1999 autobiography, *From These Roots*, that Aretha Franklin considers herself the most misunderstood of American originals. Her longtime complaint: In cataloging her many personal tragedies, we have overlooked her joy in creation. We've painted her impossibly blue when really, her music and her message, gospel and pop, were born of hard charging hope. She insists she has always been inspired by faith, even if she's singing about the most unfaithful of men. Her instrument—strong, flexible, expressive—was and is stupendous. But her importance, her destiny as an exhorter was very much dictated and amplified by her times.

Of course, she's right; it's none of our business how the good "Doctor'Ree" diagnosed and treated her own pain. Aretha has been notoriously press shy since the 1968 *Time* cover story intended to make her a star cast her as a Sad-Eyed Lady of the Ghetto, with hints at spousal abuse. And she has pulled back farther still as the sorrows piled up: Her sister, cowriter, and sometimes backup singer Carolyn died young of cancer, as did her brother Cecil, then her sister Erma. She has also borne the close personal loss of her heroes, black American men destroyed by violence: her friend and idol Sam Cooke was murdered in 1963, leaving a copy of *Muhammad Speaks* in the tomato red Ferrari that drove him to his fate. Then came the King assassination, then the loss of her musical soulmate and bandleader King Curtis, stabbed to death by a passing junkie on his own front stoop. Worst of all was her father, shot in his home by robbers; he lay comatose for five years while Aretha worked to pay for round-the-clock care, and died in 1984.

It wasn't grief that pushed Lady Soul off the charts, but something arguably worse: disco. By the mid-seventies, Atlantic's bel canto years were over; in the marketplace, the singer was subsumed by a sound. The good news—the gospel fire that had inspired the best soul music—was lost beneath the post-sixties cynicism of the Nixon years, and the preset heartbeat of the synthesizer. Aretha has had hits, collaborations with the likes of the late Curtis Mayfield and hip-hop diva Lauryn Hill. Though it could not match the intensity of her 1972, gospel album *Amazing Grace* (recorded live, with Clara Ward), Aretha produced a second gospel work, *One Lord, One Faith, One Baptism,* with invocations by Jesse Jackson. Her live appearances are increasingly rare, but there is still no more delicious anticipation than the moment when Aretha squares her shoulders over a piano bench and prepares to serve it forth. I always arrive hungry for it. Whatever is on the evening's menu, if Aretha is at the keyboards—that is to say in full, glorious control—you will tumble out the door satisfied, maybe even a little sanctified.

In measuring the stir, the revolution, the hallelujah moment of Aretha Franklin's place in American music— and in the social history of an extraordinary time—it helps to go back to New Bethel, to a passage cited in Aretha's memoir, when she is recalling the thrill of listening to her father deliver his magnum opus from the pulpit. "The Eagle Stirreth Her Nest" was based on a passage from Deuteronomy 32:11–12 that begins; "As an eagle stirreth up her nest, fluttereth over her young, spreadeth abroad her wings, taketh them, beareth them on her wings . . ."

Quoth the Reverend Franklin: "In picturing God as an eagle stirring her nest, I believe history has been one big nest that God has been eternally stirring to make man better—and to help us achieve world brotherhood. The eagle is swift . . . the eagle is strong . . ." Imagine a pause here . . . the rustle of prayer fans. "The eagle has extraordinary sight . . ."

JANE JACOBS

ROBERTA BRANDES GRATZ

JANE JACOBS IS a member of a select literary group. Only once in a great while does a popular book have an impact so profound that conventional wisdom in a given area is perceptively, permanently changed. Exceedingly small is the club of contemporary writers whose books—such as Ralph Nader's *Unsafe at Any Speed,* Jessica Mitford's *The American Way of Death,* or Rachel Carson's *Silent Spring*—have dramatically changed the way we think about our society.

Jacobs became one of these all-too-few authors upon publication, in 1961, of *The Death and Life of Great American*

Cities. Before that book, urban renewal meant bulldozers and massive rebuilding, high-rise ghettos and ever-expanding highways. After publication, different strategies took hold: community development organizations, neighborhood rehabilitation, block associations, historic preservation on a broad scale, and a growing shift in attitudes that have gradually brought residents back to old city neighborhoods and convinced others to stay. What Carson did for the environment, Jacobs accomplished for a growing urban wasteland. In the five books[1] that followed, Jacobs also redefined how to understand urban economies, analyzed how societies thrive, examined different values embodied in the separate moral codes of commerce and politics and how to apply lessons learned from nature to the ecology of economies.

Like Nader and Carson, Jacobs was a soldier-philosopher who did not shy away from the battles her work soon provoked. She has been the consummate risk taker, the gutsy city defender, the civic activist challenging the same urban targets that her writing critiques so lucidly. Her pitched battles against New York planning czar Robert Moses inspired citizens everywhere to resist totalitarian planning. She was a leader in the successful fights against Moses' plan to cut a roadway through Washington Square Park in 1955–6, against his urban renewal clearance plan for the far west side of Greenwich Village in 1961, and against his Lower Manhattan Expressway that would have cut a wide swath through Little Italy and suffocated Chinatown with exhaust fumes. SoHo would have been killed before it was born. That battle lasted through the 1960s and into the 1970s.

Jacobs had lived thirty years in New York, married and raised three children in the city she championed. In 1968, the family moved to Toronto to protest against the Vietnam War. Jacobs had been arrested earlier at an antiwar demonstration at the Pentagon. Her energetic civic actions continued in the city she described as "much like New York used to be" and her impact on Toronto has been enormous. She worked to stop the Spadina Expressway, save old neighborhoods and create new ones, like the St. Lawrence Neighborhood. Most recently, the city followed her precepts in revising development guidelines for what is now Toronto's most vibrant, reviving, district, King-Spadina, the former garment district.

Through her writing, speaking and protests, she has offered insights and wisdom regarding the nature and functioning of cities and the regions and nations that contain them. Unfortunately, her wisdom was not recognized in time to avert the worst devastation of urban renewal and highway building, and too many American cities remain crippled by city-killing projects and policies. Now, however, when destructive proposals emerge—and they still do regularly—the debate is different from what it was before Jacobs changed the way the world views cities.

Her second book, perhaps her most important, was *The Economy of Cities*, (1969). It remains the clearest explanation of how urban economies work, what gives them strength and makes them grow, how interdependent all of the often-invisible components are and how economies reflect a complex organic process that can not be created but can easily be undermined. She focused on what urban economies do well, not what they don't. This challenged—and still does—the erroneous equating of big construction projects to economic development and growth. *True economic development is about the birth, expansion, and replacement of businesses, not about construction of new buildings. Real estate does not drive true development. Development drives real estate. This is the fundamental Jacobs lesson.* She continued these ideas in subsequent books, expanding her conviction that economies need to be self-sustaining, self-renewing, and relying on local initiatives instead of centralized bureaucracies. Most recently, she has explored the similarities between the ecology of nature and the ecology of cities. In time, her economic and environmental writing will match the importance of the first book that catapulted her to prominence.

But, for now, her breakthrough writing about cities is what she is most celebrated for. In the 1950s and 1960s, so-called "experts" saw cities as full of cancers, needing to be excised and rebuilt. In contrast, Jacobs saw cities as appealing, complex organisms needing small doses of assorted medicine not massive surgery and amputation. Most importantly, Jacobs understood how cities work and lambasted planners' plans as most often counterproductive. She argued for common sense derived from direct observation and related everything to peoples' daily lives. Her message was crystal clear and totally accessible to the ordinary person.

Jacobs gave voice to what many citizens were feeling instinctively. She gave encouragement to civic activists who shared her vision and protested against slum clearance. She inspired the variety of citizen urban and environmental movements that today make the difference between positive and destructive forces. In fact, if not for Jacobs, the national community-based revitalization movement might not be as strong and productive as it is and the national historic preservation and "recycling" movement might still be overfocused on single buildings, not whole communities. Advocates of her ideas encircle the globe.

From the start, Jacobs demonstrated that what professionals labeled "urban blight" were often messy but economically or socially vibrant districts with organic rejuvenation potential. The so-called "decay" that planners and builders said needed replacing was subsequently shown to be caused more by ill-conceived government programs, redlining, insurance and mortgage-broker scams, and landlord arson to collect insurance or tenant arson to get improved public-housing accommodations. Neighborhoods declared slums often had a social fabric of familial and communal relationships tied into a local economy that sustained them. Clearance policies ignored the substance that could be found beneath physical deterioration. Announcements of "plans" to "renew" so-called "blighted" districts were guaranteed, she proved particularly in New York's SoHo, to be a self-fulfilling prophecy. It is easier today to challenge official assertions of "blight" because of her teachings.

Jacobs was the urbanists' Joan of Arc. They used her words as weapons and argued that her precepts made more sense than the professional planners' rhetoric. Her ideas eventually percolated up to the attention of people in power. Now more than ever, her name is invoked by government officials and planners to label a different redevelopment approach. Often the reference to Jacobs's precepts is misplaced and contradictory. Yet, it is significant that officials believe a Jacobs reference can strengthen their case.

Jacobs's arrest in a protest against Moses' ten-lane Lower Manhattan Expressway is the stuff of which legends[2] are made and she is often identified as Moses' most vigorous and vocal citizen opponent. In Washington Square Park, one can only identify her impact by what *didn't* happen. The West Village Houses illustrate her principle of infill housing in an existing neighborhood—even though stripped down when built by a hostile city administration—as an alternative to demolition and replacement. But it is in SoHo that one sees that transformation of a former manufacturing district, declared dispensable by experts, into the vibrant neighborhood Jacobs argues can happen in most urban districts not undermined by bulldozer planning or overrun with parking lots.

Jacobs credits the many citizens who participated in the battle, as well as the artists who moved into the vacated spaces. But she was the leader of the battle. Broad public support made it a movement, instead of a one-woman crusade. She gave the movement fire and substance. Few people understand her pivotal role in the evolution of SoHo.

The defeat of the Lower Manhattan Expressway made SoHo possible. Out of that defeat came the spontaneous regeneration of what was once and is again one of the city's most economically productive neighborhoods. With the defeat of the highway, this onetime industrial district was transformed with little loss of nineteenth-century buildings, without any suburbanizing adjustments, without any diminution of its authentic urbanism, and without large public funding. A more up-to-date, modern district cannot be found, the birthplace in recent decades of many new businesses, great creativity, and residential opportunities for artists and artisans, single and married, young and old, black and white, immigrant and native. SoHo's success led to scores of similar successes, first in and around New York and then throughout the country. Today, every downtown that has any traditional urban fabric left has a "warehouse" or "loft" district, either full-grown, emerging or with small efforts trying to plant the seed for one. SoHo today is now the most emulated rejuvenated district in the country.

SoHo became the battleground of the two conflicting urban philosophies, so clearly delineated by Jacobs and Moses. This urban battle has engulfed America ever since. Downtowns and neighborhoods most transformed in the Moses pattern are the ones struggling today to re-create themselves, often with similarly misguided plans. Surviving districts, neglected by the big visionaries and over-reaching planners, are the ones rejuvenated primarily by citizen-led efforts. Those districts are now in the best position to flourish in the twenty-first century.

While Jacobs's impact is visible in many thriving and reviving areas, the consequences of the still-dominant conventional approach are even more visible. In so many American cities, we have mistaken for regeneration the recently built big, dazzling mega-projects that attract tourists but do nothing to strengthen the cities they are in. We built big, flashy projects. We replaced messy, hodge-podge genuine urbanism with pretty, well-ordered faux urbanism, selectively picking and choosing urban elements that don't add up to urbanism. We've transformed too much of the public realm into private enclaves. We've suburbanized so many urban neighborhoods, thinned them out, and then wondered why they can't support local businesses or public transit and have minimal street life. We've erased our productive districts, the ones with small and large businesses that include producers of "things" not just "paper," the innovators large and small that might be tomorrow's Microsoft or Cuisinart.

We've replaced factory, warehouse and low-income mixed districts with stadiums, shopping malls, convention centers, cultural centers, aquariums, and lots of parking lots. We've turned city centers too often into assemblages of projects. An inventory of projects is not how to measure the health of a city. They don't add up to a city. They are not about urbanism. These are places rebuilt, not reborn through regeneration of the existing mix of people, businesses and urban fabric developed over time. This is what Jacobs referred to as "anti-city" when she accused city planning, banking and government officials of "sacking" cities instead of aiding them.

This was and remains Jacobs's fundamental challenge to establishment thinking. After World War II, viewing cities as full of problems helped popularize the suburban ideal. Cities needed to be reconfigured, the experts said. Moses showed the way. He started a trend that spread rapidly. Jacobs rejected that view. Instead of looking at the city as a problem that needed fixing, Jacobs recognized the strengths of cities and sought to build upon them. She understood the challenges faced by cities. She saw cities with problems, not cities as problems. The "experts" were studying cities in the wrong way, offering ill-considered theories and hatching destructive policies.

Much of this dichotomy remains true. In many ways

small and large, Jacobs's views have been embraced. Sometimes her teachings have modified conventional views; sometimes, they've come close to replacing them. The public as watchdog most often best reflects her wisdom. Today, where communities are engaged in local planning and development debates, where their views are honestly heard and responded to and where local people are genuine participants in the public process, the result reflects best the "Life" in the title of Jacobs's first book.

1. *The Economy of Cities* (Random House, 1969); *A Question of Separatism: Quebec and the Struggle over Sovereignty* (Random House, 1980); *Cities and the Wealth of Nations* (Random House, 1984); *Systems of Survival: A Dialogue on the Moral Foundations of Commerce and Politics* (Random House, 1992); *The Nature of Economics* (Random House, 2000).

2. The full story of this incident will be detailed in my forthcoming book currently in progress.

MARGARET SANGER

ELLEN CHESLER

"No Gods, No Masters," the rallying cry of the Industrial
Workers of the World, was her personal and political manifesto. Emma Goldman and Bill Haywood, Mabel Dodge
and John Reed were her earliest mentors and comrades.
Allied with labor radicals and bohemians, Margaret Sanger
emerged on the American scene in those halcyon days at
the turn of the twentieth century, when the country
seemed wide open with possibility, before world war, revolution, and repression provided a more sober reality.

She organized pickets and protests and pageants in the
hope of achieving wholesale economic and social justice.

But what began as a joyous faith in revolution quickly gave way to a more concrete agenda for social reform. In 1913, working as a visiting nurse on New York City's Lower East Side, she watched a young patient die tragically from the complications of a then-all-too-common illegal abortion, and vowed to abandon palliative work, devoting herself instead to single-minded pursuit of sexual and reproductive freedom for women.

Women would achieve personal freedom by experiencing their sexuality free of consequence, just as men have always done, Sanger predicted. But in taking control of the forces of reproduction, they would also lower birthrates, alter the balance of supply and demand for labor, reduce poverty, and thereby achieve the aspirations of workers without the social upheaval of class warfare. Not the dictates of Karl Marx, but the refusal of women to bear children indiscriminately would alter the course of history, a proposition ever resonant today, as state socialism becomes an artifact of history while family planning, though still contested by conservative religious forces, endures with palpable consequences worldwide.

In 1917 Sanger went to jail for distributing contraceptive pessaries to immigrant women from a makeshift clinic in a tenement storefront in the Brownsville district of Brooklyn. The nation's birthrate was already declining as a result of private contraceptive arrangements and a healthy underground trade in condoms, douches, and various contraptions, but it was Sanger who first recognized the far-reaching consequences of bringing the issue of reproductive freedom out in the open and claiming it as a woman's right. She staged her arrest deliberately, to challenge the state's anachronistic obscenity laws—the legacy of the notorious Anthony Comstock, whose evangelical fervor had captured Victorian politics and led to the adoption by the federal government and the states of broad criminal sanctions on sexual speech and commerce, including all materials related to birth control and abortion. Authorized as a special agent of the U.S. Post Office, with the power to undertake searches and make arrests, Comstock had died of pneumonia two years earlier, after repeated confrontations with Sanger and her supporters that generated widespread publicity and sympathy for her cause, transforming it from a radical local gesture to a cause célèbre.

Appeal of Sanger's clinic conviction also established a medical exception to New York law. Doctors—though not nurses, as she had hoped—were granted the right to prescribe contraception for health reasons. Under that constraint, Sanger built what became the modern family-planning movement, with independent, free-standing facilities as the model for distribution of services to women without private health care, a development that occurred largely in spite of American medical leaders, who remained shy of the subject for many years and did not formally endorse birth control until 1937, well after her clinics had demonstrated its efficacy.

By then, she and Hannah Stone, the medical director of her New York clinic, whom Mary McCarthy later lionized in the classic scene from *The Group*, where Dottie Renfrew gets her first diaphragm, had also achieved a legal breakthrough. They prevailed in a 1936 federal appellate court decision that licensed physicians to import contraceptive materials and use the federal mails for their transport. The ruling effectively realized years of effort to achieve state and federal legislative reform, though it did not override prohibitions that remained on record until the historic 1965 Supreme Court decision *Griswold* v. *Connecticut,* which established a constitutional doctrine of privacy to protect the use of birth control, a doctrine extended to abortion eight years later in *Roe* v. *Wade.*

Past eighty and confined to a nursing home, Sanger lived to learn of the Court's ruling in *Griswold* and to witness the successful marketing of the hormonal birth-control pill she had long dreamed of by a team of scientists and doctors she had encouraged and found the money to support. She died in 1966, just as Lyndon Johnson first incorporated family planning into America's social-welfare programs and committed at least a fraction of the nation's foreign policy resources to them, fulfilling her singular vision of how to advance opportunity and prosperity, not to speak of human happiness, at home and abroad.

The middle child of a large and poor Victorian family in Corning, New York, Sanger learned to dream at an early age from a magnetic Irish father who squandered away his artisan talents and his humane social vision on far too much talk and drink. From an overburdened but resourceful mother and several older sisters, however, she was lucky to absorb a powerful motivation to improve her own lot and the essential habits of self-discipline that made it possible to do so. One parent taught her to defy, the other to comport. She always warred between the two but took away from both a distinctive resolve to invest in a better life for herself and for others.

Never one to romanticize the poverty of her youth, she

took refuge as a young teenager in Catholicism, then quickly converted to a socialist catechism, jettisoning both after World War I in favor of a more reasoned confidence in the ability of science and education to shape human conduct and in the possibility of reform through bold and progressive public initiatives. Her mentor through this passage was no less than H. G. Wells, the renowned British man of letters and influence, who foresaw the development of states that would mix free markets with centralized planning for social welfare. Both became tribunes for the rational, scientific control of the world's population and its resources, with Wells giving Sanger entree to the League of Nations and enhancing her international stature.

The two shared reputations for thinking expansively about the future, but also for living brazenly in the present. Sanger left her first marriage to William Sanger, a fledgling architect and painter, and committed herself to free love. Wells was one among many liaisons during and after her second marriage of convenience to J. Noah Slee, the wealthy inventor of 3-IN-ONE household oil, who used his facilities to help her smuggle in contraceptive products from Europe before they were legal here and helped bankroll her efforts, all the while letting her work, travel and have her freedom.

Critical to Sanger's political transformation at this juncture was the maturing of her consciousness as a feminist. She lost confidence in the potential of class cohesion, but decided to invest in the collective potential of women, many of whom were oriented to activism by the suffrage movement and eager for a new cause after women finally won the vote in 1920.

Rebelling openly against conventional gender arrangements, Sanger insisted nonetheless that the price women pay for equality should not be their sexuality or personal fulfillment. Following in the footsteps of a generation of suffragists and social do-gooders who had proudly forgone marriage, she became the standard-bearer of a less-ascetic breed, intent on a broader range of satisfactions. She wanted women to have it all, and saw birth control as the necessary condition for the resolution of their often-conflicting needs.

Sanger's determined optimism about the possibilities of freeing sex from a culturally and religiously enforced shroud of mystery and myth made her a pioneer of modern sexology and one of the first to take advantage of the popular market for lovemaking textbooks that emerged in the 1920s and 1930s. An intimate disciple of Havelock Ellis, and a fervent opponent of the confining determinism of Sigmund Freud, she believed that improved communication and instruction in technique has the power to liberate human sexuality even from the yoke of the unconscious.

In no small measure, her success in this regard owed not just to the weight of her ideas but also to her considerable personal beauty and charm. She was an immensely attractive woman, small, lithe, and trim. Her green eyes were flecked with amber, her smile always warm, her hands perpetually in motion, beckoning even to strangers. By Wells's own testimony, she had a quick Irish wit, high spirits and radiant common sense. And she was, in his words, "genuinely pagan."

With an uncanny feel for the power of a well-communicated

idea in a democracy, Sanger through the 1920s wrote best-selling books, published a widely read journal, held conferences, circled the globe giving lectures, organized a network of clinics and built a thriving advocacy movement. To this end, she had no choice but to mobilize men of influence in business, government, labor, academia, science and the emerging professions, but her most active recruits always remained women. Under the best circumstances, her pioneering clinics provided a range of health and counseling services in a sympathetic environment and became laboratories for her idealism, but, as often as not, the experiments failed, and even Sanger herself grew disillusioned.

The birth-control movement stalled during the long years of the Great Depression and World War II, stymied by the cost and complexity of reaching those in need without public funding, engulfed by internal dissension and overwhelmed by a barrage of opposition. The ever-fragile alliance Sanger tried to forge with the country's social and business establishment became a distinct liability. She resigned from the American Birth Control League, which later became Planned Parenthood, because of the eugenics leanings of some of its leaders, who boldly advanced contraception as a means of slowing birthrates among the poor during the Depression. Eugenics, which addresses the manner in which biological as well as environmental factors affect human health, intelligence and opportunity, was once embraced enthusiastically by many on the left but quickly deteriorated into excuses for the sterilization and control of "undesirables" on the basis of race and class.

Sanger always disdained the idea of a "cradle competition" between rich and poor, native and immigrant, white and black. She preached an ethic of individual self-improvement that would "come from within." She advanced public-health and welfare policies fostering universal health and fitness and providing essential economic safety nets, and she spoke out against immigration prohibitions and other stereotypes. Having worked as a midwife, she was particularly sensitive to the adverse biological consequences of inadequate nutrition and health care for pregnant women.

But by bemoaning the burden of the "unfit" and by joining other progressives in refusing to condemn involuntary sterilizations of the institutionalized, Sanger left herself vulnerable to attacks of bigotry. Her reputation has been seriously compromised in recent years by an unlikely alliance of opponents of abortion on the far right and those on the far left who wholly reject her pragmatic political strategies, or condemn all family planning as covert ethnic and racial genocide.

Undermining Sanger's character as a way of undermining her message has long been an effective political strategy. Though she had enjoyed the personal friendship and professional endorsement of Franklin and Eleanor Roosevelt in New York, they refused to ally themselves publicly with her self-consciously transformed and sanitized "family planning" message when they reached Washington and became captive to the New Deal's dependence on an alliance of Catholic voters in the Northern cities and fundamentalist Protestants in the rural South.

Embittered by her failure to win support at home, and

disenchanted with the country's increasing pronatalism after years of deferred fertility during the Depression and World War II, Sanger grew increasingly irritable, conservative and rabidly anti-Catholic as she grew older. Having previously traveled to Japan, China and India, leaving rudimentary family-planning advocacy and service organizations in her wake, she again turned her attentions abroad. In 1952 she founded the International Planned Parenthood Federation, an umbrella for national associations that remain today in most countries. In recent years most of these groups have been reinvigorated by a feminist movement that has given resonance to Sanger's original claim that women have a fundamental right to control their own bodies. They are recommitted to a doctrine that once again weds population and development goals to improvements in women's status.

FANNIE LOU HAMER

Judith Coburn

THE CLOSEST I ever came to Mrs. Hamer—everyone I knew called her Mrs. Hamer—was on the boardwalk at Atlantic City. It was August 1964. The Democratic National Convention. The odor of liberal betrayal befouled the air. That month would issue forth both the Tonkin Gulf Resolution and the so-called "Mississippi compromise."

Up to then, I had revered Fannie Lou Hamer from afar. I was a lowly foot soldier in the civil rights movement up north, organizing volunteers at my girls' college for voter registration campaigns down south and in Hartford, Conneticut. Four of us comprised the total membership of the

Smith College local chapters of SDS, the Northern Student Movement, and the Student Peace Union. I had grown up lucky in America, white and upper middle class, the country club and the best schools. But I was on the run from that life and had gone far enough by then to know how lucky I was to come up against Fannie Lou Hamer that day, surrounded by SNCC organizers uniformed in their sharecropper overalls. Mrs. Hamer and her SNCC allies were turning over just how to oust the official all-white delegation of segregationist Mississippi Democrats from the convention.

I hung around the outskirts of the huddle, eavesdropping on the strategizing. I knew that SNCC pessimists saw Hamer's Mississippi Freedom Democratic Party's (MFDP) challenge and its caravan of sharecroppers towing the car in which the martyred Chaney, Goodman, and Schwerner were riding when they were ambushed as just political theater. But Mrs. Hamer and the local Mississippi folks were fired by the conviction their cause was so just it would naturally overcome. Later she described that hope: "When we went to Atlantic City, we didn't go there for publicity, we went there because we believed that America was what it said it was, 'the land of the free,' and I thought with all of my heart that [the official delegation] would be unseated . . ."

It was Mrs. Hamer's first trip out of Mississippi, a place then so brutal to blacks who lived there that simply entertaining the notion of 'the land of the free' was an act of revolutionary imagination. The youngest of twenty children of sharecroppers, the grandchild of slaves, she grew up like most Delta blacks in a shed without plumbing and electricity on a plantation in Sunflower County. Rarely was there enough to eat, and what there was was mostly collards and gravy. By the time she was twelve, Mrs. Hamer was picking cotton. But both her parents were leaders in the sharecropper community. Her father preached in local churches and ran a jook joint on weekends. Her mother worked as a maid for white people and served as a go-between for blacks who had troubles with whites.

A short, stout woman who limped from a bout of childhood polio, Mrs. Hamer suffered from diabetes, heart trouble, and the bad food and medical care to which the poor are sentenced. And she suffered from an act of racist genocide, sterilized without her consent by white surgeons during an operation to remove a cyst. Mostly unschooled, she could quote the Scriptures like a Harvard divinity student. She was shrewd, bighearted, raucous, and recklessly brave. And could she sing. She'd been singing in the choir at the Strangers Home Baptist Church since she was twelve. But she found her true voice in the movement, a voice out of slavery and the plantation, the jook joint, and the black church that pulled thousands who heard her from their despair into exultation.

Watching her on that Atlantic City boardwalk in full argument I half expected her to burst into song. There's a funny photo of her in the history books surrounded by movement leaders looking self-important—Martin Luther King Jr. natty in his fedora—they're all ignoring Mrs. Hamer, who's thrown back her head, arched her back, and is belting out one more freedom song. I was to learn how her voice was a potent political weapon, able to shut off debate and upstage conservative black ministers in their own churches.

Mrs. Hamer was already forty-four when the civil rights movement arrived in the Mississippi Delta. It was another August: 1962. Three elderly black women—the first in town—had already defied a century of fear and tried to register to vote. At a mass meeting at the Williams Chapel Missionary Baptist Church in Ruleville, after the usual prayer and freedom songs, volunteers were called to go down to the courthouse and "redish," as local folks called registering to vote in Mississippi. Mrs. Hamer raised her hand. It was news to her that black people even had the right to vote. "I felt as though I was called," Mrs. Hamer said later of that night. None of the eighteen blacks, including Mrs. Hamer, who defied their fear and tried to register the next day, were registered. Local police and Mississippi patrolmen shadowed their bus out of town and arrested the driver for driving a bus that was "too yellow."

That night the owner of the plantation where Mrs. Hamer and her husband had worked for eighteen years told her to go back and withdraw her request to register or he would expel them from the plantation. She refused and left that night. Two weeks later shots were fired into the home where she had sought refuge. She moved again and more shots followed.

She was to tell that story over and over, but never did she galvanize so many as when she told it on national television to the Credentials Committee of the Democratic Party that August in Atlantic City. But it was her tale of what happened nine months later when she was arrested after a voter registration workshop in Winona, Mississippi, that drove home to Americans what Delta blacks were up against every day of their lives. At the Winona jail, Mrs.

Hamer testified, police took her alone to a cell, forced her to lie face down on a cot and ordered two black prisoners to beat her with blackjacks:

> I was beat by the first Negro until he was exhausted and I was holding my hands behind me at that time on my left side because I suffered from polio when I was six years old. After the first Negro had beat me until he was exhausted, the state highway patrolman ordered the second Negro to take the blackjack. The second Negro began to beat and I began to work my feet and the state highway patrolman ordered the first Negro . . . to sit on my feet . . . I began to scream, and one white man got up and began to beat me on the head and tell me to 'hush.' One white man—my dress had worked up high—he walked over and he pulled my dress down and he pulled my dress back, back up. . .

But only the Credentials Committee heard Mrs. Hamer describe her torture. President Lyndon Johnson, monitoring Hamer's live testimony on national television, quickly called a press conference to divert the cameras' eye away from her. But her account of the beating made the evening news.

The beating left Mrs. Hamer with permanent scars: kidney damage and a blood clot that damaged her eyesight. But it didn't slow her down one bit. When people would ask her if she hated the men who had beaten her, she always said her mother told her that hating made you as weak as those filled with hatred. She kept right on cajoling neighbors to step up, testifying in song and speech, shaming everyone to register to vote and turn out for the MFDP's own statewide convention. In early August, [1964,] more than 800 MFDP voters elected sixty-eight delegates (including four whites) to represent Mississippi in Atlantic City.

That convention week, the politics of the MFDP challenge surged across the boardwalk, from the tawdry Gem Motel where the MFDP was quartered to the Union Baptist Church where SNCC workers slept on the floor, to suites at the grand Pageant Motel, the White House's convention redoubt. I rushed back and forth trying to keep up. I was a minor MFDP agent working undercover as an LBJ hospitality girl at the convention, wearing my "Part of the Way with LBJ" badge hidden under my collar. It was my official job to dress up spiffily (in a tight black minidress and an LBJ souvenir cowboy hat) and do menial tasks for the Missouri delegation at their night and day cocktail parties in their hospitality suite. What I was really doing was lobbying delegates to support the MFDP, stealing floor passes when I came across them, or trying to persuade delegates to lend them to me so MFDP lobbyists could get on the convention floor to talk to other delegates.

Meanwhile, over at the Pageant, MFDP sharecroppers, clergymen, and moderates like Aaron Henry were being whipsawed by pleas from liberals like Hubert Humphrey and Walter Reuther (and veiled threats from LBJ emissaries) to withdraw their challenge in the service of party unity. (A ubiquitous Martin Luther King Jr. at first deferred to the MFDP then later argued to accept a compromise with the Democratic Party.) The boardwalk grapevine reported that when Humphrey tried blackmail, claiming LBJ wouldn't make him Vice President if the MFDP didn't accept just two seats on the convention floor, it was Mrs. Hamer who stood up to him. "Senator Humphrey, do you mean to tell me that your position is more important to you than 400,000 black people's lives?" Both of them reportedly wept.

I came to understand at the Gem Motel that Mrs. Hamer and the delegation's community people resisted liberal paternalism because their cry for justice wasn't just a political opinion, it was a physical necessity. They had risked their lives to register to vote and come to Atlantic City. They were going back there to live with their neighbors in the dire poverty and segregation enforced by gun and club. To them and their SNCC supporters, letting Democratic Party leaders dictate a deal for a couple of seats and who would sit in them was akin to being pushed again to the back of the bus. Before he upstaged her testimony, President Johnson was reportedly so incensed by Mrs. Hamer's down-home speechifying that he decreed she couldn't be one of the two MFDP delegates seated in proferred compromise. "The President will not allow that illiterate woman to address the convention," Humphrey told MFDP negotiators. Bob Moses called him a racist in reply.

"We didn't come all this way for no two seats," was Mrs. Hamer's verdict on the compromise. The MFDP agreed and told the President no. That afternoon was frenzied. Those of us with floor passes rushed on and off the floor borrowing floor credentials from other delegates and spiriting them out to the MFDP delegation. That night it was my job to lead a procession of sharecroppers into the upper balcony above the Mississippi delegation to be in position to cheer when the MFDP delegates staged a sit-in on the floor. I hitched up my skirt and climbed over the barricade into the VIP section, waving gaily to Katherine Graham and Alfred Friendly of the *Washington Post*, whose daughters I had hung around with at boarding school. They started to wave back, noticed the black sharecroppers, thought better of it, and simply gaped.

But the regular segregationist Mississippians had already stormed out in protest, and FBI agents posing as reporters with NBC credentials had removed the delegation's chairs. So Mrs. Hamer and the others had no seats at all on the bus. They filed back out after a while and joined a vigil on the boardwalk where Bob Moses and others wore black placards with JFK's silhouette and his "ask not what your country . . ." slogan, or held up portraits of Mississippi martyrs. Mrs. Hamer lifted up her voice for a woebegone "We Shall Overcome," and we all joined in while LBJ's birthday fireworks detonated red, white, and blue across the boardwalk.

At the next Democratic convention—the infamous Chicago 1968—Mrs. Hamer finally got her seat as an officially elected Mississippi delegate. But this radical turnabout in American political life wasn't witnessed by many of us who'd gathered to support the MFDP on the Atlantic City boardwalk. We were battling cops on the streets of Chicago. The war in Vietnam—which Mrs. Hamer opposed from the get-go—had blown back home and crushed so many hopes, both liberal and radical. The wreckage of the civil rights movement—black power, infighting over the meager rations of the poverty program, and the politics of ego—weighed heavily on the still desperately poor Delta. Mrs. Hamer and the MFDP went on to challenge five Mississippi congressmen on grounds that blacks had been denied the right to vote and that Mrs. Hamer and other MFDP candidates had been denied a place on the ballot. The challenge failed. She ran for the Mississippi State Senate and lost. Her lawsuit, *Hamer v. Sunflower County*, demanded the county integrate its schools. And in 1971, Mrs. Hamer, sticking to the openness to working with whites she had shown since SNCC days, helped found the nearly all-white National Women's Political Caucus.

But unlike so many of her compatriots in the movement, Mrs. Hamer continued to live with and fight for the poor Delta blacks, the stock from which she came. Mrs. Hamer's national celebrity couldn't protect her family from the persistent harsh reality of life in the black Delta. In 1966, her daughter died because there was no hospital near Rulesville that would care for blacks. She threw herself into creating a pig bank[1] and "Freedom Farm," a cooperative where poor blacks could live and raise their own food. The effort received more support from Northern whites than it did the middle-class blacks, most of them men, who had wrested control of the civil rights movement from grassroots organizers like Mrs. Hamer and SNCC. She grew increasingly bitter, railing at "house niggers," whom she thought lacked respect for poor people and their struggles. She understood as few did how reform could integrate the political structure without changing the lives of poor people.

But "Freedom Farm" and the pig bank failed, victims of the lack of money, know-how, and self-confidence they were created to change. And poverty finally killed Mrs. Hamer: After two mental breakdowns, she died of diabetes, heart failures, and cancer, and the diet of a lifetime of poverty.

Toward the end of her life, Mrs. Hamer told a reporter she was "sick and tired of being sick and tired." I think of that often, decades later when I feel sick and tired of how America's idea of freedom has become corrupted into an imperial right to anything we want as long as we're well off and when I feel sick and tired of not knowing anymore how to change that. Then I think of Mrs. Hamer and feel ashamed and marvel at how she kept on.

What kind of moxie drives a black sharecropper with a sixth grade education out of rural Mississippi to jump up out of that lot and turn history around?

"Ain't gonna let old Jim Crow turn me 'round, turn me 'round, turn me 'round," Mrs. Hamer used to shout out. She turned him around and us too.

¹ Hamer's pig bank "loaned" a sharecopper a pig, which was then paid back in a piglet which could then be "loaned" to someone else in turn.

SAMUEL FULLER

J. HOBERMAN

THE B-MOVIE master of visual pow and hard-boiled gibberish, Samuel Fuller (1912–1997) was the most dynamic,
genuinely radical, and authentically underground Hollywood filmmaker of his generation.

Over the course of his forty-year movie career, Fuller
directed a total of twenty-three, mainly low-budget,
mostly action, films. He scripted or coscripted all of them
and produced nearly half, opting at every opportunity for
creative freedom over commercial success. From the stand-
point of artistic freedom, Fuller was our Ingmar
Bergman—albeit one who knocked out movies for the

bottom half of a double bill and thus, for the most part, flew beneath the radar of critical awareness. It was only after he was discarded by Hollywood—churning out countless unproduced scripts during the 1960s and 1970s— that Fuller became an inspiration, first to the directors of the French nouvelle vague, then the German neue kino, and finally the American independent movement.

Fuller famously used to fire a starter's gun in lieu of shouting "action!" on the set and there's a sense in which each of his movie is a combat saga. As a World War II infantryman, he fought in North Africa, Sicily, Normandy, and Czechoslovakia: "I hate phony heroics," he once said. "The reaction I would like to my pictures is 'only an idiot would go to war.' " Be that as it may, it's difficult to imagine a more visceral, confrontational filmmaker. Fuller's love scenes are nearly as violent as his fights; his heroes are mostly abrasive sociopaths; America, his constant preoccupation, is invariably defended by its outcasts and they usually don't know why. Fuller's dialogue is so packed with oppositions it can stop the brain cold. His classic line occurs halfway through *The Steel Helmet* (1951), when the lumpish hero Sergeant Zack, shoots an unarmed POW point-blank. Realizing that he faces a court martial, Zack grabs the aspiring Korean by the throat and screams, "If you die—I'll kill you!"

Although justly celebrated for his use of extreme close-ups and choreographed action sequences, Fuller considered himself to be primarily a writer: "I direct mainly because I don't want any other banana-head to spoil what I've written." This pugnacious Jewish street kid had been a newsboy and a teenage crime reporter for the notorious *New York Graphic*. ("It taught me creative exaggerating," he would later maintain.) There has never been another American filmmaker has ever been more devoted to journalism. Fuller always went for the scoop. The movies that he called "great yarns" and "front-page material" addressed issues of racism and national identity, war and corruption, with a political cartoon's iconic, mind-boggling bluntness.

Fuller made the first Korean War film in *The Steel Helmet*, a ten-day wonder that suggests *Waiting for Godot* as it might have rewritten by Mickey Spillane; *China Gate* (1957) was the first Hollywood movie about Vietnam, opening six months before the original version of *The Quiet American*. Although set during the final months of French rule, the cast of characters effectively prophesy the war's next stage: One of the Americans fighting with the French Foreign Legion is Gene Barry, a loudmouthed white supremacist; the other (played by Nat "King" Cole) is a black man under the delusion that if he can only rid the world of commies, America will become a safe place for him to live. (One need only bracket *China Gate* with John Wayne's *The Green Berets* for Wayne's epic to blow up in its own face.)

Park Row (1952) was Fuller's great labor of love. He lost his own money on this re-creation of 1890s New York newspapering. The movie opens by dollying smack into the statue of Horace Greeley and, typically, takes literally the notion of a circulation war. But *Pickup on South Street* (1953) is Fuller's great love story. Confining itself largely to moody reconstructions of the crime reporter's beat, this masterpiece of low-life lyricism takes place half in the New York City subway or beneath the Brooklyn Bridge, with the rest mostly unfolding in police stations, Bowery flophouses, and all-night Chinese noodle joints.

Fuller's mash note to New York resonates with urban detail and is rich in underworld slang. "That muffin you grifted, she's OK—stuck her chin way out for you," Thelma Ritter's stool pigeon tells the cynical pickpocket played by Richard Widmark. That none of the movie was actually shot in New York—Fuller used a mix of detailed studio reconstructions and well-selected parts of downtown Los Angeles—gives *Pickup* an additional hallucinated poignance, enlivened by the director's zest for orchestrated mayhem. "I liked the idea of Widmark pulling [the villain] downstairs by the ankles," he said of the fight in a near-perfect replica of a specific Lower East Side subway station that provides *Pickup*'s action climax. "The heavy's chin hits every step. Dat-dat-dat-dat: It's musical."

Pickup on South Street was Fuller's second effort for 20th Century–Fox studio boss Darryl F. Zanuck, and it was very much Zanuck's kind of film. A onetime boy wonder, the mogul had launched the gangster cycle—as well as other fast-paced, slangy, urban-set topical movies—at Warner Brothers in the early 1930s. Zanuck made Hollywood's first attack on anti-Semitism with *Gentlemen's Agreement* (1947) and, always interested in current material, reaped considerable publicity for producing the original Cold War anti-Communist thriller, *The Iron Curtain*, a year later. *Pickup on South Street* was Fuller's contribution to the Red Scare—a movie in which, for reasons that have nothing to do with patriotism, a pickpocket, a stoolie, and a temporarily reformed hooker named Candy confound a Communist spy ring. "Are you waving the flag at me?" the pickpocket mocks an FBI agent in a scene that J. Edgar Hoover found particularly offensive.

Fuller thrived on brutal ironies and ate contradictions for breakfast. He was obsessed with America and saw it scummy-side up. His films typically used neurotic loners and loudmouthed lumpenproletarians to test society's official pieties (freedom, democracy, integration). The protagonist of *Shock Corridor* (1963) is a Pulitzer-obsessed newspaper reporter who, in Fuller's parlance, decides to "pull a Nelly Bly." Like the nineteenth-century reporter who feigned madness in order to report on conditions in New York's Wards Island asylum, he has himself committed to a mental hospital to solve a mysterious killing. To get him in, his stripper girlfriend poses as his sister and informs the police that he has been molesting her. She's genuinely troubled, but what's really bugging her is the reporter's insane ambition: "I'm fed up playing Greek chorus to your rehearsed nightmare," she cries in Fuller's wildly empurpled prose. "Hamlet was made for Freud, not you!"

You might say that Fuller practiced a form of narrative manifest destiny. Every situation is pushed to the limits. We lost a lot when his Hollywood career stalled for some fifteen years after *The Naked Kiss* (1964). Sam was just hitting his stride—making an exposé in which a hooker goes straight and moves to an all-American town only to discover the goody-goody millionaire who romances her is a child molester—and, as American social reality approached the lunacy of *Shock Corridor*, moving left. Indeed, the controversy and misunderstanding that surrounded Fuller's final studio film, the ferociously antiracist *White Dog* (1982), which centers on a pet programmed to attack African-Americans, demonstrates that he never lost his ability to confront and trouble audiences.

"Young writers and directors, seize your audience by the balls as soon as the credits hit the screen and hang on to them!" Fuller advises in his memoirs. "Smack people right in the face with the passion of your story!" Feisty wasn't the word for this guy. As anyone who ever met him knows, Fuller gave the impression of being weaned on a stogie and raised by a teletype machine. He was great copy. Wildly enthusiastic, Fuller savored his words and spit them out as leads: "To kill a human being is hard," he informed me when I interviewed him in 1980. "About as hard as it is to dig up a man to finance a picture. The object is similar [pause to draw on cigar]—an accomplished act to continue to survive!"

A dogged anticareerist, Fuller consistently turned down offers to direct big-budget, star-studded best-seller adaptations—passing up an earlier chance to make his autobiographical war film *The Big Red One* because he didn't want John Wayne to star. (The movie was finally made in 1980; albeit butchered by his studio.) Zanuck proposed that Fuller reconfigure *Park Row* as a Technicolor musical for Gregory Peck and Susan Hayward; Fuller insisted on shooting the movie his way, in black and white with Gene Evans. It flopped.

Some called Fuller a primitive. Others were enchanted by the idea of him. But Jean-Luc Godard and Martin Scorsese loved his movies—and I did too, even (or perhaps especially) the crazy McCarthyite tract, *Pickup on South Street*. Like the newspaper cartoonist Chester Gould, inventor of *Dick Tracy*, and the press photographer Weegee, Fuller elevated tabloid hysteria to something that resembled art. The man was our skid row Eisenstein, our 42nd Street Brecht, Hollywood's greatest abstract sensationalist.

MILES DAVIS

LUCIUS SHEPARD

MOST OF WHAT we know about the life of Miles Davis is either anecdotal or a matter of official record, and thus not absolutely reliable; but by all accounts, most pertinently by his own, Miles Davis was a bad man. *Live-Evil. Bitches Brew. Dark Magus. Sorcerer. Black Devil.* The titles of those albums tell the story he needed us to hear. They—and the music whose nature they reflect—embody an admission of perfidy, malice and vengefulness, and further convey the prideful glorification of those transgressions. Like all of us, Miles invented himself from the chaos he was given to interpret; unlike many of us, he never bothered with reinvention. He hewed to his original self-conception with unrepentant ferocity, engaging in a type of human alchemy, changing himself into an imaginary creature who lived in place of the ordinary man. The fanfare that opens *Bitches Brew* contrived the formal announcement of this change and, thereafter, he inculcated his music with a churlish, occult presence that refined it into something other than music, a brooding and often brutish form of intimacy that gladdened no hearts and lifted no spirits, speaking instead to the body and the hindbrain.

Critics like to enthuse about Miles Davis in the 1950s and 1960s and disregard his output during the 1970s, a creative period after which he retired for several years. Some see this electric music as a dissolute phase and some perceive it as tired, evidence of an aging talent attempting to be contemporary. But Miles never had to work at being contemporary. He proclaimed no cosmic evangel, as did Coltrane, and he was neither a Blakean visionary like Albert Ayler nor a mad scientist poet like Ornette Coleman. The information he relayed when playing never seemed dated as sometimes is the case with poets and preachers. Elegance was a suit he wore, but inside it he was sinewy, funky, raw. Passion was a language he could speak, but passion bored him and he employed it only when it served to pay the bills. Essentially, he was on the lookout and streetcorner-talking about what he saw coming. Not the long view, but the way things looked a few storefronts down, next week, a couple months from now. He wanted to be the coolest monster on the corner, the one who got raised up yet stayed with the street no matter what marble halls surrounded him. That may not be all he was, just who he wanted to be, but he wanted it with such genius intensity, he became the star of his own personal Blaxploitation movie, acting the role of a sinister, magical hustler who when he played was checking things out and reporting back to himself. He included us in the conversation because we gave him the money and attention he had hustled us for, and he bought into his own con so completely, he left behind a standard street hustler's legacy of embittered ex-friends and maltreated women.

All great artists pander a little—they feel they have to tell us something good about ourselves, offer a connection that'll make us believe we're complicit what they do and give us something to talk about afterward. Miles outgrew that tendency during the 1970s. He turned his back on the audience and muttered into his horn as if pronouncing a curse he didn't want anyone to understand. He played mean, he played nasty, he played coolly sneering blurts of sound, and even when he played beautiful, it seemed he was commenting on beauty rather than lending it voice, that at the core of every melody was a disaffection that rendered beauty irrelevant, an attitude increasingly informed by a politics compounded of anger and heroin and egomania. During those years, his face shriveled from a griot's aloof mask to a black wizard's skull with a Sphinx hairdo. His music was distilled down from innovative melodic phrasings which played like luminous blue branches forking among the rustlings of the rhythm section, into something dread and basic, dark oceans. Chords opened over a snaky, slithering cymbal hiss, a cluttered rumble of bass, followed by the sinuous trumpet line, a snake-charmer whine rising from a storm of thunderheads and scuttling claws, as plaintive and elusive as a muezzin's call. It seemed to have the freedom of jazz, yet at the same time it had the feel of heavy, ritual music.

I remember how, after seeing Miles in the 1960s, I walked out of the club thinking about his technique and the particularity of his invention and his ostensibly offhanded yet astonishingly precise enunciation of the notes. His 1970s music—as, for instance, the Carnegie Hall recordings released under the title *Dark Magus*—doesn't provoke any similar intellectual reaction, which explains why it is dismissed by intellectuals. It breeds images in your mind. Static red flashes and black mountains moving. Mineral moons in granite skies. A thread of fire outlining a distant ridge. Then it washes over you and shuts you down. It's not art, it's not beauty, it's a meter reading on the state of the soul, a registering of creepy fundamentals, a universal alpha wave, God's EKG, a base electric message crackling across the brain. It suggests that what Miles saw on his immediate horizon was a figure of terrible promise.

That's what I heard, anyway. A reedy alarm mounted against a crawl of background radiation, a whisper of melody leaking out through a crack in death's door, filling all the air with its singular disturbance. Miles ultimately wanted less to entertain than to unsettle his audience, and this music was as much a statement of that policy as it was one of blighted conviction.

There was nothing Promethean about Miles. Transfiguration and transcendence were not among his concerns. Like Rimbaud and Bukowski, Céline and Mishima, he was a hero descending, moving ever downward into a spiritual bottomland, never flinching from the experience, wallowing in the stuff that tarred the floor of his soul. His music is a record of that descent, a sonic diary that tagged the walls with an enduring graffiti, and, at the same time, a fiction he was telling the street, the environment whose demiurge he sought to be. During the '70s, however, he seemed to have become an oneiric figure in whom fiction and truth comingled. Dressed in flashy silks; his face grown somewhat wizened, the sort of ancient face you see emerging from the rough textures of tree bark or an avocado pit; standing still in the noise of the storm he orchestrated. Watching and listening to him, I had the idea that his arrogance and defiance were no longer merely part of a costume, but served to deflect fear—that he had seen the shadow of the myth he made and it was coming to claim him, an awful conclusion that, if we could see it, big, burly and spitting flame, would frighten us as well.

In the 1980s, when Miles returned after his retirement, his style was slicker and, though some of the music was good, it no longer seemed possessed by that furious entity. He was, for all intents and purposes, done. It's hard to sum up what a musician leaves behind. Though the recordings remain, the sounds have been vacated to a degree by the death of the player. But when I put on *Dark Magus* or *Pangaea* or any of his music from the 1970s, one thing comes clear: Miles didn't bring us much good news on his way down to death, but for a time he showed us how the Devil might have sung while he fell through the floor of Heaven.

THELONIUS MONK

STANLEY CROUCH

THERE WAS NO one at all like him. Unlike most important jazz musicians in the line that stretches from Louis Armstrong to Ornette Coleman, he was not a small man. He was a big guy and his intensity was such that it could immediately be felt at one's back. Whether or not one knew *who* was close, surely *someone* was there because it felt as if the door of some kind of human furnace had suddenly been thrown open. Upon turning around, the sight that struck the eye was a man who appeared to be all darkness and sweat. There was, perhaps, an unfiltered cigarette protruding from his lips. His body was not quite still or it was turning in a circular motion. An arm suddenly jutted out then seemed to be sliding into or pulling itself from an invisible sleeve. There he was. That was him. The inimitable. The unique. The one and only. In his case, all such clichés obtained.

He had such uniqueness that it became a fetish to his fans and something of an event in itself. What kind of unusual hat would he wear? Might he have on his sunglasses with the bamboo frames? Would he suddenly stand up and introduce the members of the band? What arrangements and what songs would he play? Would he chose to extemporize with great velocity and shock those who didn't know he could? Would he abstract essences from the reams of notes flying through his mind, improvising as though he was concerned in his long pauses with playing only the most telling two or three notes or the most shocking chords dropped at the most unpredictable places in the swing of the rhythm section? Who knew?

Since Monk seemed to function on such an Olympian level of whim, he might have it in him to sit alone at the piano and give an interpretation of some song that everyone had known for what seemed forever, but that sounded as though he had actually written it and was both reclaiming it for his kingdom and extraditing it to a place within the borders of his aesthetic nation. He achieved this extradition by using his expansive array of individually crafted keyboard effects developed in order to make the piano produce colors and textures that were neither expected nor exactly precedented—even in a music known for moving away from the common consensus. Yes, among the uncommon, he existed on a level of individuality that was extreme to the point of eccentricity but that never intruded or misdirected the scope of his musical mind. Because of that, Monk is, doubtless, one of the most important influences on jazz over the last sixty years.

Once upon a time, shortly after the war years in which Germany, Italy, and Japan had to be brought down, it would have seemed quite odd to say such a thing about Thelonious Monk. In the era of bop glasses, berets, and faux submissions to Islam, he seemed a shadow figure existing outside of the winner's circle of controversial and celebrated innovators. At the point when bebop added some fresh, stupefying, and thrilling interpretations to the language of jazz, Monk did not have the influence on piano players that Bud Powell had. His approach to the piano was not recognized as having any relationship to Kenny Clarke, who had brought about a dramatic shift in the stylistic possibilities of playing jazz drums. Few would have mentioned Monk's name with those of Charlie Parker and Dizzy Gillespie, who were thought as the two essential fountainheads of the new style.

Yet the facts of the matter were quite a bit different. Monk had been the one who worked out the new chords with Dizzy Gillespie at Minton's Playhouse up in Harlem. He, with bassist Oscar Pettiford and drummer Kenny Clarke, had reinvented the jazz rhythm section. His songs were the most profoundly beautiful—and difficult—to arrive within the time period of that movement. In fact, he went his own way with such certitude that his vision comprised a movement all its own. In that personal movement, which could be reduced to two words—Monk's

Point—conceptual ideas about harmony, melody, rhythm, architecture, and motific improvising continued to influence the direction of the music, even in the work of players who seemed to have little to do with his manner of making music.

That is, doubtless, the most important thing about the great thinker: He or she can contribute a *vision* that transcends the specifics of technical methods. That is what Monk actually did, and the impact of his thoughts was profound in method and even more profound in the variety of its influence. No, Monk did not influence many people in terms of how he, personally, executed his vision. He had influenced the shaping of their individuality. He helped players and writers to revamp their thinking or to think in ways that took them in the direction of bringing greater continuity and order to their improvising and their composing.

This becomes quite obvious when we look at the work of his most amazing protégés. Miles Davis began his career imitating Dizzy Gillespie and stood, night after night, next to Charlie Parker, as often as not responding to Parker's florid genius with melody lines and rhythms derived from Lester Young and Billie Holiday. But under the influence of Monk, Davis learned that one could pick the most explosive harmonic notes in short units of melody. Davis related this to Wallace Roney in Montreux in 1991. Sonny Rollins learned from Monk the power of improvisational architecture and the depth of organization that motific improvisation could bring to improvising. When John Coltrane worked with Monk at New York's Five Spot in 1957, he learned one song, "Trinkle Tinkle," which forever changed his approach to rhythm and remained with him to his death ten years later. Coltrane also picked up on the motific approach and one of his most successful examples is his improvisation on the title track of his *Crescent* album, where the material with which he begins his improvisation is expanded and contracted throughout the performance, a favorite technique of Monk's. Ornette Coleman developed an original take on Charlie Parker but tended to improvise, as Monk always suggested to musicians. Coleman built his playing on the melodies he wrote, improvising with the phrasing and tonal freedom heavily implied in Monk's improvisations, which had, as Winton Marsalis observed, a much larger range of note values than anyone else who had come forward during his era. In short, unlike so many of those who came to notice during the bebop era, he was not one who used the eighth note as a basic value in his playing.

It is almost as though Monk understood more quickly than anyone else how the bebop style could be reduced to mannered chord-running and rhythms that were far less varied than those of the various jazz approaches that had preceded it. He seemed intent on underlining what Kenneth Clarke reminds us about "two aspects of a masterpiece." It is "a confluence of memories and emotions forming a single idea" and possesses the "power of re-creating traditional forms so that they become expressive of the artist's own epoch and yet keep a relationship with the past." Quite often in Monk's work we hear the single idea, the form created by recurring and reimagined motives. Through that approach to improvising we experience the extended development of those memories and emotions that were expressed with power but that did not break loose from aesthetic clarity.

Much of the problem that Monk's music presented when it arrived full blown by the end of the 1940s was that its creator was the first Picasso of jazz. He was the first black musician to develop a style that willfully shunned overt virtuosity in favor of a control of the central elements of the music in fresh ways. That Monk's methods were chosen, not stumbled upon, was revealed to pianist Walter Davis, Jr. who had been told by Bud Powell that of all of the jazz pianists, Monk had the greatest mind. In the early fifties, Davis once heard Monk sit down to the piano and play a number of choruses on "Nice Work If You Can Get It" at high speed, executing his own language with the clarity Davis expected from Powell but had no idea was within Monk's capacity. "I knew it then, baby! He wasn't doing what he did because he couldn't play the piano. It was a *choice.*"

So Monk may have been a great aesthetic chef, but he was not a waiter. He might have cooked the food, but the customer had to be ready for some self-service. Just as Picasso demanded that a viewer do something other than peruse a photograph or an *impression* of a photograph, Monk demanded that the listener play the song along with him, fill in the holes he left, figure out where he was, understand what he was doing with the beat, or at least *sense* more than the ordinary. His vision was one of freedom, of comprehensive reliance on his predecessors such as Jelly Roll Morton, James P. Johnson, Duke Ellington, and Count Basie. He even incorporated the drive and the relaxation of Charlie Christian, which included some of his dissonances echoing the tone and the attack of the great, doomed guitarist (who rose to flaming significance in his youth but had his candle extinguished by tuberculosis almost as soon as he was noticed).

Finally, for staying the path and never relinquishing his vision, Thelonious Monk symbolized a kind of integrity we rarely encounter today, when musicians either sell out to the esoteric and to a critical establishment that demands any contrivance so that it can have something to write about. At the other end, there are too many musicians who suffocate their talents inside a security blanket called "relating to the public" or "using the pop music of *our time.*" Monk was never concerned with academic acceptance and he was always above the lowest developments in the popular arena. He knew too much and believed too deeply in what he knew. In his work we hear the now-mythic glamour of the dance hall and the flirtations with the beat and the tempo that are central to the great Afro-American dance tradition. We hear the blues at its most basic and at its most ambitious. We hear those ballads that project as much courage as they do romance, as much deep, deep sentiment as high-minded flair and superb structure. We hear the rhythm called swing delivered with protean intensity, as if willed mutation within the empathetic context of a band is somehow one of the most pure ways of standing up to existence and providing the moment with meaning, as opposed to shallow gestures. We think of all of those things when we think of Monk because, once we understand him, he leaves us with no other choice.

THEODORE DREISER

RICHARD LINGEMAN

THEODORE DREISER'S CAREER was one of the most
obstacle-ridden in our literature. As he once said, "Like a
kite I have risen against the wind—not with it." He picked
his way through a minefield of censorship, snobbery, and
polite euphemisms.

During the first quarter of the twentieth century,
Dreiser dominated the American literary landscape. He
was American literature, the only novelist who wrote
with the mature seriousness and tragic sense of life of
the great Europeans. Born in Indiana to a poor German
immigrant family, with a ninth-grade education, he

seemed almost sui generis, bulking against the sky like a new- formed volcano.

Dreiser had taken his education in newspaper offices, the common school for many writers of his generation. "I went into newspaper work," he recalled, "and from that time dates my real contact with life——-murders, arson, rape, sodomy, bribery, corruption, trickery and false witness in every conceivable form. The cards were put down so fast before me for a while that I was rather stunned. Finally, I got used to the game and rather liked it." It was a prime education in the realities of American life—which he discovered were not reflected in the novels of his day— and he graduated magna cum laude. As Norman Mailer said, "Dreiser came closer to understanding the social machine than any other American writer who ever lived."

But he was not only a novelistic seismograph of social forces, he was a literary innovator whose novels erected a bridge between the Victorian and the modern sensibilities. As his critical champion H. L. Mencken wrote, "American writing, before and after Dreiser, differed almost as much as biology before and after Darwin."

If Dreiser had written nothing after his first novel, *Sister Carrie* (1900), his place in American literature would be secure. But he did write others, including his monumental "Trilogy of Desire"—*The Financier* (1912), *The Titan* (1914) and *The Stoic* (revised and published in 1947)—in which he traced the rise of finance capitalism in America through the career of the ruthless, predatory, philandering transit magnate Frank Cowperwood, who was based on Charles T. Yerkes, the "traction king," who played Monopoly with Chicago's street railroads. Dreiser's autobiographical novel *The "Genius" (1915)* remains a clumsy but passionately honest chronicle of the artist in a business society, torn professionally between creativity and commerce, and in his personal life between sexual happiness and the conventions holding him in an arid marriage.

These and other novels, plays, essays, travelogues, and short stories were battering rams against the critical establishment, still mired in the Victorian mores of the genteel age. Sherwood Anderson summed up what Dreiser meant to the younger writers starting out in the 1910s and 1920s: "The man has . . . pounded his way through such a wall of stupid prejudices and fears that today any man coming into the craft of writing comes with a new inheritance of freedom."

Dreiser was the first major author to challenge the official and tacit censorship of his day. In the second part of the nineteenth century the audience for novels was largely feminine, and white male publishers exercised a paternalistic self-censorship, banning "immoral" subject matter and demanding idealistic stories. Novels featuring heroines who sinned and went unpunished were verboten. The "sex question" was taboo, and the nation's moral policeman, Anthony Comstock, head of the New York Society for the Suppression of Vice, hounded pornographers and abortionists to suicide and threatened reputable publishers with jail if they violated the strict obscenity laws he helped write. *Sister Carrie*, the story of a young woman who falls from virtue and rises socially and economically, threatened to undermine the religious-moral assumptions on which censorship was based.

As the Chicago lawyer-poet Edgar Lee Masters summed up in a letter to Dreiser;

When you wrote Sister Carrie there was just one way in which
to write the novel about a woman. It was to prove that as a
matter of Christian sin, not even cause and consequence . . .
the woman was punished. . . . . You cleaned up the country and
set the pace for the truth and freed the young, and enlightened
the old where they could be enlightened.

The costs to the truth teller could be high, though, as
Dreiser discovered at the beginning of his career. *Sister
Carrie*'s publisher, Frank Doubleday, branded it immoral.
He brought it out only because Dreiser held him to an oral
contract and did all he could to suppress it. Dreiser's fears
that his second novel, *Jennie Gerhardt*, would also be
unpublishable because the heroine has an illegitimate child
and becomes the mistress of a wealthy man, rendered him
incapable of finishing it. He sank into a deep depression
and ended up on the streets, shabby and hungry like Hurst-
wood in *Sister Carrie*. His famous songwriter brother Paul
Dresser ("The Banks of the Wabash") met him by chance
on Broadway and helped him regain his health.

Abandoning novel writing, Dreiser turned to magazine
editing to earn his bread—succeeding at it so well that he
rose to become the handsomely paid editor at Butterick
Publications, a stable of genteel ladies' fashion magazines.
In 1911 he completed *Jennie Gerhardt*. It was banned spo-
radically because of objections to its deterministic view of
its characters' "immoral" behavior and veiled call for a
more open treatment of sexuality in novels.

By then Dreiser had lost his magazine job because of a
love affair with a much younger woman and returned to full-
time writing. He was gaining a following among the young,

but in 1913, his publisher heavily bowdlerized a book about his European tour, which contained frank discussions of sexuality and prostitution. The following year, the second novel of his "Trilogy of Desire," *The Titan*, was withdrawn by Harper & Brothers because the publisher feared Dreiser's muckraking portrait of financial chicanery and lawless capitalism would offend the J. P. Morgan Bank, to which the company was heavily mortgaged.

In 1916, *The "Genius"* appeared, and was banned by Anthony Comstock's successor, John S. Sumner, who believed that Dreiser, the leader of the movement for realism in literature, was a threat to feminine purity. He complained to Dreiser's publisher that the novel's passages describing the hero's sexual awakening were obscene. Threatened with legal action, the publisher quickly took the book off the market.

Despite the successful campaign of H. L. Mencken to persuade leading American authors to sign a petition protesting the ban, the book remained in a legal limbo for seven years. This dealt Dreiser a cruel financial blow. On top of this he was branded as an immoral writer and a German sympathizer because of his pro-German and anti-British views at the beginning of World War I. Publishers and magazine editors shunned him. He abandoned his next novel—*The Bulwark*, the story of a pious Quaker whose strict old-fashioned morality drives his modern-thinking children to rebel—for fear it would be branded seditious in the repressive wartime climate.

In the freer moral air of the 1920s, Dreiser's fortunes improved. A liberal publisher named Horace Liveright reissued *The "Genius"* without censor problems. But ten years elapsed between the publication of that novel and Dreiser's next one, *An American Tragedy*, in 1925. This novel is generally conceded to be Dreiser's masterpiece, a somber, massively documented critique of the destructive impact of class differences and the American dream of wealth and social success on a sensitive youth.

The story of a poor young man who clumsily plots the murder of a factory girl he has seduced and made pregnant stirred up the religious moralists. Boston's puritanical censorship group, the Watch and Ward Society, brought a criminal complaint against it and it was banned under the city's sweeping antiobscenity laws.

That was not the end of the *Tragedy*'s problems with the moralists. In the early 1930s, a movie adaptation of the book, which was to have been filmed by the Russian director Sergei Eisenstein, was canceled by Paramount after complaints by right-wing groups that the script was lewd and full of Communist propaganda. Josef von Sternberg directed a timid version that complied with the Hollywood code in 1931. (In the early 1950s, George Stevens created a bold script based on the novel but excised the social content from the filmed version, *A Place in the Sun*.) The filming of *Sister Carrie* was held up for years by the Hays Office, on the moral complaint of an earlier day— the heroine goes unpunished for her sinful life.

In the late 1930s, Dreiser ran into political censorship because of his support for leftist causes. The Federal Bureau of Investigation kept a dossier on him, interrogated him on one occasion and placed him on a secret list of radicals to be rounded up in a national emergency. Sympathetic with the aims of communism, Dreiser shrugged off party discipline. In a symbolic gesture he joined the party shortly before his death in 1945.

Dreiser fought all his life for artistic and sexual freedom. He had a stubborn, rebellious, at times truculent temperament. His stubbornness was his great strength, but it also led him into foolish actions. His insistence, for example, that Frank Doubleday honor his contract and publish *Sister Carrie* was a mistake, for he could have found a more supportive publisher.

His battle against the de facto ban of *The "Genius"* was ahead of its time, but Dreiser was unable to mount a legal challenge to it because the courts ducked the issue. Mencken, his friend and critical champion, became disillusioned with him when in the middle of the petition campaign, Dreiser wrote a tragedy about a child molester, *The Hand of the Potter* (1919). Mencken begged and hectored him to destroy the inflammatory work, saying it would set back the campaign. But Dreiser refused to budge. No artistic subject was per se immoral, he told Mencken: "as long as I am in possession of my senses current mores will not dictate to me where I shall look for art. My inner instincts and passions and pities are going to instruct me."

Until the end of his days Dreiser waged a fight for the right to say what he believed, artistically and politically. In 1940, he composed a cranky, wrongheaded isolationist tract. The publisher who commissioned it backed out. Then the printer refused to set it in type, and its lawyers demanded changes to tone down the radical message. In the midst of this fight, Dreiser lamented, "I hate . . . to be once more suppressed." Those words were the leitmotif of his entire career.

JOHN STEINBECK

Robert W. Snyder

Years after he slogged through the fields of California to chronicle the struggles of migrant farmworkers from Oklahoma mired in the Great Depression, John Steinbeck set down his thoughts on another American who gave voice to the Okies and their American exodus: Woody Guthrie. Steinbeck praised Guthrie's tough songs and raspy singing, but added that there was something even more important in his music: "the will of a people to endure and fight against oppression. I think we call this the American Spirit."

The same could be said for Steinbeck. In the 1930s, when capitalism collapsed and insurgents of all sorts fought to set the world a-right, Steinbeck honored unsung Americans and their struggles for decent lives. His journalism looked inside the tents of starving migrant workers. His novels, above all *The Grapes of Wrath*, gave the dispossessed unforgettable names and voices—Ma Joad, Tom Joad, Preacher Casey. In later years, critics would call his literary reputation inflated. Old admirers would recoil at his attacks on Vietnam War protesters. But in the 1930s, when dissent was slandered as a Bolshevik plot, John Steinbeck made the fight for a decent place of your own seem downright American. That's why he's worth remembering, celebrating, and learning from decades after he wrote about starving people filled with wrath in a land of plenty.

The rough outlines of Steinbeck's early years recall those of many word-struck young men. Born in 1902, he grew up in Salinas, California, in modest but comfortable circumstances. He vowed to become a writer at fourteen, graduated high school, and was in and out of Stanford University, without earning a degree, from 1919 to 1925. He then did a stint in New York City—first as a construction laborer on the Madison Square Garden, then as a cub reporter for the *New York American*. Returning to California, he worked for a time as a caretaker at a Lake Tahoe estate. He published his first novel in 1929—*Cup of Gold*, based on the life of the buccaneer Henry Morgan.

For a writer who arguably did his best work during the Great Depression, the crash of 1929 had limited initial impact on Steinbeck's writing. Economic disaster churned in the background while the details of his life fell into place. In 1930 he married his first of three wives, Carol Henning, a woman of radical politics who supported and encouraged his writing. Together they settled into the coastal California town of Pacific Grove. Steinbeck befriended Edward F. Ricketts, a marine biologist whose organic, ecological thinking would echo powerfully in Steinbeck's writings. In 1933 he met Lincoln Steffens, who lived nearby in Carmel, California. The old muckraker, then a mentor to young journalists and writers, encouraged Steinbeck and others to investigate the agricultural strikes and trials that rocked California farm labor.

When 1934 began, Steinbeck was still a struggling free-lancer who gave no strong sign that he would produce the most celebrated socially conscious novel of the decade. His course soon began to change, though. Supporters of the Communist-organized Cannery and Agricultural Workers' Industrial Union brought to Steinbeck's area two men fresh from a strike in the San Joaquin Valley. They went by the names of Carl Williams and Cecil McKiddy. The goal of their trip was to spread the word and gain support for their struggle.

Plans to bring McKiddy to Steffens's home fell through, probably because of fear of arrest. Instead, a secret meeting with Steinbeck was arranged. Enthralled by McKiddy, and sensing a good story, Steinbeck decided to work with him to produce a first-person account of a strike leader. He never wrote the story. The episode, however, fostered Steinbeck's first major novel—*In Dubious Battle*, a fictional account of a strike published in 1936. It was followed by *Of Mice and Men* in 1937 and *The Grapes of Wrath* in 1939. The three novels—foremost among them *The Grapes of Wrath*, which also became an acclaimed motion picture—form the bedrock of Steinbeck's reputation as the writer who told the stories of Dust Bowl refugees.

It's a reputation that has been battered in the decades since the Depression. Among literary critics, Steinbeck is often seen as a sentimental writer of leaden prose, uneven output, and murky philosophy. The women in his books seem limited to evil temptresses or sustaining mothers. His emphasis on native-born Okies as symbols of agricultural labor could obscure the toil and strikes of Mexican, Chinese, Filipino, and Japanese workers. Over time, as the scholar William Stott observed of much documentary writing produced in the '30s, Steinbeck's work moved from identifying America's failures to celebrating its strengths.

There is something to all of these criticisms, but they shouldn't be allowed to obscure the vitality of Steinbeck's best work. In *The Grapes of Wrath*, he united fact and feeling, the story of a general crisis and an individual family, to scald America's injustices and affirm the strength of its working people. He wrote as a reporter, a novelist, and a radical democrat. A lifelong journalist, Steinbeck brought to *The Grapes of Wrath* a detailed knowledge of migrant struggles and poverty gained while reporting the workers' crisis for *The Nation*, the *San Francisco News*, and the *Monterey Trader*. (The *Trader* picked up a Steinbeck piece originally written for *Life* that was too hot for the Luce publication.) Describing a starving three-year-old in a piece for the *News*, he wrote: "He sits on the ground in the sun in front of the house, and the little black fruit flies buzz in circles and land on his closed eyes and crawl up his nose until he weakly brushes them away."

Steinbeck—a prolific and versatile writer—was fully alive to the media of his time. In *The Grapes of Wrath* he wrote with the imagery of films and newsreels ("the last rains came gently, and they did not cut the scarred earth"), the attention to the individual that distinguished documentary photography, and the dialogue of radio drama. Although the novel's emphasis on home, family, and the prospect of a small farm seemed nostalgic in a time when most Americans lives in cities, Steinbeck understood the depths of the agricultural depression and the deep resonance of rural life in American culture.

He also looked forward. Thanks to his friend Tom Collins, who ran New Deal Farm Security Administration camps for migrant workers, Steinbeck gained a close look at the kind of lives Okies could live if government action lifted their worst burdens. Standing in Collins's Arvin Sanitary Camp, better known as Weedpatch, Steinbeck sketched something like an American social democracy: self-government, decent living conditions, and a Saturday night square dance. ("This here's a nice place," says Ma Joad. "We could be happy here awhile.")

The Grapes of Wrath resonated with other works of the 1930s, such as Woody Guthrie's songs, Dorothea Lange's photography, and Carey McWilliams's book *Factories in the Fields*. Together, they helped to foster a political stance that brought radicalism, liberalism, and a faith in "the common man" into a complex but fruitful alliance. There were problems and limits to this bloc. (Among other weaknesses, it never fully incorporated African-Americans and projects like Collins's Weedpatch Camp were too few.) Still, it sustained the Popular Front and the broader, longer-lived New Deal order. For decades, it protected Americans from the worst depredations of laissez-faire conservatives.

It all began to come apart, and with it some of Steinbeck's

reputation, during the Cold War. Steinbeck never joined the Communist Party, and his skepticism about the Machiavellian tendencies of party organizers was abundantly clear in his novel *In Dubious Battle*. But he attended enough John Reed Club meetings, met enough radicals, and said enough about the fascist tendencies of California vigilantes to attract the attention of the Federal Bureau of Investigation. Security checks dogged him into World War II. In the '50s, Steinbeck was an Adlai Stevenson Democrat with a healthy contempt for both Communist orthodoxy and the anti-Communist witch-hunters in Congress. His reputation among leftists and liberals suffered in the '60s, though. Some of his worst wounds were self-inflicted.

In 1964, President Lyndon Baines Johnson invited Steinbeck into the White House to work on his nomination acceptance speech. As the Vietnam War and the President grew more unpopular, Steinbeck continued to endorse the American military effort. His popularity and credibility suffered. Communism brought out the skeptic in Steinbeck, but anti-Communism led him into dubious battles—especially when it combined with his eager loyalty to American fighting men. In World War II, that allegiance made sense. In Vietnam, it led him to a cockeyed support for a mean war. A tour in Vietnam as a *Newsday* columnist from late 1966 into 1967, while his son served there in the Army, produced pieces that lauded the power of American weaponry and the good character of American soldiers. Back home, antiwar critics howled. In private, Steinbeck developed questions about the war. None of them, however, took the form of a firm public statement before he died in 1968.

The centennial of Steinbeck's birth in 2002 highlighted

signs of enduring and even resurgent interest in the author: conferences, the Center for Steinbeck Studies at San Jose State University, the National Steinbeck Center in his native Salinas, and a project to read and discuss *The Grapes of Wrath* throughout California. More attention came the summer 2003, when Oprah Winfrey selected *East of Eden* for her book club and made the novel a bestseller.

In fact, even without Oprah, Steinbeck's books still sell well—about 2 million copies a year. Some academics and literary critics may shake their heads at Steinbeck—even question his Nobel Prize for Literature in 1962—but plenty of ordinary people like him. Students read Steinbeck in their introductions to American literature. Westerners see him as one of their own in a literary culture dominated by the East. Readers with an ecological sensibility recognize his fascination with people and their environment. Professors of American Studies assign *The Grapes of Wrath* because it illuminates the radical politics and fiction of the '30s. Professors of journalism cite his articles on migrant workers to show how reporting can invigorate literature. Internationally, he remains one of the most popular of American authors.

Steinbeck may have died with a reputation as a supporter of a bad war, but his bequest is bigger than that. As Steinbeck's friend Arthur Miller wrote in a centennial tribute, the man's life was a struggle: first to be recognized, and then to fight off "easy and shallow popularity and the wiles of show-business values." And when Steinbeck was wrong, as Miller felt he was about the Vietnam War, he didn't take the easy way out. "In a word," Miller concluded, "he was not outside the battle, safe in his fame, but in it to the end."

The author of *The Grapes of Wrath* still inspires liberals and the left. The John Steinbeck Award of the Steinbeck Center at San Jose State has gone to Bruce Springsteen, John Sayles, Arthur Miller, Jackson Browne, Studs Terkel, and Joan Baez. Not a conservative, compassionate or otherwise, in the bunch.

Steinbeck's best work echoes through his successors in American culture. You can read it in Terkel's oral histories and in Barbara Ehrenreich's reports on working life. You can see it in Milton Rogovin's photographs of the forgotten people of Buffalo, New York. You can hear it in David Isay's radio documentaries about America's neglected voices and in the Springsteen album *The Ghost of Tom Joad*, with its stories about immigrants from Vietnam and Mexico straining for the American dream.

In the battles of memory against forgetting, Steinbeck helps us recall a time when the solidarity of American working people, aided by government action, met the worst of the Great Depression. And he does more. Harry Hopkins, who led some of the New Deal's best work at the Works Progress Administration, grasped the problem that Steinbeck confronted. "You can pity six men," he wrote in his 1936 book *Spending to Save*, "but you can't keep stirred up over six million." Steinbeck taught us how to see the few and the many. After *The Grapes of Wrath*, the victims of the Depression had unforgettable faces and voices. Steinbeck's words made plain people's struggles against injustice part of the American spirit.

MARIO PUZO

NICHOLAS PILEGGI

WHEN *The Godfather* was first published in 1969, word spread quickly among the nation's literate wiseguys that there was something to read beside subpoenas. Here was a book filled with bits of authentic street gossip that could easily be compared to live dons, band singers, and casino bosses.

For instance, was Don Corleone based on Carlo Gambino or Joe Profaci? Profaci was in the olive oil business and had politicians in his pocket, but Carlo Gambino was the don who first forbade the sale of narcotics.

And when the crooner, Johnny Fontane, got his contract

release from a bandleader in the back room of a New
Jersey roadhouse, everybody knew it was Giuseppe "Joe
Adonis" Doto, not Luca Brasi, who made the offer Tommy
Dorsey could not refuse.

What was Puzo doing? What did he really know? Who
was he talking to? What were his sources?

"I'm ashamed to admit that I wrote *The Godfather*
entirely from research," Puzo later said in the foreword
to *The Godfather Papers*. "After the book became
'famous,' I was introduced to a few gentlemen related to
the material.

"They were flattering, but they refused to believe I had
never been in the rackets. They refused to believe that I
had never had the confidence of a Don. But all of them
loved the book."

Puzo recalled how bottles of champagne would arrive at
his table unordered from men with sunglasses and diamond pinkie rings.

The truth about Puzo, however, was that he did not have
to go to a don or the cops for any secrets. He already knew
them.

Born and raised in Hell's Kitchen, along a stretch of
Manhattan's Tenth Avenue in the West Thirties, Mario
Puzo grew up in the kind of Italian immigrant neighbor-
hood that Columbia University sociologist Dr. Irving
Spergel defined as a "Racket subculture."

It was a neighborhood in which storefronts were converted into "members only" social clubs and the local men,
including off-duty waiters, burglars, construction workers,
bookmakers, truck drivers, hijackers, civil servants, and
loan sharks, would spend hours playing cards, arguing

about the prizefights, and getting away from their wives and kids upstairs in the tenements.

There were candy stores with stale pretzels and lunch-eonettes with more guys taking numbers than flipping burgers. It was a neighborhood in which the rackets—and racketeers—were considered a normal way of life.

Growing up in this kind of insular and suspicious neighborhood, Puzo saw how the grim immigrant residents and their first-generation children shunned the entire law-enforcement structure: the police, who might interfere with their wine cellars; the judges, who confused justice with honor; and the lawyers, who could steal more with a briefcase than a hundred men with guns.

Community problems—from getting resident visas for bakers named Enzo, to justice for undertakers named Bonasera—were solved in the storefront social clubs where "men of respect," very much like Vito Corleone, doled out nineteenth-century Sicilian justice in the twentieth-Century New York.

Mario Puzo grew up in a community where pigheaded-ness was considered a virtue and where a good discussion lent itself to arguments rather than answers. Puzo had seen the old dons soothe bruised egos, calm the hysteric and, when necessary, chill the intractable with deathly fear. It was through these clubs that order was imposed on the community. In return, the community responded by sounding the alarm whenever anything suspicious turned up in the neighborhood. Of course, not everyone in these clubs was a racketeer, but they all knew each other. They had grown up together. They knew who lived where, who worked where, what time they went out, when they'd get home. They knew each other's parents, as well as each other's sisters and brothers.

Puzo grew up in an area where the mob watched out for the neighborhood and the neighborhood watched out for the mob.

To write *The Godfather*, Mario Puzo really didn't have to interview anyone but himself.

Born in 1920, and raised in a sixth-floor railroad flat overlooking the "black iron gardens" of the New York Central Railroad, Puzo says he always dreamed of being an artist or a writer.

When his father died before his teenage years, Puzo's dreams seemed distant, except he spent hours reading in the library at the nearby Hudson Guild Settlement House. After serving in the army during World War II, Puzo studied writing at Columbia University and the New School.

His first novel, *The Dark Arena*, was published in 1955. His second novel *The Fortunate Pilgrim*, published in 1964, was called a "small classic" by the *New York Times*. Between novels, Puzo married and moved to Long Island with his wife and children, but the themes of his work always came from his neighborhood roots.

"Nearly all the Italian men living on Tenth Avenue supported their large families by working on the railroad," Puzo later wrote. "Their children also earned pocket money by stealing ice from the refrigerator cars in summer and coal from the open stoking cars in winter.

The older boys, the ones just approaching voting age, made their easy money by hijacking silk trucks that loaded up at the garment factory on Thirty-first Street. They would sell the expensive dresses door to door, at bargain prices no discount house could match. From this some graduated into organized crime, whose talent scouts alertly tapped young boys versed in strong arm. Yet, despite all this, most of the kids grew up honest, content with fifty bucks a week as truck drivers, deliverymen, and white-collar clerks in the Civil Service.

I had every desire to go wrong but I never had a chance. The family structure was too formidable. I never came home to an empty house. My mother was always there to greet me, sometimes with a policeman's club in her hand (nobody ever knew how she acquired it) . . . My father had access to the fruits coming off ships, the produce from railroad cars, all before it went through the stale process of middlemen . . .

The fact that much of the food on the Puzo table "fell off a truck" and that he never remembered his mother using anything but the finest olive oil or Italian cheeses, was the reality of his neighborhood. There was no condemnation on Tenth Avenue for larcenies involving food, shelter, and warmth. In fact, they were looked upon as enterprising.

Puzo had an uncle, an assistant chef in a famous New York restaurant, who tucked six eggs, a stick of butter, and a small bag of flour under his shirt every day, six days a week.

"By doing this for thirty years," Puzo said, "he was able to save enough money to buy a fifteen-thousand-dollar house on Long Island and two smaller houses for his son and daughter . . . My mother and her friends did not thing this stealing. They thought of it as being thrifty."

While compared to *Sesame Street*, this might look like a colorful neighborhood in which to grow up, but Puzo saw it differently:

I dreaded growing up like the adults around me. I heard them saying too many cruel things about their dearest friends, saw too many of their false embraces with those they had just maligned, observed with horror their paranoid anger at some small slight or a fancied injury to their pride They were, always, too unforgiving.

. . . I never heard an Italian singing. None of the grownups I knew were charming or loving or understanding. Rather they seemed coarse, vulgar, and insulting. And so later in my life when I was exposed to all the clichés of loveable Italians, singing Italians, happy-go-lucky Italians, I wondered where the hell the movie makers and storywriters got all their ideas from.

Puzo straightened them out. He drew upon those Old World threads of neighborhood suspicion and spun them back as gold.

In *The Dark Arena* and *The Fortunate Pilgrim,* Puzo wrote about the difficulties such a grim world presented to its powerless and impoverished inhabitants. These earlier books got excellent reviews, but racked up modest sales.

It was not until 1969 that things changed. Suddenly, with the publication of *The Godfather,* Puzo's neighborhood insights touched universal themes. The book attracted a huge national and international audience. It sold over 20 million copies. It is one of the best-selling books ever.

The book arrived at a time when many Americans were feeling cynical and powerless about their government. Assassinations wounded the country. Street crime was rampant. Drugs were uncontrollable. A divided country was fighting an unpopular war in which more than fifty thousand young men had died while one hundred thousand others returned to meager benefits, no parades, and a taste for drugs.

When Don Corleone disparages Michael's Marine Corps heroics with "He performs those miracles for strangers?" the sentiment was not lost on an anti–Vietnam War generation.

Turning mobsters into empathetic characters, however, was not easy, but Puzo lulled us into feeling for the Corleones as skillfully as Clemenza might slip into the rear seat of your car as you set off on a one-way ride for cannoli.

Puzo accomplished this, in part, by making sure we understood that Vito Coreleone was shot because he refused to deal in the dirty business of narcotics. That Sonny Corelone, his impetuous son, was killed in an ambush because he tried to save his pregnant sister from a brutal husband. And, that Michael Corleone, the godfather's college-educated war-hero son, assumed his father's Mafia mantle not out of greed, but from a sense of responsibility to his father, who, for all his illegal activities, was a far more honorable man than all the crooked cops, venal judges, corrupt politicians and perverted businessmen who peppered the plot and, for that matter, America.

When Amerigo Bonasera went to the godfather for justice and revenge against the college boys who abused his daughter, the don asks why he didn't come to his earlier?

"I went to the police like a good American," Bonasera says. "America has been good to me. I wanted to be a good citizen. I wanted my child to be an American."

"Then you have nothing to complain about," the don says. "The judge has ruled. America has ruled. Bring your daughter flowers and a box of candy when you visit her in

the hospital. That will comfort her. Be content . . . Give me
your word that you will put aside this madness. It is not
American. Forgive. Forget . . ."

But when Bonasera vacillates, the Don continues:

> You go to the law courts and wait for months. You spend your
> money on lawyers who know full well you are to be made a
> fool of. You accept judgment from a judge who sells himself like
> the worst whore on the streets. Years gone by, when you
> needed money, you went to the banks and paid ruinous
> interest, waited hat in hand like a beggar while they sniffed
> around, poked their noses up your very asshole to make sure
> you could pay them back.
>
> But, if you had come to me, my purse would have been
> yours. If you had come to me for justice those scum who ruined
> your daughter would be weeping bitter tears this day. If by
> some misfortune an honest man like yourself made enemies
> they would become my enemies and then, believe me, they
> would fear you.

That was it. At that moment, millions of legitimate,
churchgoing, white-bread Americans, people who had
never heard of godfather or cannoli, but had felt the sting
of injustice, stood ready to turn their backs on the Constitution and its Yankee Doodle courts and join Bonasera for
a little visceral justice.

Mario Puzo had written much more than the mob's
Forsyte Saga. He wrote a book that planted the seeds of
Sicilian revenge in the hearts of Middle Western Americans, and ended forever the myth of "loveable, singing,
happy-go-lucky Italians."

DOROTHY DAY

WAYNE BARRETT AND CHRIS BARRETT

IN THE FINAL days of Rudy Giuliani's term as mayor of
New York, three months after the heroism of 9/11, he quietly approved a politically wired project to build twenty-
five multimillion-dollar mansions on Staten Island. An
expediter for the project's mob-tied developer was already
under indictment for forging the demolition permit that
had cleared the site illegally. Nonetheless, Giuliani's
deputy mayor secretly summoned his reluctant planning
commission chairman to City Hall to read him the riot act
over delaying it, forcing the final go-ahead.

The forged permit—which later led to a conviction—

authorized an ambush on a sanctuary. The Catholic Worker movement owned the three wooden cottages destroyed by bulldozers in the dead of night. One had long been occupied by its founder, Dorothy Day, who spurned personal property, ate the same gruel served now in her 200 Worker hospitality houses worldwide, wore the same discarded clothes she gave the poor, and carried only a prayer book and a coffee jar on her pilgrimages across America.

Nominated for canonization by Cardinal John O'Connor in 1998, Day was buried near the bungalow in 1980. She'd converted to Catholicism in 1927, while living in another bungalow a short distance down the Raritan Bay beach. She'd started the first Catholic Worker farm nearby.

The memory of her on the island, and across the city, was so strong that church and preservation groups had been petitioning Giuliani's Landmarks Commission for three and a half years to designate the cottages as landmarks, even cornering the mayor himself at a Town Hall meeting. While landmark officials had refused to make the designation, they had also barred demolition as negotiations with the builder continued. That's why the developer and his partners, who had contributed $41,000 to Giuliani and his GOP allies, needed a phony permit to level them— just the sort of lawlessness that former prosecutor Rudy ordinarily went bonkers about.

Not this time.

Giuliani had launched his putative Senate campaign against Hillary Clinton in 2000, before prostate cancer and a public mistress cut it short, by attempting to make himself the Catholic candidate in a very Catholic state. He'd shut down a Brooklyn Museum art exhibit because it featured an arguably profane painting of the Virgin Mary with elephant dung. But by 2001, when the Day controversy exploded, the Catholic posturing by the rare churchgoer was over.

Dorothy Day was hardly Rudy Giuliani's kind of Catholic, anyway. With the $57 she and four friends put together in 1933, partly from an article she published in *America* magazine, they printed an eight-page tabloid called *The Catholic Worker* and handed out 2,500 copies at the May Day Communist rally in Union Square. With only the $5 she had to her name a few months later, she rented a vacant apartment to provide emergency shelter for six homeless women after hearing that one of their friends had thrown herself in front of a subway. These two acts launched one of the most elegantly simple revolutions in history.

Feeding the hungry, giving drink to the thirsty, welcoming the stranger, and sheltering the homeless were seen by Day "as the very ground of the Christian life." Day chose for herself a life of voluntary poverty, a call not only to serve the poor but to join them in their poverty. In a radical shift of Catholic tradition, Day mothered a lay movement in which Christ's counsel to be poor in spirit became a physical reality, in the everyday form of voluntary rather than vowed poverty. Her lay ministry with the homeless, as well as the creation of a lay community with the impoverished, departed from the centuries-old Catholic custom of using vowed, celibate religious orders to meet the needs of the church and the world.

While the church norm, going back to St. Benedict in the fifth century, had been the establishment of highly regulated and legalistic celibate communities, Day created an anarchistic lay community dedicated solely to service. Hostels were her cathedrals. Rags were her vestments. Bread was her eucharist, soup her wine. Even as her Worker network of houses and farms spread across America and the world, she gave it no overarching rules or creed, leaving it amazingly free of Catholic formalism, as much a structural challenge to orthodoxy as it was an activist rebuff of clerical complacency. Her message made her the most influential and inspirational leader of Catholic outreach since St. Francis of Assisi in the twelfth century, who, like her, called the church back to its "communistic" roots of radical redistribution of wealth to ensure that none were in need.

Despite her radicalism, she was never a Church pariah. "Though she is a harlot at times," Day wrote of the Church in one of her eight books, "she is our mother." Her devotion to its essential teachings was beyond question—a daily communicant, she also recited the Psalms each day, explaining to a fellow prisoner and drug addict in the Women's House of Detention that they were her "fix." Weathering an abortion in her twenties, she came to share the Church's pro-life beliefs, converting when she later baptized her only child, even at the cost of her marriage to a confirmed atheist. The University of Notre Dame, for example, gave her its highest honor, the Laetare Medal, recognizing her as one "who comforted the afflicted and afflicted the comfortable." The Vatican announced on March 16, 2000, that it had started the canonization process, triggered by O'Connor, who said of her: "She is not a 'gingerbread' saint or a 'holy card' saint, but a modern-day devoted daughter of the Church."

Her difficulties with the hierarchy, especially Cardinal Francis Spellman of New York, revolved around her peace advocacy, not her work with the poor. Adamant opposition to all war and preparation for war—"gospel nonviolence"— were a hallmark of her life. "We believe that Christ went beyond natural ethics . . . and taught nonviolence as a way of life," she wrote, confronting the willingness of church leaders like Spellman to find "just war" rationales for every nationalist military adventure.

Her Worker organizations never paid federal income taxes or sought tax exemptions. Most of her six or seven jail terms were a result of acts of antiwar civil disobedience. Her opposition to the Spanish Civil War, World War II, the Korean War, Vietnam, the cold war, and the nuclear arms race aligned her with the early Church fathers, who universally opposed Christian participation in war, but pitted her against more recent prelates. Her views helped move the Church, leading to the condemnation of indiscriminate warfare and nuclear weapons at Vatican II in 1965, and paving the way for the Pope's current critique of Bush's "war on terror."

In the January 1942 issue of the *Catholic Worker*, the first after the Pearl Harbor attack, she wrote: "Our manifesto is the Sermon on the Mount. . . . We will print the words of Christ who is with us always—even to the end of the world. 'Love your enemies, do good to those who hate you.' " A Worker newspaper ran the same piece—under the same headline ("We Continue Our Christian Pacifist Stand")—almost sixty years later, in the first issue after September 11, 2001.

In her last public appearance, on August 6, 1976, she

questioned the Church's reluctance to condemn nuclear weapons. Asked to address the International Eucharistic Congress in Philadelphia at a mass to honor the military, she noted that it was also the anniversary of the bombing of Hiroshima. "Here we are on the day the first atomic bomb was dropped. Our Creator gave us life. . . . But we have given the world instruments of death of inconceivable magnitude. Today we are celebrating—how strange to use such a word—a mass for the military. . . . Why not a mass for the military on some other day? I plead that we regard the military mass, and all our masses today, as an act of penance, begging God to forgive us."

This fierce pacifism was linked to her voluntary poverty by the common bond of her life: love. "The measure by which we will be judged," love in action, was to her, as it was to Father Zossima in *The Brothers Karamazov,* "a harsh and dreadful thing compared to love in dreams." The "revolution of the heart" that Day invoked was a life of loving sacrifice that was its own pained reward.

Her radicalism was determinedly Catholic, a conscious rejection of secular activism. She had grown up with Jack London, Peter Kropotkin, Charles Dickens, and Upton Sinclair. She'd found work early in life at the socialist magazines, *The Call* and *The Masses.* But she went from cutting religion out of her life to making it the core. One of her best friends, Mike Gold, a writer at the *Daily Worker,* introduced her to Eugene O'Neill, who would recite Francis Thompson's famous religious poem, "The Hound of Heaven," to her in the back room of the Hell Hole, a tavern where they'd often meet. It made her feel "so great a need to reverence, to worship, to adore." She became a mystic on a pilgrimage from God, of God and toward God, one of history's great spiritual athletes.

The communist and socialist movements were insufficiently individual to her, wedded to the abstraction of the masses. She was drawn to the work of a French Catholic named Emmanuel Mounier, who inspired the personalist movement through his journal, *Esprit*. Two papal encyclicals—"On the Condition of Labor" by Pope Leo XIII in 1891 and "After Forty Years by Pius XI in 1931"—led to the founding of her Worker network. As Day's lieutenant Eileen Egan wrote: "The core of the movement was the recognition of the importance of each person."

Seventy years after the first Catholic Worker community opened in New York, two followers of Dorothy Day, Bill and Sue Frankel-Streit, opened one of the latest Worker homes in rural Louisa County, Virginia, just in time for last Christmas. They called it the Little Flower Catholic Worker Farm, named after Saint Thérèse of Lisieux ("The Little Flower"), whose autobiography was a Day favorite. Located in a dilapidated antebellum farmhouse with primitive heating, the Worker farm feeds and succors the country poor just as Day did among the tall stalks of Manhattan decades ago. As Bill Frankel-Streit stoked the wood stove around which a dozen Day descendants gathered for the mass of dedication with Bishop Walter Sullivan of Richmond, he joked that this new house of love was "a diamond in the rough."

So was its inspiration.

BENJAMIN MAYS

ROGER WILKINS

BENJAMIN ELIJAH MAYS—devout Christian minister, uncompromising advocate for justice, career educator and longtime president of Morehouse College in Atlanta—was called the "Schoolmaster of the [civil rights] Movement" by the historian Lerone Bennett, Jr. Indeed, among the thousands of proud black men who were shaped by Mays, there were many who played key roles in that movement, including Martin Luther King, Jr. and Julian Bond. Bond, once communications director of the Student Nonviolent Coordinating Committee and now a university professor and chairman of the board of the NAACP, remembered Mays in a recent interview: "He was the embodiment of everything we wanted to be, and even though we knew we could never achieve his greatness, we strove to be like him. I revered him."

Bond was not alone in his reverence. In recalling Mays's influence on her husband, Coretta Scott King wrote in *My Life With Martin Luther King, Jr.*, that her husband's decision to go into the ministry

> was largely due to the example of Dr. Benjamin E. Mays. . . . From first to last, Dr. Mays took a great interest in Martin. It was not so much that he deliberately guided him toward the ministry as that he influenced Martin by his own example. For although Dr. Mays was brilliant, he was not removed from the heart of the people. In the pulpit he talked a great deal about social justice; you might say he preached a social gospel. This conformed exactly with Martin's ideas, and it helped to form them. . . . At Morehouse, listening to Dr. Mays preach . . . Martin came to see that the ministry could be intellectually respectable as well as emotionally satisfying.

Andrew Young, once King's trusted lieutenant, then congressman, ambassador to the United Nations and mayor of Atlanta, made the point that the leading black professionals in every city in the country and "most certainly one of the key preachers and probably most of the black elected officials owe where they are to Dr. Mays."

I am not a Southerner, but I began to sense the power of this extraordinary man when I first stepped onto the lowest level of the national stage. Proud of my two degrees from the University of Michigan, I joined the State Department in 1962 and was mentored by Bob Kitchen, an elegant black For-

eign Service officer and a Morehouse graduate. "Too bad you
didn't go to Morehouse," he said after I had confided uncer-
tainties about my ability to function in Washington. "You
could have been raised up by Benny Mays." Over the years, I
learned from a number of other "Morehouse Men" that a
central element of Mays's gift to them was a conviction that
their minds and their determination to do right would prevail, no matter how many of the antiblack booby traps
embedded in American culture might blow up in their paths.

Considering his inauspicious beginning, no one could have
foreseen that Mays would become a shaper of strong men and
of events. The year of his birth was 1894; the place, a few
miles outside the village of Ninety Six; the state, South Carolina; the parents, former slaves; the race, Negro. Despite all
that, the baby born black, poor, and Southern would confound
stereotypes drawn by a wide variety of Americans; early-twen-
tieth-century white academics, 1960s Black Power advocates
and 1980s conservatives. Six years after Mays's birth, Paul Bar-
ringer, who was faculty chair at the University of Virginia, lectured that anything more than "Sunday-school training" was
wasted on the black because his lot in life was to be a "source
of cheap labor for a warm climate; everywhere else he is a fore-
ordained failure, and as he knows this he despises his own
color." Many decades into Mays's astonishing life as a pillar of
black education and constructive and active citizenship, he and
his kind were derided by Black Power advocates of the late
1960s as hopelessly docile and out-of-date. In the 1980s, as
Mays's life was coming to a close, conservatives—black and
white together—were claiming to have invented a new
remedy for black ills: self-help.

Mays's powerful, devout and astonishingly constructive

life as a world traveler, civil rights stalwart, writer, minister, citizen-activist, educator-mentor and confidant to a wide range of influential national figures, including presidents, contradicted all these sloppy stereotypes. He was as brilliant as anyone who ever taught at the University of Virginia, a far more effective and long-lasting instrument of black advancement than any of the Black Power leaders, and a man for whom black self-help had settled into the core of his moral compass at about the time many of the 1980s conservatives were being born.

Mays was born in the era of the white terror in the South. Blacks were pushed back on all fronts by whites who were determined to "redeem" as much of pre–Civil War dominance as possible and therefore sought to impose black subservience across the board. To this end, the Ku Klux Klan and other night-riding terrorists, aided and abetted by many local law-enforcement agencies, did everything possible—including lynchings—to slam blacks back into the "place" whites believed appropriate. The cast of mind of the majority of South Carolina whites in the days of Mays's youth is best exemplified in the comment made by Senator Benjamin Tillman after President Theodore Roosevelt had invited Booker T. Washington to dine with him in the White House: "The action of President Roosevelt in entertaining that nigger will necessitate our killing a thousand niggers in the South before they will learn their place again."

The story of how Mays traveled the road from "Pitchfork" Ben Tillman's South Carolina to the fullness of his maturity, when he had become an important factor in our national life, is a many-faceted example of the black self-help tradition at work at its highest level. That tradition runs back to the time before the United States was a country, when blacks on plantations took care of one another as best they could and began transforming Christianity into a liberation theology. Then, during the Revolution, each side had blacks in its ranks soldiering for, among other reasons, their own freedom as they simultaneously tried to figure out how to purchase liberty for their families as well. In 1787, as great white founders were drafting the Constitution in Philadelphia, the great black founders, Richard Allen and Absalom Jones, were also at work in that city, creating the Free African Society, the first formal black self-help group in the country. The tradition continued in the nineteenth century, with Nat Turner's attempt to wrest freedom forcefully from his owners; through Harriet Tubman's and Frederick Douglass's freedom and abolitionary crusades; by black soldiers fighting for the Union and slaves attaching themselves to the conquering Union armies; and finally through the postwar educators—most notably Booker T. Washington—who in the late nineteenth century dedicated their lives to providing education to the newly freed slaves and their children.

In his autobiography, *Born to Rebel,* Mays wrote that even as a child surrounded by South Carolina cotton fields, "I really wanted to learn. . . . Vaguely, yet ardently, I longed to know, for I sensed that knowledge could set me free." But education was hard to come by in Ninety Six, where black cotton-pickers were far more highly prized than black readers. Thus for many years Mays could attend school only in the months from November through February. Another obstacle was his father's skepticism about the value of an education. But, encouraged by his mother and carried through by a supernatural level of persistence and grit (which included cleaning latrines in the wee hours to pay his keep), Mays managed to finish high school at twenty-one. He then made his way to Bates College in Maine.

As usual, he worked his way through school, graduating with honors, having been a debater and a football player. Bates provided Mays with his first opportunity to make friends with whites. His graduation from Bates began a work-study journey toward a Ph.D. in philosophy from the University of Chicago, a journey that was punctuated by the ministry as pastor of the Shiloh Baptist Church in Atlanta; his apprenticeship as an educator at Morehouse and the South Carolina high school, from which he had graduated; and community-service work with the Tampa Urban League and later as national student secretary of the YMCA. During this period, Mays married and then suffered the loss of his wife, Ellen, and subsequently married Sadie Gray, who had been a high-school classmate.

This rich tapestry of experiences gave Mays deep, firm roots in the Southern black community and a certain ironic knowledge of life in the liberal North, where he encountered the legendary racism of Chicago—including from some of his professors at the university who would not speak to him outside the classroom. A few months before the award of his doctorate, Mays was appointed dean of the school of religion at Howard University, a job that he held with great distinction for six years until, in 1940, he assumed the presidency of Morehouse.

Mays brought his profound faith in God, his deep understanding of the Bible and of the Negro church, and his experience as an educator to Howard. During his six years there, the school gained accreditation by the American Association of Theological Schools—the second black seminary to achieve that status. While Mays was dean, Howard Divinity School sent forth a large number of men who would become major leaders of the church and of society. During that period, Mays broadened his perspective by traveling a good deal—most significantly to South Africa and to India, where he and Gandhi had deep exchanges on the philosophy and tactics of nonviolent social activism.

Mays needed all his faith, his deep learning, his passion for rendering service, and his enormous energy when he became president of Morehouse, which was then the impoverished weak sister of black higher education in Atlanta and was falling rapidly toward junior-college status. As president, he set out to correct all the institution's problems; by the time he retired twenty-seven years later, both he and the college were legendary. Mays left a solvent college with an excellent faculty and many buildings that hadn't been there when he took over. But most important of all, he made Morehouse Men—legions of them—whom he sent out into the world in the mold of Benjamin Mays.

When I told Washington businessman and civic activist James Hudson, Morehouse '61, the story about my State Department colleague Bob Kitchen from Brunswick, Georgia, Jim said: "That's what he did. He went around to all those little towns in Georgia—and other states too— and found these smart small-town boys with limited futures and brought them to Morehouse. Some of these kids hadn't even finished high school, but he had developed a special program for any really promising students

he discovered." (Martin Luther King Jr. entered Morehouse in 1944, when he was fifteen.)

"Mays got to us through those Tuesday chapel sessions,"
Hudson said. "He told us, 'Yes there is segregation, but
your mind is free. Your job is to cultivate your mind to its
fullest extent. Now segregation is a reality, but it is not an
excuse. What is important is to make your mind work.' "

Both Hudson and Bond describe a Morehouse that was
suffused with the personality and drive of this energetic,
religious, loving, service-giving man. He worked ceaselessly
to drive the hesitation and self-doubt that segregation was
designed to implant in the black spirit right out of every
man who came to Morehouse. The Morehouse Man was to
be a man of dignity and pride and intellect and faith and
commitment to justice—in a word, he was to be like Mays.
Everyone I have ever known who went to Morehouse in his
time carried a large dose of Benjamin Mays in his spirit.
Mays made sure that he knew each and every Morehouse
Man very well and that each of them had felt his expectations of them, both individually and through his weekly
appearance at chapel, where he addressed them all.

"You knew, if you let yourself down, you were letting
him down," Hudson said. "You know, in all father-son relationships there's bound to be some friction generated by
family stuff and household intimacy. With Mays, it was
like a clean father-son relationship." Both Bond and
Hudson describe an indefatigable model that was as clear
in both word and deed as a human being could be. "The
big reason people trusted him," Hudson said, "was the way
he lived his life; no women, no money problems. And the
interest in you was real. Long after you had left, he would

follow you, check on you, see how you were doing and give you encouragement."

That comment reminded me of a remarkable encounter I had with Mays in Washington sometime in the late 1970s, long after he had left Morehouse. After some major African-American event had ended in a Washington hotel and most of the people had left, I spotted him sitting alone at a large table looking thoughtfully toward the door through which the last stragglers were drifting away. I had met Mays briefly and casually a couple of times over the years, so I went over to pay my respects to him and, to my surprise, he invited me to sit down.

I was somewhat stunned that he remembered me and that he knew what I was doing for a living. After we talked about journalism a bit, he gave me a searching look and asked, "Has being Roy Wilkins's nephew been a burden to you?"

My eyes widened at his directness and his perceptiveness, but I answered. "It has been—sometimes more than others, but yes—a burden along with the blessings."

Mays smiled and said, "Cherish the blessings and ignore the burdens. Just do your work—your best work." I remembered my old friend Bob Kitchen then, and his comment that "Benny Mays could have raised you up." Indeed.

Mays's life was full of activities beyond the campus. Most notably, he served a term in the 1970s as president of the Atlanta Board of Education, where he led the effort to devise a program to desegregate the schools without sending the white population fleeing to the suburbs. He was a force in the National and the World Council of Churches, a member of the board of the NAACP, and committee member of the NAACP Legal Defense Fund. He was one of the black leaders to whom Presidents Kennedy and Johnson turned during the turbulent 1960s. Kennedy intended to nominate him to a seat on the U.S. Commission on civil rights, but the move was blocked by Georgia senators who charged that he was a Communist because of his memberships in organizations fighting lynching and seeking to improve black education in the South. Mays denied being a Communist. "They don't believe in God," Mays said. "I couldn't belong to a group that doesn't accept God." Kennedy appointed him to the Peace Corps Advisory Council instead, and later included Mays in the U.S. delegation that attended the June 3, 1963 funeral of Pope John XXIII. Though he received fifty-five honorary degrees from colleges and universities in the United States and abroad, Mays said that the renaming of a black church in Ninety Six, South Carolina—Mays United Methodist— was the most touching honor he had ever received.

"I have never done anything for the purpose of being honored, to have my name on the front pages of the newspapers," Mays once said. "I have done what I believe I was sent into the world to do: worship my God and serve my fellow man." This view was embedded in a homely understanding of life: "We all travel the same road from our mother's womb to the grave. So there's no need of anybody getting chesty. We travel the same highway."

Well, maybe. Julian Bond observed, "First he built himself, then he built Morehouse Men." Benjamin Mays would be entitled to become a little chesty about the fact that so many Morehouse Men try hard to travel that highway in the way they were taught by the incomparable "schoolmaster of the Movement."

BELLA ABZUG

PATRICIA BOSWORTH

"I'VE BEEN DESCRIBED as a tough noisy woman—a prize-fighter—a man-hater . . . a Jewish mother with more complaints than Portnoy. There are those who say I'm impatient, impetuous, uppity, rude, profane, brash, and overbearing. Whether I'm any of these things or all of them you can decide for yourself. But whatever I am—and this ought to be made very clear—I am a very serious woman."

Bella Abzug said that about herself in her memoir, *Bella!*, which was published in 1972, not long after she'd been elected to represent the 19th Congressional District on the West Side of Manhattan. She was the first woman elected to Congress on a women's rights/peace platform. Her slogan: "This woman's place is in the house . . . the House of Representatives!"

She was already instantly recognizable to the public thanks to her large, colorful hats and a voice Norman Mailer said that "could boil the fat off a taxicab driver's neck."

I interviewed her right after she was elected. I was a young journalist at *McCall's*, caught up like most working women my age (I was twenty-seven) in the excitement of the women's movement, and Bella was my heroine. She seemed part of every skirmish and every standoff in our struggle for equality. Plus, she was not only a celebrated feminist, antiwar activist, reform Democrat and lawyer—she was a wife and mother of two girls. How did she do it all? That's what I wanted to write about.

We met at her headquarters in Greenwich Village—an office right next to the Lion's Head bar. The place was staffed mainly by female volunteers, some of whom had brought their squalling babies. For a while, Bella and I talked about the importance of women's networks and then about how women define power. "Sure we define it differently from men," she told me. "We define power as the ability to use our gifts—our creativity. Our power—women's power—is about being able to control our lives." Finally we got around to how she was able to juggle so many roles—wife-mother, lawyer-activist—successfully. "For starters you gotta marry a man like my husband, Martin Abzug. That's my secret." She grinned.

Martin Abzug was a woman's dream. The two had met on the way to a Yehudi Menuhin concert in 1944. Martin wanted romance. Bella wanted to be a lawyer. She was then on scholarship at Columbia Law School, where she already had a reputation for being forceful and brilliant; she was an editor of the *Law Review.* Martin would meet her at midnight at the Columbia Law Library. When she began to practice law, representing union workers, Martin would type her briefs for her. (She couldn't type.) He promised her she could always keep working even after they had children (that had been her major hesitation about marriage), and she did continue practicing law after their two daughters were born. Meanwhile, Martin was a stockbroker and wrote two novels. He wasn't interested in politics, but he supported Bella in all her aspirations. He adored her. And she adored him. They were married for forty-two years.

Bella served in the House from 1971 to 1977, and she was a huge galvanizing force in Washington. Working an eighteen-hour day, she was scrupulously prepared on all the issues. She became an expert in parliamentary law— cutting through red tape and also tangling up red tape to suit her purposes. She knew how to strategize—she could sniff out opponents' agendas—and she understood the complexities of leadership, the importance of forging alliances. She kept a journal of what it was like to be a freewheeling woman of New York confronting the genteel Southern male establishment that ruled Congress at the time. She would write, "I spend all day figuring out how to beat the machine and knock the crap out of the power structure," and in another entry she wrote, "I'm not being facetious when I say the real enemies in this country are the Pentagon and its pals in big business."

Vehemently opposed to the war in Vietnam, she was the first member of Congress to call for Nixon's impeachment—

and she was an early supporter of the Equal Rights Amendment. She initiated the Congressional Caucus on Women's Issues and helped organize the Women's Political Caucus; she was the chief strategist for the Democratic Women's Committee, which achieved equal representation for all elective and appointive posts, including presidential conventions. She introduced pioneering bills on child care, family planning and abortion rights. In 1975 she introduced a bill in support of gay and lesbian rights.

"She was absolutely indefatigable," said her former assistant Esther Newberg. "Yes, she was difficult to work with and yes she yelled and got angry a lot but it was because she cared so deeply about what she wanted to accomplish."

She would always credit her parents—Jewish immigrants from Russia—for encouraging her to be a forceful, dynamic, opinionated person. She was born Bella Savitzky on July 24, 1920, in the Bronx; her mother thought she could be President. Her father, Emanuel (whom Bella described as "this humanist butcher"), ran the Live and Let Live meat market on Ninth Avenue, in Hell's Kitchen. By the time she was eight, Bella excelled in her ability to read Hebrew—she was one of the best students in the Torah school she attended. She was also a graceful swimmer ("like a dolphin" someone said), a cardplayer and a talented musician—she sang and played violin. At eleven she joined a left-wing labor Zionist group at her school and got caught up in politics raising money and making speeches for a Jewish homeland, arguing about the importance of peace and justice.

When she was thirteen, her father died, and that's when

she made a crucial choice. Forbidden by religious tradition from saying Kaddish (the prayer for the dead) for her father in synagogue, Bella did it anyway. For an entire year, every morning before she went to school she'd march into synagogue and daven (pray). People were shocked, but they didn't stop her. She did what she believed she had to do for her father, who had never had a son. "I made that choice," she said, and it was a lesson she never forgot. Always be true to your heart. People may not like it, but no one will stop you. It became her philosophy.

She always remained impatient with the demands of conforming to a restricting feminine ideal. She refused to mask her strengths with wiles, abhorring the double standard applied to powerful, larger-than-life women, who were invariably penalized for being ambitious or outspoken whereas powerful, larger-than-life men were invariably admired and praised. So Bella was often disruptive when she was expected to be deferential. As when she barked "Fuck you!" to Carl Albert and Hale Boggs after they voted no to her resolution to end the Vietnam War. As when she was invited to the White House and in the receiving line informed President Nixon that her constituents wanted him to stop the bombing.

As the chair of the Subcommittee on Government Information and Individual Rights, Bella co-wrote three crucial pieces of legislation: the Freedom of Information Act, the government "Sunshine law" (which required government bodies to meet publicly) and the Right to Privacy Act. She was "one of the most exciting, enlightened legislators that ever served in the Congress," said Manhattan Representative Charles Rangel. By 1977 the Gallup Poll had named Bella one of the twenty most influential women in the world.

In the following years, I kept in touch with Bella. We'd bump into each other at rallies and marches. I was part of a large contingent of journalists who helped her celebrate her fifty-seventh birthday at Studio 54. I reviewed her fine book *Gender Gap*, which she wrote with Mim Kelber in 1984. In it she very succinctly explains how women can achieve political power in America—through coalition building and bringing a sense of female values to the political process.

After she left Congress she tried to run for mayor of New York but lost to Ed Koch in the primary. Her last campaign was in 1986, for a House seat in Westchester. She lost. It was during this campaign that Martin died. Bella never recovered. "I haven't been quite the same," she admitted to me once over the phone. Even so, she fought her depression and later cancer, and she worked tirelessly to fulfill a vision of an international women's movement. The result was WEDO (Women's Environment and Development Organization). In November 1991 WEDO convened the World Women's Congress for a Healthy Planet in Miami. Fifteen hundred women from eighty-three nations came together to produce the Women's Action Agenda 21.

The last time I saw Bella was in 1995, just before she left for China for the Fourth World Conference on Women in Beijing. I wanted her to do an oral history so her entire amazing political journey could be recorded. I wanted to hear her talk about founding Women Strike for Peace with Cora Weiss, and how they lobbied for nuclear disarmament. I wanted to hear her describe in depth one of her early landmark cases, in the 1950s—when she represented

Willie McGee, a black Mississippian who had been convicted of raping a white woman and was sentenced to death. (She argued the case in Mississippi when she was eight months pregnant; white supremacists threatened her and refused to allow her to stay in a hotel, so she slept in the bus station.)

But Bella had no interest in an oral history about her career. She was too caught up in the present and in WEDO. "We're gonna have 35,000 members of nongovernmental organizations covering this conference," she enthused. "Our Plan of Action is earmarked for the twenty-first century— we're gonna stop poverty and crush corporate greed and stomp on defense spending . . . women are being mobilized like crazy all over the world." Suddenly she looked at me with narrowed eyes. "Didn't you once ask me about networking?" I was amazed she could remember something from thirty years earlier. I admitted I had, and then she burst forth with how important international networking was for women, an international network of women working all over the world for peace, justice, health, and human rights—a "global sisterhood," she called it.

Bella Abzug died in 1998 after heart surgery. She was seventy-seven years old. When I read her obituary I discovered that former President Bush had paid a private visit to China that coincided with the Beijing conference. During his stay, Bush commented to a group of food executives, "I feel somewhat sorry for the Chinese—having Bella Abzug running around. Bella Abzug is the one who has always represented the extremes of the women's movement."

When told of Bush's remark, Bella snorted. "He was addressing a fertilizer group? That's appropriate."

FATHER MYCHAL JUDGE

TERRY GOLWAY

WALK ALONG WEST 32nd Street between Sixth and Seventh Avenues and you will have some sense of the life and work of Mychal Judge. You will hear very little English, for it is a street of immigrants. You may be asked to spare some change, for it is a place where the poor and homeless congregate. Your brain may be rattled by the blast of a fire engine's horn, for just around the corner is the quarters, now under repair, of Engine 1 and Ladder 24. And if you are in any way spiritual, or even just curious, you may be drawn inside the St. Francis of Assisi Church, attached to a Franciscan friary and just a few steps, and a few thousand miles, from the glamour of Madison Square Garden and the bustle of Penn Station.

Here was Father Mychal Judge's world, or certainly a good part of it, before he became Victim Number 0001 on September 11. He lived in the friary with his brother Franciscans for fifteen years, and celebrated mass in the church. He worked with the poor who line up outside the friary every day to be fed at the church's soup kitchen. He ministered to men and women suffering from AIDS, to immigrants who were unsure of their rights, to alcoholics whose demons he knew all too well. And he served as a chaplain for the Fire Department of New York.

Those were the people who knew him best. Had he survived September 11, had he been out of town when disaster struck, he would have remained a fairly obscure, complicated, and beloved Roman Catholic priest who sought inspiration and solace from the son of a wealthy Italian merchant, Francis of Assisi. His good works and spiritual example surely would have continued to inspire a startling array of New Yorkers, from writers and drunks to firefighters and gay and lesbian Catholics. But they would never have commanded attention of magazine writers, biographers, and politicians. And it is unlikely, although possible, that a movement would have sprung up among lay Catholics to begin the long process of canonization—to have Father Mychal Judge declared a saint of the Roman Catholic Church. That is not to say that Father Judge, or Father Mike as he was known to his firefighter friends and others, would have minded the attention, if not the rituals of canonization. As his biographer, Michael Ford, has pointed out, Father Judge rather enjoyed his occasional forays into the spotlight. Though he dressed in the plain brown robes that mark a Franciscan, he appreciated glamour and bright lights and at least some of the trappings of power and celebrity. He could hardly contain his joy and wonder when he was invited, along with more than 100 other clergy, to the Clinton White House for a breakfast with religious leaders. (That he was invited at all suggests that while Father Judge was not particularly famous before his death, somebody, somewhere, was aware of his good works.)

As Ford recounts in his book, Father Judge wrote a long essay about his day at the White House, taking pains to point out that he had met Clinton twice before. Also not surprisingly, when the breakfast was nearing an end and the President said he could take just one more response from his guests, Father Judge rose and delivered a longish address that touched on his immigrant Irish parents, the power of prayer and the strength he drew not only from his faith, but from the support of his friends in Alcoholics Anonymous.

It was a very human moment. And that's what made this priest so popular—and, let's not forget, so holy. He was a man of God who was as flawed as any of us, and knew it, which is why he spoke so openly about his battle with alcoholism, and why he was able to relate to others—sinners like him, flawed human beings like him—as a minister, a pastor, a teacher, and a comforter.

Father Judge was also was a gay man, which came as a surprise to many who knew him. His sexuality was not especially hidden while he was alive, nor was it flaunted. After his death, the media made much of this, because, obviously, of the Roman Catholic teachings on homosexuality. But those who knew Father Judge well enough to know his sexual orientation insist that he never broke his vow of celibacy. But he did act on the sympathy he felt for gay Catholics who wished to retain a connection to a church and a faith they treasured. Through the tumultuous 1990s, a time of sometimes-bitter confrontation between gays and Cardinal John O'Connor of New York, Father Judge was a familiar figure in St. Clare's and St. Vincent's hospitals in Manhattan. There he ministered to patients with AIDS and counseled their relatives and loved ones. And, all too frequently, he presided over the funerals of those who died of AIDS. Ford's biography of Judge is filled with stories from Catholics and non-Catholics alike who remembered the priest's kindness, spirituality, humor, and humanity during those years.

His pastoral outreach was extended to gay Catholics who formed a group called Dignity. Eventually, Cardinal O'Connor banned the group from the New York Archdiocese's parishes, but Father Judge—who, as a Franciscan, answered to his order but not to the cardinal—continued to minister to gay Catholics. In the late 1990s, he became an important liason between the cardinal and Dignity when O'Connor quietly signaled if not a change of heart, then at least a better appreciation of the sincerity of gay Catholics who treasured their connection to the Church. Informal meetings resulted, but ended when the cardinal became ill with cancer in late 1999. He died in May 2000.

In the months after September 11, the media focused both on Father Judge's sexuality and his work with gay and

AIDS groups. But, while that work was admirable and indeed brave, Father Judge's ministry contained multitudes. It included an extraordinary relationship with Steven McDonald, the New York police officer who has been in a wheelchair since being shot and paralyzed below the neck in 1986. Father Judge accompanied McDonald to Northern Ireland, where the two men offered the prayer of St. Francis of Assisi for that tormented land, where religion has been used to divide people. It included a touching and lovely ministry to New York's firefighters, active and retired, and their families and survivors. I met Father Judge at such a gathering on Staten Island several years ago, when I spoke at a meeting of the department's Emerald Society. Several almost stereotypical firefighters—big guys with Staten Island accents and rough hands (and, by the way, with college degrees)—stopped by our table to shake his hand, to ask for prayers, or just to talk shop. He spoke their language, understood their burdens—and their fears.

A couple of years later, on the morning of September 10, 2001, Father Judge was in the Bronx at the newly renovated quarters of Engine 73 and Ladder 42. He celebrated Mass on the apparatus floor, and when it came time for his homily, he looked directly into the eyes of the dozens of firefighters and their family members. And he talked like a man who knew every one of the worshippers in that makeshift house of God:

> You do what God has called you to do. You show up, you put one foot in front of another, you get on the rig and you do the job, which is a mystery and a surprise. You have no idea when

you get on that rig, no matter how big the call, no matter how small, you have no idea what God's calling you to do.

You love this job. We all do. What a blessing that is. . . . Isn't He a wonderful God? Isn't He good to you, to each one of you? And to me. Turn to Him each day, put your faith and your trust and your life in His hands, and he'll take care of you, and you'll have a good life.

His good life would end in twenty-four hours. But only in death would the world know about his remarkable minstry, his deep faith, and his extraordinary humanity.

JUSTICE WILLIAM O. DOUGLAS

NAT HENTOFF

Since when have we Americans been expected to bow submissively to authority and speak with awe and reverence to those who represent us? The constitutional theory is that we the people are the sovereigns—the state and federal officials only are our agents.

—William O. Douglas, *Statement on unfair arrests for disorderly conduct, 1972*

In a time in our history when the administration is conducting an increasingly accelerating war on the Bill of Rights, the life and work of the William O. Douglas, the most plainspoken of all the Supreme Court Justices, are acutely relevant.

On the bench, Douglas pursued his unwavering conviction that each of us has the fundamental right to his or her own views, even if those views go against the moral or political conclusions of the majority. But like William Brennan, another Justice of equally passionate commitment to the individual liberties guaranteed by the Bill of Rights, Douglas was continually aware that, as Brennan told me in one of our last converstations, "We've always known—The Framers knew—that liberty is a fragile thing."

Douglas knew that fragility at an early age, growing up in Yakima, Washington. The family was so poor and isolated that, as Douglas recalled, he, his brother and his sister were never invited to a single children's party. "We grew up never seeing the inside of another home."

As a teenager, during vacations from school, he worked with harvest crews in the wheat fields of eastern Washington. Alongside him, as well as on other jobs he had, were members of the IWW (Industrial Workers of the World, also called "Wobblies"). They believed in true socialism under which hunger and want would be abolished.

He also rode the rails with the Wobblies, earning an acute distrust of police dedication to justice that never left him. Working and riding with the Wobblies, "We were all treated as outcasts or vagrants. We were even fired on by the police in railroad yards."

No other Supreme Court Justice in history ahd that kind of life experience to sharpen his understanding of the rule of law.

Douglas worked his way though Whitman College in Walla Walla, Washington, not quite an Ivy League school; taught in a Yakima public school for two years; and was accepted at Columbia University's Law School. He worked as a freight hand, handling two thousand sheep halfway to New York; and traveled the rest of the way as a hobo, riding the rails. When Douglas got to New York, he had six cents in his pocket.

He wound up second in his class at law school, and his education outside of class included seeing the New York police, on a small building near the main branch of the public library, operating a dentist chair to extract confessions from resistant arrestees.

Douglas worked for a time for elite Wall Street law firms, and hated the experience. "I looked around at the older men there, and I knew I didn't want to be like any of them. They couldn't climb a mountain, couldn't tie a dry fly; the knew nothing about the world that was closest to me—the real world, the natural world."

He became a professor at Yale Law School, building a national reputation as an expert in financial matters, and that led to his 1934 appointment to the Securities and Exchange Commission, of which he became chairman two years later. Summarizing Douglas's tenure there, the *Washington Post* noted that the mountaineer from the Far West "brought the giants of Wall Street to heel."

During poker sessions at the White House, he and Franklin D. Roosevelt got to respect each other a great deal, and in 1939, FDR appointed Douglas to the Supreme Court. Douglas was forty years old. Douglas had been much influenced by Supreme Court Justice Louis Brandeis—known as "the people's lawyer"—before being appointed to the Supreme Court, a position almost denied him because of the virulent anti-Semitism of some senators.

In the spirit of Brandeis, Douglas—nine years after he came onto the Court—wrote in a characteristic dissent: "Power that controls the economy should be in the hands of elected representatives of the people, not in the hands of an industrial oligarchy."

In 1944, Roosevelt told the Democratic National Convention that either Douglas or Harry Truman would be acceptable to him as vice president. The party leaders decided that Truman, having come up from the party machinery, would be much less dangerous to the status quo than this wild card from the West. Journalist and lawyer Sidney Zion, a friend of Douglas, said ruefully that if Douglas had become president, "there wouldn't have been any loyalty oaths, and the atomic bomb wouldn't have dropped on Hiroshima."

Remaining on the Supreme Court, Douglas continued to be its most fervent protector of freedom of speech and thought. As he wrote for the Court in *Terminello* v. *Chicago* in 1949:

A function of free speech under our system of government is to invite dispute. It may indeed best serve its high purposes when it induces a condition of unrest, creates dissatisfaction with conditions as they are, or even stirs people to anger.

Speech is often provocative and challenging. It may strike at prejudices and preconceptions and have profound unsettling effects as it presses for acceptance of an idea.

In a dissent, when the Supreme Court confirmed a conviction of Southern students arrested in a small Florida town for assembling at the jail in protest of official segregation policies, Douglas wrote:

The right to petition for a redress of grievances is not limited to writing a letter or sending a telegram to a congressman; it is not confined to appearing before a local city council, or writing letters to the president or the governor or mayor. Legislators may turn deaf ears; formal complaints may be routed endlessly through a bureaucratic maze; courts may let the wheels of justice grind very slowly.

Those who cannot afford to advertise in newspapers or circulate elaborate pamphlets may have only a more limited type of access to public officials. Their methods should not be condemned as tactics of obstruction or harassment as long as the assembly and petition are peaceable, as those were.

As an environmentalist before the term was known, Douglas, in dissent, fought against any further exploitation of forests and streams even claiming that all the forms of natural life should have a representative standing before the Supreme Court to defend their right to exist—"the pileated woodpecker as well as the coyote and bear, the lemmings as well as the trout in the streams."

After suffering a stroke on New Year's Eve, 1974, Douglas continued, in intense pain, his work on the Court until very reluctantly resigning in November 1975. He tried to stay on as "the tenth justice," but finally was persuaded to withdraw entirely. On January 19, 1980, William Orville Douglas died at Walter Reed Army Medical Center in Washington, D.C. He was eighty-one.

His Court opinions fill 118 large volumes, and they testify to his credo: "The conscience of this nation is the Constitution." He was its keeper, and no one on the Court before or since, has matched his fierce devotion to everyone's freedom of conscience.

In 1976, a group of young lawyers in Washington State invited him to come to speak. In his letter of acceptance, Douglas wrote:

The Constitution and the Bill of Rights were designed to get Government off the backs of the people—all people. Those great documents . . . guarantee to all of us the rights to personal and spiritual self-fulfillment. But that guarantee is not self-executing. As nightfall does not come all at once, neither does oppression. In both instances, there is a twilight when everything remains seemingly unchanged. And it is in such twilight when everything remains seemingly unchanged. And it is in such twilight that we all must be most aware of change in the air—however slight—lest we become unwitting victims of the darkness.

Since September 11, 2001, the changes in the air have become increasingly more ominous under the Bush administration, as Attorney General John Ashcroft—while assaulting the Bill of Rights—accuses his critics of "scaring peace-loving people with phantoms of lost liberty."

Our liberties are dissolving, and Douglas knew that. Thomas Jefferson was right when he reminded Americans to come that, "The People are the only sure reliance for the preservation of Liberty."

The people are now resisting—with more than 200 towns and cities passing the Bill of Rights—telling their member of Congress to roll back the unconstitutional laws and executive orders of Bush and Ashcroft. Three state legislatures—Alaska, Hawaii, and Vermont—have also passed those resolutions and Congress is beginning to listen and act.

I. F. STONE

VICTOR NAVASKY

SIDNEY HOOK, THE Marxist philosopher-turned-neoconservative who once mistakenly listed I. F. Stone among those who had defended the Moscow purge trials, wrote a book titled *The Hero in History*. In it he distinguished between eventful men (like the Dutch boy who put his finger in the dike), people who happened to be in the right place at the right time—and event-making men, the ones who make things happen.

To me, I. F. Stone, né Isadore Feinstein, known to his friends as Izzy, was an event-making man. He was event-making not because Izzy and his little newsletter, *I. F.*

Stone's Weekly (later biweekly), were right about McCarthyism, right about the war in Vietnam (he was one of the first to raise questions about the authenticity of the Gulf of Tonkin incident), right about the Democrats' repeated failure to live up to their own principles, right about what he called, long before the U.S. invasion of Iraq, the "Pax Americana." Writing in *The Nation* (which he served as Washington editor in the 1940s), he was prophetic about the Holocaust, which in 1942 he called "a murder of a people" "so appalling . . . that men would shudder at its horrors for centuries to come." He was even, by the way, prescient about the meltdown of the Soviet Union. In 1984, seven years before it happened, he told Andrew Patner, the young Chicago journalist who had the wit to debrief Izzy on tape, that "all these dictatorships look so goddamned powerful. [But I think] one day they [will] just collapse. They're rigid, and rigid structures crack."

It's the way he was right, the way he lived his life, the way he did his journalism that magnified his influence, made him something of a role model for the most idealistic of the next generation. This college dropout who couldn't see without his Coke-bottle glasses, and who couldn't hear without his hearing aid (which he turned on and off strategically), was something of a pariah among his peers in 1953, the nadir of McCarthyism, when he founded *I. F. Stone's Weekly*. His name was on a Senate Internal Security Subcommittee list of the eighty-two "most active and typical sponsors of Communist-front organizations" (which in Izzy's case meant mainly popular-front, antifascist organizations or civil-liberties groups upholding the Bill of Rights against those who would undermine it in the name of combating a phantom domestic Red Menace).

When Izzy founded the weekly, with the help of a $3,000 loan from a friend and a 5,300-name subscription list inherited from the defunct *PM* and its successor progressive papers, also defunct, he was unemployed and some thought unemployable, including by *The Nation.* (*The Nation*'s editor, Freda Kirchwey, who had fired him as Washington editor when he didn't notify her that he had signed on with *PM* to become the first journalist to travel with the Jewish underground to the Holy Land, was reluctant to reemploy him.)

But in short order, although he never attended presidential press conferences, cultivated no highly placed inside sources, and declined to attend off-the-record briefings, time and again he scooped the most powerful press corps in the world.

His method: To scour and devour public documents, bury himself in the *Congressional Record,* study obscure congressional committee hearings, debates, and reports, all the time prospecting for news nuggets (which would appear as boxed paragraphs in his paper), contradictions in the official line, examples of bureaucratic and political mendacity, documentation of incursions on civil rights and liberties. He lived in the public domain. It was his habitat of necessity, because use of government sources to document his findings was also a stratagem. Who would have believed this cantankerous-if-whimsical Marxist without all the documentation?

And as he gleefully explained to a group of Swarthmore students in 1954 (I know, because I was one of them), if you didn't attend background briefings, you weren't bound by the ground rules; you could debrief correspondents who did, check out what they had been told and, as often as not, reveal the lies for what they were.

Despite his poor eyesight, Izzy saw what others missed, even though it was often in plain sight. Partly it was a matter of perspective. Izzy was always looking for evidence of the great forces and trends that shaped our history—"the fundamental struggles, the interests, the classes, the items that become facts." And he was not merely a Marxist; he wanted to synthesize Marx and Jefferson. How many Jeffersonian Marxists, after all, had penetrated the periodical galleries of the House and Senate? Izzy, by the way, had to sue to get his press card.

But Izzy also got and made news by reading the dailies, the wire services and such, and then following up where others had not thought to tread. He once told David Halberstam that the *Washington Post* was an exciting paper to read "because you never know on what page you would find a page-one story."

One of his favorite scoops, he told a conference of investigative journalists in Amsterdam, of which more below, had to do with our capacity to monitor underground nuclear tests. It happened in the fall of 1957, when he spotted a "shirttail" in the *New York Times*. A shirttail, Izzy explained to the foreign journalists, is usually some wire-service information run as a little paragraph hanging down ("like a shirttail") at the end of the main story.

The main story, about the first underground nuclear tests in Nevada, had quoted experts forecasting that they would not be detectable 200 miles away. The distance was important because at that time test-ban negotiations between the United States and the USSR were under way, and Dr. Edward Teller, whom Izzy regarded as a Strangelovian mischief maker, was raising questions about whether a test ban could be enforced. If the tests were in the atmosphere or underground, could they really be detected? Teller asked.

When he got home, Izzy noticed that the city edition of the *Times* had a shirttail from Toronto saying that underground tests had been detected there. He went downtown to get the late city edition and saw more shirttails from Rome and Tokyo saying the same thing, so he clipped them and squirreled them away in his files. By the time the Atomic Energy Commission put out its report the following spring, saying that the tests hadn't been detected more than 200 miles away, Eisenhower's disarmament negotiators had gotten the Soviet Union to agree to monitoring posts every 1,000 kilometers (620 miles). Izzy jumped into his car and drove down to the seismology branch of the Commerce Department's Coastal and Geodetic Survey, who were happy to see and cooperate with a reporter since, other than during earthquakes, the press ignored their work. There he learned that we had listening posts as far away as Fairbanks, Alaska—2,600 miles from the Nevada test site—that had picked up the tests. Why do you want this information? they asked. He told them. They called the AEC. The AEC called Izzy, and after listening to what he had to say, changed their press release.

Izzy clearly got as much pleasure telling the story of how he got the story as he did getting the story in the first place. And that's another thing to admire about him. Izzy lived a life against the grain, but he believed in having a good time, leading the good life. When we invited him to speak at Swarthmore in the 1950s, he agreed to come, but requested a club-car ticket. At the time, this seemed like an extravagance and out of keeping with my image of Izzy as radical conscience of his cohort. But as he once put it, "I have so much fun, I ought to be arrested."

It wasn't until the 1980s when *The Nation,* along with the Dutch weekly *Vrej Nederlander,* invited Izzy to keynote an international conference of investigative journalists (who better to attract idealistic, progressive, investigative reporters from all over than the by-now-famous one-man band, I. F. Stone?), that I came to fully appreciate the significance of his lifestyle.

When I called to ask Izzy if he would be available, he said not only did it sound like a valuable event but he had a sentimental reason for being interested. He and his wife, Esther, had taken their honeymoon in Amsterdam many years ago. When our publisher, Hamilton Fish, made a follow-up call to pin Izzy's participation down, and Izzy responded, "We'd love to do it." Hamilton, correctly concerned about matters budgetary, stuck his head into my office and asked, "Who is this 'we'?"

I explained that Izzy prefers not to travel without Esther, don't worry about it. Izzy's presence would guarantee the success and gravitas of our conference.

As it turned out, not only was Izzy ready to join us, but he made it clear that he understood no fee would be involved—a good thing, since, as Ham had unnecessarily pointed out, we had no fee in our tight budget.

In fact, our budget was so tight that we had arranged

with a nonscheduled airline for budget round-trip tickets, at $400 per person, and at the other end our friends at *Vrej Nederlander* had negotiated a group rate at a modest hotel on the outskirts of town. (We would commute to the conference center by a chartered bus that had agreed to give us its lowest rate.)

A couple of days later, Ham stuck his head into my office again to say we might have a problem. Izzy had called and explained that over the years he and Esther "have found that it's too much of a strain to fly going east, so we take the boat," and it seemed the boat they always took was the *Queen Elizabeth II*. Once again I started to tell Ham not to worry when he interrupted to tell me, "Izzy has already told me that. And he put me in touch with a travel agent in Jacksonville, Florida, who he says always takes care of them. In fact, he even knew which cabin they favored."

So when, the next day, Ham appeared with some new news, I said, "Don't tell me," but he did.

Apparently, when Ham called to tell Izzy that the *QE II* was going to dock in England a few days prior to the conference, he couldn't have been more pleased. "At our age," he explained, "we need a couple of days to get our land legs, and we have this little hotel in London which makes a nice base."

So Ham was not surprised when, a few days later, his phone rang again. "You know, Hamilton," Izzy confided, "I'm a romantic," and he proceeded to explain that on their honeymoon they had stayed "at a small pensione on the canal that ran through the center of town, not very expensive, and if you could just locate that . . . ," and we did.

It was more of a joke than a problem when Izzy called again to tell us that by happy coincidence one of his children, along with the family and in-laws were going to be in Europe at the same time and if they could stay in the cottage by the canal . . .

Also, Izzy had an idea. There was a famous cathedral in Amsterdam that operated as a sort of agora, a public forum. If we could arrange for Izzy to speak (he had done this many years ago and seemed to have something of a following in Amsterdam), he would be pleased to donate his fee to help defray the costs of the conference.

In the end, close to a thousand Dutch men and women showed up to hear Izzy speak, and forty activist-journalists from all over Europe came to the conference. From the opening session Izzy peppered journalists with questions, and shared observations and anecdotes from the audience. His own keynote was truly inspirational, and the conference led to follow-up conferences in London and Moscow attended by hundreds of investigative reporters, activists, and scholarly resource people. At a farewell session at a local bar, we consumed caviar and vodka, and he raised a toast: "Comes the revolution, we will all live like this."

It was, then, part of Izzy's charm that he never accepted the idea that in order to be a heretic, a maverick, a solo practitioner, it was necessary to be a martyr or a monk. As Peter Osnos, who had worked briefly for Izzy at the start of his own distinguished journalistic and publishing career, pointed out, it was not only on *The Nation*'s ticket that he danced his way across the Atlantic. He and Esther used to go out dancing twice a week. More significantly, his insistence on his perks had less to do with hedonism than a sense of dignity, of self-confidence, of earned entitlement. He wasn't about to allow a priggish journalistic establishment to marginalize him. He once said, "You may just think I am a red Jew son-of-a-bitch, but I'm keeping Thomas Jefferson alive." He embodied the romantic idea of one man pitted against the system.

Who else but a romantic college dropout would have thought to teach himself ancient Greek in his sixties in order to write a history of human freedom, "because Athens was where it all began"? His quirky revisionist history of Socrates became an unlikely best seller, but his commitment to freedom of thought remained his constant companion. Once when *The Nation* ran an editorial condemning some act of speech suppression by the Sandinistas, Izzy called to cheer us on, as if to say he had learned the hard way not to treat socialist sins more sympathetically than capitalist ones. He was calling to give us his blessing, but also his legitimacy.

One night in the mid-1980s, after dinner in New York, I was walking Izzy back to his hotel, the Tudor, where he liked to stay when in town. Izzy said he had an idea he thought might be appropriate to his energy level.

He would write a weekly paragraph, maybe 150 words, under the heading "Izzy Says." He said every week he had at least one thing to say. We contacted the great caricaturist David Levine, who provided the perfect logo: Izzy holding a life-size pen the way a medieval warrior might carry his spear.

And sure enough, the next week Izzy sent in a 150-word item on the Reagan Defense Department. A few hours later, though, he called again. It seemed the story was bigger than he thought. He had gone down to the press building and read the wire reports. He had another 200 words.

Our production person remade the page, and here we were on press day when Izzy called again. "I think we have something of a scoop," he chirped, and proceeded to dictate his "final" adds.

Over the next few weeks Nation readers were treated to a number of "Izzy Says" items, at least one "Stonegram," and a few "I.F. Stone Reports." And the young staff, increasingly impatient with Izzy's cheerful but deadline-oblivious modus operandi, looked skeptical when told how grateful they would be in some distant future for having had the privilege of working with this legendary maverick.

And then one day Izzy called apologetically to say he had better stop. "I'm an old war horse," he said, "and once I get started I can't stop. I have to go downtown and read the wires. I have to follow up. Let's go back to the old system, and I'll just do occasional pieces as they occur." And he did.

A few weeks before he died, Izzy called—as I expect he called many of his friends—just to say how much "I have appreciated your friendship."

Even after he died, they still didn't quite know how to handle him. In a classic example of the sort of on-the-one-hand, on-the-other-hand journalism against which I. F. Stone fought all his life, the lead paragraph of his obituary in the *New York Times* neatly balanced his "admirers" against his "critics."

Although in the course of its nineteen years the weekly's circulation rose from a few thousand to 70,000 at his death, someone still called it "a fleabite of a journal."

So what did it matter that Izzy was an event-making man if the event was a fleabite? Andy Kopkind, the gifted radical journalist, who took inspiration from Izzy, had answered the question some years before, when he wrote of the weekly that it "organized the consciousness of its readers somewhat in the way a community action group organizes a neighborhood: for awareness, understanding, action." In other words, it mobilized and nourished a community of resistance.

It also inspired a generation of would-be Izzy Stones. Whether Alexander Cockburn's *CounterPunch* or Jim Hightower's *Lowdown* or Tris Coffin's (later Ben Franklin's) *Washington Spectator,* or even many of the latter-day so-called bloggers, they all were inspired by Izzy!

And by the time he passed on his newsletter to the *New York Review of Books,* for which he had written a series of highly influential early anti–Vietnam War pieces, this man of the Old Left had become a moral exemplar for such early New Lefties as Paul Booth, Dick Flacks, Todd Gitlin and Tom Hayden. Izzy was "a spiritual eminence on early SDS," is the way Gitlin put it.

After he died, some latter-day cold warriors tried unsuccessfully and preposterously to frame him—based on some newly released cables from Soviet spymasters to their American confederates—as a Soviet agent. The charges were discredited quickly. But the long-run answer to such nonsense may be found in his *Who's Who* entry. Others take the occasion to list their worldly accomplishments. Izzy chose to print his credo: "To write the truth as I see it; to defend the weak against the strong; to fight for justice; and to seek, as best I can, to bring healing perspectives to bear on the terrible hates and fears of mankind, in the hope of someday bringing about one world, in which men will enjoy the differences of the human garden instead of killing each other over them."

FRANK SINATRA

SIDNEY ZION

A talent like Frank Sinatra comes along once in a century.
Why did he have to come along in mine?

—Bing Crosby

I **PLAY A** game: What if Sinatra had been born later in Bing's century—say, December 12, 1945 instead of December 12, 1915? This would have made him the classic baby boomer, in the prime of life today. But nobody would be wondering where or when they fell in love with that voice before.

The generation that brought us Elvis and the Beatles

and those crazy old Stones would have left Frank Sinatra without a song. Unless you believe he'd have captured the collective hearts of the world with "Hound Dog" or "Why Don't We Do It in the Road" or "Sympathy for the Devil."

The boomers did not disdain Sinatra; many of them loved him. "New York, New York" became an anthem in the 1980s that had kids dancin' in the discos and jumpin' in the aisles of Yankee Stadium. But if he'd been born when they were born, the only shot he'd have had to be Chairman of the Board would have been the board of the Gambino family.

Well, he had the luck of the draw, and lucky for the world that he did. Maybe not for Crosby, but for us. Frank Sinatra came on the scene when the great American songbook was flying to the moon. He had the pick of the crop of the best composers and lyricists ever to come together in any century in any place.

Irving Berlin, Cole Porter, Rodgers and Hart, Jerome Kern, Dorothy Fields, the Gershwins, Harold Arlen, Harry Warren, Johnny Burke, Oscar Hammerstein, Frank Loesser, Lerner and Lowe, Yip Harburg, Burton Lane, Gus Kahn, Vincent Youmans, Cy Coleman . . .

One could write a book of lists and still miss some of the great songwriters of the Sinatra Century. All but a few of whom were left for dead by the boomers and buried by the record industry and radio and the theater.

Nobody understood this better than Sinatra, who retired in the early 1970s because nobody was writing songs he could sing. And nobody was writing because nobody was listening no more.

Of course, he came back, and when he did, he went back to the stuff that gave him the world on a string. "All they want to hear are the old standards," he told me, "and that's all I want to sing."

He never sang a song onstage or in a saloon without crediting the guys and dolls who wrote the words and music. When I congratulated him for this, he said: "Where the hell would I be without them?"

An engineer, which his old man wanted for him? A hard sell for a kid who didn't bother to graduate from high school. I'd like to think he would have gone into politics, given the boost his momma, the great Dolly, Democratic ward leader in Hoboken could have given him.

But there were few spots open to Italian-Americans in those days in Jersey and surely no room at the top, where of course Sinatra needed to live.

Which leaves the Mafia, and I don't think I insult his veil by making this the best bet. Sinatra spent a good part of his life at once dodging and cultivating the image of a godfather.

There were plenty of people in law enforcement—most notably Bobby Kennedy—who were convinced that if he wasn't of the mob, he sure as hell was *with* them.

But while Bobby and others jammed him up now and again, they never nailed him. The heat actually added to his celebrity, his glamour. The world now had the Dark Sinatra to go with The Voice, the sad balladeer, the swinger; at whose feet, presidents, statesmen, pols, and godfathers dropped like so many bobbysoxers at the Paramount.

He was hands down the greatest entertainer of the twentieth century, eclipsing his old hero Crosby, just as Bing eclipsed Al Jolson.

But just as he couldn't have done it without the songwriters, he needed the life he so famously and notoriously led.

Sinatra used to say, "I'm a classic manic-depressive." True or not, it was a metaphor for his career. In ten years, 1939–1949, he went from nobody to a household name— and then to a guy hustling for a buck and singing "The Hucklebuck" to empty tables.

"My year of Mondays," he called it, but it was more like five years when he had to take the back of the bus to such as Eddie Fisher, Frankie Laine and Guy Madison. He hit bottom when he recorded "Momma Will Bark" with Dagmar.

His marriage to Nancy was kaput, because here came Ava Gardner. Even Mr. Webster had no words to describe this love affair. Leonora Hornblow, who knew Sinatra since the Tommy Dorsey days, explains it best: "Frank and Ava were either making love or throwing ashtrays, right in front of you. You ducked—out of embarrassment or fear."

It didn't help that she was riding high while he was sinking. Except that it was Ava who got Harry Cohn to audition him for Maggio in *From Here to Eternity*. Cohn told him, "You ain't no actor," but when Eli Wallach dropped out of the running, Sinatra ended up with the Oscar.

The movie changed everything for Sinatra. He had lost his record company, his agent, his money—and finally Ava.

She left his bed, but never his heart. "The only woman I ever loved," he told me one night, thirty years after they split. Long before, everybody alive to Sinatra knew it. He couldn't have broken all our young hearts with *In The Wee Small Hours*, if Ava hadn't done him in.

But if Ava hadn't set him up with Harry Cohn, the manic Sinatra might never have emerged. Maggio, the loser, brought forth the swaggering Sinatra, who turned the children of the bobbysoxers into swinging lovers.

Or at least wannabes, which was a big deal in those ultra-dull Eisenhower years, when Perry Como ruled the airwaves and college boys dreamt of Madison Avenue, and life in the suburbs with Debbie Reynolds.

Sinatra, on top again, let us feel that anything was possible; to hell with boredom and Brooks Brothers and nice girls in gingham.

Nobody could sing "Come Fly with Me" like Frank— because nobody had the plane and the broad to make it come true—but we could hope.

And even when he got loaded and threw a drink in some bum's face, or belted an enemy at Toots Shor's, we cheered because he was our urban Huckleberry Finn.

Once he got barred from Australia—a whole continent. But who cared, because who else could do that and still be loved. And who else could swing, from being a left-wing Democrat, beloved by FDR; from Jack Kennedy to Nixon and finally to Ronald Reagan and still and still. Let's go to the videotape.

Joe Kennedy called him to Hyannisport on the eve of the West Virginia primary, 1959. Jack Kennedy's problem was his Catholicism. No Catholic had ever been elected to the presidency of the United States.

At his Palm Springs compound in 1984, Sinatra told me what happened.

"Joe Kennedy said it was up to me, I could get Jack the nomination. 'Hubert Humphrey has played into our arms. He thinks he has a lock on West Virginia because the labor unions love him. But of course the unions are run by some of your friends. So talk to them, Frank, and you'll make Jack president.' "

Humphrey made a catastrophic mistake by entering the West Virginia primary. He was not only a lifelong promoter of the labor movement, he was a Protestant. If he beat Kennedy, the victory would have meant next to nothing, because he was supposed to win and win big in this Protestant workingman's bastion.

Conversely, if JFK could beat him here he would dispel the notion that a Catholic couldn't become president. So Sinatra called on his mob pals, and poor Hubert was left with Pete Seeger strumming labor songs.

Of course, there was still November, and nobody in the Kennedy camp was foolish enough to believe that as goes West Virginia so goes the nation. Sinatra and his friends in the Mafia did more than a little to elect Kennedy—indeed, in their minds they put him in the White House.

When an election is won by a hair, everybody goes to the winner's dressing room, seeking credit. But the mob is not your usual creditor. Unlike ordinary politicians looking for jobs, all they wanted was to be left alone.

The appointment of Robert Kennedy as attorney general sent shock waves through organized crime. He had been their nemesis for years; they were his book, *The Enemy Within*.

Bobby turned all his guns on the mob and their union satellites (see Jimmy Hoffa) and nothing was ever the same again for La Cosa Nostra. They felt betrayed and they put plenty of heat on Sinatra, the guy who took them to this dance of death.

He survived it, but not JFK, whose assassination was laid

completely on Lee Harvey Oswald by the Warren Commission. The underworld never believed it and to this day those who are still around say it was the mob who set Oswald up. Joined by plenty of journalists and revisionist historians.

Sinatra was the first to get the message that Bobby would have nothing to do with his father's markers. Shortly after the election, Bobby got his brother to cancel a visit to Frank's Palm Springs compound, rubbing it in by substituting Bing Crosby's house for the weekend.

Crosby, who hadn't done a thing for JFK, was a fucking Republican! It's become a received opinion that this slight turned Sinatra from a Roosevelt Democrat to a right-wing Republican. But to buy it, you have to forget that he backed LBJ in 1964 and heavily supported Humphrey in 1968.

Yeah, he backed Nixon in 1972, but so did plenty of Dems who got turned off by George McGovern. In Sinatra's case, I think it was more vanity than philosophy—Nixon was smart enough to invite him to the White House.

His support of Ronald Reagan was old Hollywood connections, combined with wanting to be with a winner. The old underdog Sinatra had gotten fat, to be sure, but I'm sure it had more to do with the old crowd dying and the young crowd out there with the Rolling Stones.

As I write about the Political Sinatra, I smile. What other singer in his time would rate even a paragraph about politics? Perry Como? Eddie Fisher? Nat Cole? Dean Martin or Sammy Davis or the rest of the Rat Pack?

It comes out this way. Francis Albert Sinatra was a commotion. As such, he refused to live backstage. It was not enough to be the best singer in the world. He had to be the most loved and most hated, if that's the way it crumbled.

His friends and enemies were legion.

It has been said that if Frank Sinatra was your friend, you needed no others. He was the most generous, loyal guy in the world if he loved you. He could also cut you dead, and sometimes you didn't know why, and then maybe bring you back and you didn't know why.

What good is it to be a manic-depressive if you can't do that?

In the end, the music survives, and in the end, that's all he cared about.

"I just don't want them to sing 'My Way' at my funeral," he told Leonora Hornblow.

You didn't have to worry about that, Frank. The whole world ran out and bought all your stuff, sold out the house. Or as they used to say, "It's Sinatra's world—we only live in it."

JOHN GARFIELD

MICKEY KNOX

A TEENAGE DREAM of becoming an actor like my film
hero, James Cagney, was interrupted by the screen
appearance of John Garfield. Friends in high school who
had seen Garfield in his first film, *Four Daughters* (1938),
all told me I looked like that new actor . . . y'know . . .
what's his name?

I played hooky and saw the movie. Finally, a bitter
piano-playing wanderer appeared—John Garfield. The
man was magnetic. The audience was dead silent, absorbed
by Garfield's striking screen presence. It was a rare
moment in film history: The sighting of a new film star.

I forgot about James Cagney—so much for teenage loyalty—and although I didn't think I looked that much like Garfield, he intrigued me. Yeah! I superimposed my image over his as he played the piano and allowed the smoke from the cigarette dangling out the side of his mouth to curl up to his dark, angry eyes. And that's the day I began to smoke.

Four Daughters flashed the news around the country that a star was born. He came before Brando, Jimmy Dean, Al Pacino, and the other superb young actors of the next generation. He was the first authentic film rebel. For the moviegoer, he was the real article; tough, taking no crap from anyone, his fists ready to defend his bruised dignity . . . yet there was that damn vulnerability . . . unlike Cagney, who was really tough, on or off the screen and had to fake vulnerability on the walk to the hot seat after being convinced by a priest that the gang of kids who idolized him wouldn't be impressed by his courage unless he faked being a phony tough gangster, crying and collapsing until the final jolt of juice. Cagney had to use all his talent to act a coward.

Garfield used his authentic vulnerability, and it always paid off. He would evoke a twinge of pity in the audience, but the combination of passion and fierce intensity usually would overcome that twinge. No matter what part he played, no one ever doubted he was really that character up on screen.

What an actor!

He was often cast as a hard-luck, tough-but-honest bloke; or a gangster, or a revolutionary and once a lovesick Mexican in John Steinbeck's *Tortilla Flats* (1942). He was loved by the working stiff, the poor and by the marginal. They identified with his resistance to authority, his immutable battle against injustice.

Garfield was born Jacob Julius Garfinkel. He spent his youth on the mean streets of the Bronx during the Great Depression. He was a little kid when he was orphaned and somehow had survived while openly bearing that maligned chip on his shoulder. That chip was there in most of his film roles and anchored the reality of whatever character he had created.

As a young actor in New York, he changed his name to Julie Garfield. When Warner Brothers brought him to Hollywood, he became John Garfield. However, he was always "Julie" to his friends and coworkers.

We first met in 1947 at the home of Morris Carnovsky, one of the nucleus of actors that formed the Group Theater in 1931. But it wasn't John Garfield the wary movie star, or the tough-talking character—no, it was Julie Garfield, boyish, immediately friendly. And restless. He hardly sat; he paced, a slight bounce in his step. And he spoke a lot—we had both found a new friend.

Robbie Garfield, Julie's wife, was there. They were married barely out of their teens. Robbie was quick as a whiplash, smart and funny, her Bronx accent thick and lovely. First meeting and damn, it was almost like family.

The historically important Group Theater that lasted through the 1930s in New York City was home to a band of actors thoroughly influenced by the writings of Stanislavsky, the Russian actor, stage director, and father of what became known in America as The Method.

Harold Clurman, one of the founders of the Group Theater and a noted stage director, wrote a book, whimsically titled, *All People Are Famous*, subtitled *Instead of an Autobiography*. This is a quote from his book:

> . . . Garfield, was a thoroughly sweet boy. Orphaned young, he became a problem child. A wise educator, Angelo Patri, the principal of a Bronx high school, took him in hand, so successfully that Jules Garfield endeared himself to everyone in the theater, first to Eva Le Gallienne and later to all of us in the Group.
>
> The total absence of malice in him, his love of laughter and his capacity for friendship won him the confidence of all sorts of people everywhere. Even his constant malapropisms charmed everyone . . .

For those who never saw Garfield on stage or screen, the Clurman quote will give his character some definition. But the fact of the matter is that Garfield surely suffered psychic and physical pain as an orphan. However, the affection he got from the Group's members warmed his heart, and the sweetness Clurman refers to was clearly unaffected.

Garfield was in the Group Theater during much of the thirties, acting mainly in plays written by Clifford Odets, the Group's talented resident playwright (*Waiting for Lefty, Awake and Sing*). Odets wrote his most successful play, *Golden Boy*, about a violin-playing boxer, with Garfield in mind. But the Group's leadership screwed

Garfield royally and gave the part to Luther Adler, a more experienced actor.

He was reported to be good in the part, but given the emotional power Garfield would have brought to the play he would have set the stage aflame.

Garfield was deeply pained by the Group's rejection and he took the Hollywood offer to appear in *Four Daughters*. His most touching and effective scene was his anger at destiny for abandoning him. As an actor, I have no doubt he used the hurt he suffered by the Group for the way he played that scene.

Stanislavsky would have approved.

Warner Brothers had Garfield under contract for seven years (1938–1946) and cloned the part Garfield played in *Four Daughters* in many of his subsequent films. The one saving grace of most of them was Garfield's performance.

Burt Lancaster was interested in acquiring the film rights to Norman Mailer's *The Naked and the Dead*. They were both friends of mine and they arranged to meet at my home. I also asked Julie to join us because I knew he was interested in playing the part of Sergeant Croft, one of the main characters.

Never able to resist an opening to get a laugh, during a moment of silence, I said, "If Julie plays Sergeant Croft, you'll have to change the name to Sergeant Kraft." Stung, Julie was visibly hurt. I got a small laugh, not at all worth the remorse I felt, but I was struck by Garfield's lack of social armor.

After running out his contract with Warner Brothers, Garfield formed a production company. For his first independent film, *Body and Soul* (1947), Abe Polonsky, wrote the screenplay and Bob Rossen directed it. Garfield played an acclaimed boxer, finally flattened by arrogance and mindless extravagance. One can argue that it wasn't Garfield's finest performance in his best film, but it would be a feeble argument.

Both Polonsky and Rossen were eventually blacklisted. Polonsky remained an unfriendly witness before the House Un-American Activities Committee, but Rossen kissed ass and named names. At a dinner party, he chose me to tearfully tell his sad tale: He was rich enough to live without working, but his life was meaningless without the ability to work. I made no comment.

In 1951, thirteen years after *Four Daughters,* destiny nailed Garfield. He appeared before the House Un-American Activities Committee and refused to name his friends as Communists. He was duly declared an unfriendly witness. The film industry, spineless—no surprise there—blacklisted Garfield.

Garfield was a political innocent. He loved the Group Theater for accepting him, encouraging him, loving him, and training him to use his talent fully as an actor. Yes, he listened to the talk of the time, the politics of the Great Depression, the hopes for the success of the Russian Revolution, the fear of Fascism.

Most of the Group were on the left, and some were members of the Communist Party—but Garfield was not a member. The House Un-American Activities Committee knew that, but they were convinced that he knew those in the Group who were or had been Communists.

The last acting for Garfield was onstage, a revival of *Golden Boy*. Finally, he got to play the golden boy. I was out of the country and didn't see it, but later, speaking to friends who had seen Julie's performance, I got no joy in hearing that he had lost some of the zest and energy of his beautiful talent. The blacklist had done its deadly work.

I, too, having been blacklisted, was on my way to Italy late in 1951 to be in a film of *Othello*. I stopped first in New York. When I called the Garfields, Robbie invited me to dinner. They then had an apartment on the West Side, off Central Park. Julie was not his lively self, in fact he was uncharacteristically silent. Robbie wasn't a bundle of laughs either.

After dinner, Julie said, "come on for a walk in the park." (Those years, you could stroll safely in the park.) Walking slowly, Julie wailed over and over again softly: "What do they want from me? What did I do? What do they want from me? What did I do? . . ."

I couldn't say a word. He was in the grip of bewildered frustration and didn't have the strength to break out of it. His was a desperate cry for destiny to save him from death.

It was the last time we ever saw each other.

In Rome I stayed with Stan Swinton, bureau chief of Associated Press. By definition journalists are heralds of disasters. Swinton, had journalism in his blood and knowing I was a friend of Garfield's, tried his best to contain his excitement when he called from his office to report the rotten news—Garfield was dead. The year was 1952—Julie was thirty-nine.

Harold Clurman writes that Garfield's lawyer was meeting with a representative of the House Committee to clear Garfield, since he was proven not to be a communist. The phone rang, the committee rep answered, put the phone down, and announced that Garfield had died. He laughed and said, "Easy come, easy go." Garfield's lawyer walloped him.

REVEREND NORMAN EDDY

DAN WAKEFIELD

THE GROWING PLAGUE of heroin addiction in the 1950s was brought to the attention of Eisenhower America by *The Man With the Golden Arm*, the 1955 film based on Nelson Algren's hard-hitting novel, starring Frank Sinatra as a junkie poker dealer. The problem was brought to the attention of a young minister in East Harlem in a more immediate way by a seventeen-year-old Puerto Rican boy who belonged to a storefront church on 100th Street. Louis "Pee Wee" Leon told the Reverend Norman Eddy that the lives of his friends and neighbors were being destroyed by the drug, and asked "What are we going to do?"

"Like all good Americans," Norm recalled many years later with a wry smile, "we formed a committee."

The Narcotics Committee of the East Harlem Protestant Parish was not like most committees, though, for its members, guided by Norm Eddy, did not just meet and "study the problem." They actually did something about it.

"When 'Pee Wee' Leon came to me for help in 1956," Norm told me, "there was not a single hospital or doctor in New York City or State to treat adult addicts."

The courts could send addicts under twenty-one to Riverside Hospital on North Brother Island for detoxification treatment, but the only option for adults hooked on heroin was to kick the habit cold turkey—on their own or in jail. They could petition the court to spend thirty days at the Riker's Island prison or check into the Federal Narcotic Facility in Lexington, Kentucky.

So what could be done to change all this by the minister of a storefront church, the church's secretary, the mother of an addicted young woman, and a high-school kid? They enlisted a few other neighbors and soon had seventy-five to a hundred people coming to meetings to learn about the subject that up until then, Norm said, had been "very hush-hush." Doctors, sociologists, jazz musicians, cops, and social workers came to talk, exploding myths of addiction that flourished when the subject was taboo.

Talk became action as the EHPP Narcotics Committee and their allies picketed Metropolitan Hospital to open beds for addicts withdrawing from the drug, and state hospitals followed. The committee provided counseling, referrals, and a "wild, rich" weekly Bible study Norm led in his living room where people argued, shouted, vented, and found inspiration and support. Usually a warm, smiling man, Norm turned red with anger if a visitor got "too intellectual." I was there when he kicked out a visiting social worker who was making pretentious comments.

The people of 100th Street between First and Second Avenues, dubbed "The Worst Block in the City" by the *New York Times,* trusted this prematurely white-haired young white minister who lived on the same block. Rebelling against the "Country Club Christianity" of Eisenhower America, when bigger churches with taller spires were symbols of religious "success," Norm and his fellow ministers of the East Harlem Protestant Parish took literally Jesus' message of service to the poor. Like Dorothy Day and her followers in the Catholic Worker movement, they lived where they preached and what they preached.

Like most of his "group ministry," Norm served in World War II (he drove an ambulance and saw action in the battle of El Alamein), graduated from Union Theological Seminary, and grew up in a middle-class community (Hartford, Connecticut). Norm's parents, like those of his colleagues in the parish, were shocked and dismayed that he and his wife (the Reverend Margaret Eddy) not only lived in a drug- and crime-ridden neighborhood, but intended to raise their son and two daughters there. As it turned out, none of the children of the parish ministers got into drugs or crime, as so many of their suburban counterparts did.

I met Norm in 1957, when I went to East Harlem to write my first book, *Island in the City,* and I brought James

Baldwin up to meet him and hear about his work. The novelist asked the minister why he had come to live in that neighborhood, and Norm explained it was not to "save souls" or "do good" in the way outsiders assumed, but rather to realize a dream: "I want to help create Plymouth Colony in East Harlem."

Baldwin said immediately, "I understand."

Norm told me later that Baldwin was "the first person who knew what I was talking about."

Norm also understood the dream of a young minister in the South named Martin Luther King the moment he heard about it. He went to Montgomery, Alabama to meet Dr. King in 1956, sensing he was the man to lead the nation in the civil rights struggle. Norm felt his instinct was confirmed when he learned that King had hired a former addict from 135th Street and Lenox Avenue to be his driver.

"In those days, addicts were considered 'beyond hope,' " Norm said. "The fact that King put his trust in such a man showed he believed that people could grow and change."

That belief is a cornerstone of Norm's life and work, proved by the grassroots, inner-city groups he helped coordinate with his wife and fellow minister "Peg" Eddy that began on East 100th Street. The EHPP Narcotics Committee changed the laws for treatment of drug addiction, The Christian Economics Group of ten young adults saw their neighbors ruined by loan sharks and established the first inner-city credit union, while the Metro North Citizens Committee launched the neighborhood's first community housing project and rebuilt the tenements on 99th Street from Second Avenue to the East River.

Norm calls these groups that began in the 1950s and 1960s "the great-grandparents" of changes that still benefit people in New York City and State, and beyond. Norm himself is a great-grandparent who still lives in the neighborhood and carries on his work at age eighty-three, devoting himself in recent years to improving East Harlem's schools. With his "spirit-guided" grassroots activism, he has proved that ministers can build more valuable legacies than church spires.

WALT WHITMAN

RICHARD GAMBINO

IN 1848, TWENTY-nine-year-old Walt Whitman was for three months a reporter for the *Daily Crescent* in New Orleans, writing fluff pieces about local color and charm as seen through Yankee eyes. But he also saw darker spectacles there—streetside auctions of slaves—and six years later put his emotions into ironic verse:

I help the auctioneer, the sloven does not half
know his business . . .
Have you ever loved the body of a woman?
Have you ever loved the body of a man?

Do you not see that these are exactly the same to all in all
  nations
and times all over the earth?
If any thing is sacred the human body is sacred.

When he returned to New York, he became the editor
of the *Brooklyn Daily Freeman*, the nation's foremost
voice of the Free Soil movement, whose motto was,
"Free soil, free labor, free men!" He continued his advocacy of the movement, because of which, just before
going to New Orleans, he had been fired as editor of
the *Brooklyn Daily Eagle*. But intimacy with those
in the movement had its effect. Whitman came to hate,
on the one side, the abolitionists for their fanaticism, most
of which went into infighting among themselves, and on
the other, the hypocritical and corrupt men of the
Democratic Party, all of them "born freedom sellers of
the earth." He resigned from the *Freeman*, despondent.
His faith rested in the sympathy of the human heart,
which had failed.

I have said that the soul is not more than the body,
And I have said that the body is not more than the soul,
And nothing, not God, is greater to one than one's self is,
And whoever walks a furlong without sympathy walks to his
  own funeral drest in his shroud.

Whitman's faith in democracy flowed from the same
source. It was not a faith resting on constitutionalism,
legalisms, political science schemes, natural law, or laws
of history. It was rooted in a belief in the best of the

human souls of ordinary citizens, often dismissed as his "mysticism." But when he was answering the challenge of whether the soul exists, his response did not depend on abstractions or esoterica but on the perceived experience of personal and historical growth. "No reasoning, no proof has establish'd it,/Undeniable growth has establish'd it." His faith in democracy rested on a distinctly American populism of pragmatic human experience. So in a twentieth century obsessed with ideological convictions that politics—and especially economics—determine human behavior and history, he was brushed aside as a quaint American naïf whistling in the dark.

Another common error is to take Whitman's faith in free humanity as a bombastic Pollyannaism, or softheaded narcissistic, mystical messianism. Yes, he tells us that as a boy he was electrified by hearing a sermon by Elias Hicks of the Quaker Church on Joralemon Street in Brooklyn. (Hicks's faith in the human spirit was so radical that even his fellow Quakers denounced him as a heretic.) Whitman was captured by the idea that "the fountain of all . . . truth . . . [is] namely in *yourself* and your inherent relations," and that in this, Hicks was "a brook of clear and cool and ever-healthy, ever-living water." But young Whitman, who'd been pulled out of school at age eleven, developed his own pragmatic, experiential populism, so would not become a Quaker. "Logic and sermons never convince,/The damp of the night drives deeper into my soul." His mature populism was not of a Mary Sunshine kind.

Whitman's *Democratic Vistas* (1871) should be read by

all Americans. It is a lengthy, scathing critique of American democracy's flaws at the time, and in ours—the flaws being the failings of its people and culture:

> I would alarm and caution . . . against the prevailing delusion that the establishment of free political institutions, and plentiful intellectual smartness, with general good order, physical plenty, industry &c., (desirable and precious advantages as they all are,) do, of themselves, determine and yield to our experiment of democracy the fruitage of success. . . . I say we had best look our times and lands searchingly in the face. . . . The spectacle is appaling. We live in an atmosphere of hypocrisy throughout. The men believe not in the women, nor the women in the men. A scornful superciliousness rules in literature. . . . The great cities reek with respectable as much as non-respectable robbery and scoundrelism. In fashionable life, flippancy, tepid amours, weak infidelism, small aims, or no aims at all, only to kill time.

Whitman's enduring lesson about American democracy: "O I see flashing that this America is only you and me." No better, no worse. "The genius of the United States is not best or most in its executives or legislatures, nor in its ambassadors or authors or colleges or churches or parlors, nor even in its newspapers or inventors . . . but always most in the common people."

Whitman's brand of populism mandated that he seek the liberation of people and culture, in a liberated poetic form. He did not invent free verse but embraced it and advanced it, against the ornamental, parade-ground regularities of meter and rhyme, which constrained his early poems to the point of banality:

Rhymes and rhymers pass away, poems distill'd from poems
   pass away . . .
America justifies itself, give it time, no disguise can deceive it
or conceal from it, it is impassive enough.

In naturalism, freed from pie-in-the-sky otherworldliness:

And a mouse is miracle enough to stagger sextillions of infidels.

In exquisite sensuality:

Out of the rolling ocean . . . came a drop gently to me,
whispering *I love you, before long I die,*
I have travl'd a long way merely to look on you to touch you.

In sexuality:

Without shame the man I like knows and avows the delicious-
   ness of his sex,
Without shame the woman I like knows and avows hers.

And in sexual orientation. Although he resisted admit-
ting his homosexuality, even to absurdly claiming he had
six illegitimate children, he did so to avoid, as with regard
to all matters, being pigeonholed, and thus vulnerable to
easy dismissal. But his "Calamus" poems are frankly
homosexual, even celebratory in the sexual orientation
(Calamus is a plant with a phalluslike head):

O here I last saw him that tenderly loves me, and returns again
   never to separate from me,

And this, O this shall henceforth be the token of comrades, this
calamus-root shall,
Interchange it youths with each other! let none render it back!

Whitman's sexual poems, like many others, were coura-
geous. He was fired from a badly needed job as a clerk at
the Interior Department in Washington by none less than
the Secretary of the Interior himself. Secretary James
Harlan stole Whitman's personal copy of *Leaves of Grass*
from his desk, and noted, ironically, some of the hetero-
sexual poems of the "Children of Adam" section as
"obscene."

The female form approaching, I pensive, love-flesh tremulous
aching . . .
The face, the limbs, the index from head to foot, and what it
arouses,
The mystic deliria, the madness amorous, the utter abandon-
ment.

Whitman's courage, and humor, extended to his last days.
Wheelchair-bound, sleeping on a water bed "like a ship or
a duck" to relieve constant pain from multiple ailments,
including pervasive TB and strokes, he described himself
as "some hard-cased dilapidated grim ancient shellfish or
time-bang'd conch (no legs, utterly non-locomotive) cast
up high and dry on the shore-sands." (Years before, after
suffering a stroke that left him paralyzed except for his
head and one arm, he had brought himself back to complete mobility through his own efforts, including wrestling
with saplings in woods.) He struggled against pain and

paralysis to complete a ninth edition of *Leaves of Grass.*
And succeeded.

Whitman saw in the risky experiment of a free people
possibilities for a great polity, culture, and morality.
Three years before his death, in 1888, when he was sixty-
nine, he wrote that there had been in his life one "purpose enclosing all, and over and beneath . . . Ever since
what might be call'd thought, or the budding of thought,
fairly began in my youthful mind, I had had a desire to
attempt some worthy record of that entire faith and
acceptance . . . which is the foundation of moral
America."

His challenge to us, again typically American, is that the
faith is to be fulfilled with each person and generation in
the future:

Dear camerado! I confess I have urged you onward with me,
and still urge you, without the least idea what is our destination,
Or whether we shall be victorious, or utterly quell'd and
defeated.

FREDERICK WISEMAN

STUART KLAWANS

LIKE A LATTER-DAY Jacob Riis outfitted with movie equipment, Frederick Wiseman made his name by exposing scandalous conditions, in a work that became scandalous in itself.

His debut film, *Titicut Follies* (1967), laid bare the brutalities practiced in the state prison for the criminally insane in Bridgewater, Massachusetts. The horrific events he recorded in this documentary—such as the force-feeding of a crazy old man—seemed all the more terrible for the matter-of-fact, Riislike ungainliness of Wiseman's images, which he presented without comment or explanation. Whether he had studied *How the Other Half Lives,* I can't say; but if he had, he surely knew that the book's power resided in its mute photographs, far more than in the loquacious and judgment-laden text. So Wiseman chose to convey his truth about Bridgewater through a combination of reticence and naked force, which so shocked the State of Massachusetts that it obtained a court order preventing public screenings of *Titicut Follies.* Its success thus guaranteed, the film went on to become a prized item on the film-society circuit, securing Wiseman's fame as a muckraker.

Within a few years, though, faithful viewers began to place him in a different tradition, one that runs back not to Riis but to August Sander, or maybe Balzac. As Wiseman went on creating his portraits of institutions, it became clear that his ambitions were encyclopedic. He was out to describe the full range of American society in the late twentieth century: its public-education system *(High School)*, military *(Basic Training)*, police *(Law and Order)*, commerce *(The Store)*, religion *(Essene)*, urban space *(Central Park)*, human-animal relations *(Zoo)*, treatment of the poor *(Welfare, Public Housing)*, treatment of the disabled *(Adjustment and Work)*, treatment of the aged and terminally ill *(Near Death)*, and favorite nourishment *(Meat)*. In their running times, these documentaries began to stretch out, almost languorously. Their images became more composed, even when animated by grief or outrage. The beautiful, meditative *Belfast, Maine* (2000) seemed to bring together all these facets of Wiseman's filmmaking and of American life, in a documentary that summarized not just the title city, but his career as well.

But then, there was still more. To the titles of muck-raker and encyclopedist, his followers had to add that of dramatist.

Wiseman's interest in the theater—or, perhaps, the theatrical presentation of self—at last became obvious when he directed for the stage his adaptation of a chapter of *Life and Fate,* a novel by Vasily Grossman, and then put the production onto film as his 2002 release *The Last Letter.* In substance, both the play and the film represent the testimony of a Jewish doctor in the Ukraine, who is about to be murdered in the Holocaust. In emphasis, though, the movie becomes a close-up study of the acting technique of Catherine Samie, then the senior member of the Comédie-Française.

She comes before the camera without makeup, dressed in a shroudlike gown, as if stripped of everything except her formidable skill. Wiseman focuses intently on the artfulness of each tremor of Samie's hands, each nuance of her face, during the hoarse inflection of each deliberately cadenced phrase. The film monumentalizes her performance, in ways that a stage production cannot. But, beyond that, *The Last Letter* helps make sense in retrospect of Wiseman's documentaries *La Comédie-Française* and *Ballet* (in which he demonstrated his interest in the work that goes into a performance); of the scene in *Belfast, Maine* in which an amateur troupe rehearses *Death of a Salesman*; and even of *Titicut Follies,* which takes its title from a show performed by the hospital's inmates.

Are all of his films performance recordings?

In an interview conducted in the late 1990s by critic Gerald Peary, Wiseman declared that ordinary people have no ability to act for the camera. Maybe so; but in the next breath, he also insisted that drama is inherent in everyday life. His job is to reveal the drama—in effect, to get social reality to perform itself. He does this not by coaching people or inciting them to play to the camera (as his detractors charge) but by moving quickly and fluidly during the filming and by putting in long, long hours afterward in the editing room. During the shoot, Wiseman handles the boom mike, darting in or backing off continually, always responding first of all to the voice. Already, he's imagining the edit: While the camera rolls, he positions and repositions his longtime cinematographer, John Davey, getting the shots he'll need to piece together the sequence. Later, at his Steenbeck, he'll reduce an hour and a half of such footage into perhaps five minutes of screen time, in a compression that turns rambling events into scenes and normal people into actors.

For the most part, the art in this process remains hidden. Wiseman famously rejects all framing devices and explanatory apparatus—voice-overs, interviews, texts, postproduction music—so that the events in his films may seem to unfold transparently. The effect is deceptive. Although you're absent and uninvolved, watching from a seat in the movie house or a living-room chair, you get the privilege of enjoying a surrogate presence through the camera. (Think of a point-of-view shot in which the viewer is nobody in particular.) And although the only information available to you is what your eyes and ears can pick up, Wiseman's editing offers subtle cues, which allow you to understand situations as if you knew their context.

Of course, almost all movies involve you in this process

of prompting and identification: encouraging you to imagine your way into the picture, hinting at how you should respond. If Wiseman's films differ, it's because their apparent purity denies the effect of his direction yet reveals him to be the sole shaper of these realities. Before the great Iranian filmmaker Abbas Kiarostami began to shift the border between documentation and fiction, in his now-epochal *Close-Up* (1990), Wiseman was already playing at being inside and outside the film simultaneously, performing for the audience and making himself invisible.

Not that he thought all this up on his own. When Wiseman was living in Paris in the late 1950s, toying for the first time with an 8-millimeter camera, the people who talked most vividly about movies were excited by the idea that the world would disclose itself to the camera of its own accord, given a long enough take and a steady enough gaze. (As Godard said, film might allow us to call things by their right names.) Later, when Wiseman returned to the United States, he might have seen this principle put to the test in a political context in the 1960 documentary *Primary*, whose roster of filmmakers included such proponents of direct cinema as Richard Leacock, Albert Maysles and D. A. Pennebaker. The availability of portable, synch-sound equipment was opening new subject matter to filmmakers; it permitted the individual an unprecedented level of control, but at the same time encouraged some of these new-made authors to concentrate less on themselves and more on the actualities before them. Shirley Clarke was already working in this vein in 1963 in her fiction film *The Cool World*, produced by Fred Wiseman as his first foray into professional moviemaking. (For his day job, he was still teaching law in Boston.) In 1967, when Wiseman came out with *Titicut Follies,* Clarke matched him by releasing *Portrait of Jason,* her feature-length, direct cinema interview with a gay African-American man. It's another film that is as much a performance piece as a documentary.

So Wiseman was not alone—at least, not at the start. Through steady work, extraordinary consistency, and a useful relationship with the Public Broadcasting Corporation, he has achieved solitude. I can think of no filmmaker other than Wiseman who so combines an outraged conscience, a hunger for knowledge, and a conviction that our lives ought to be respected as works of art.

As of this writing, he has completed the second feature-length installment of *Domestic Violence* for a total of thirty-two documentaries. Should future generations have the heart to look back on us, they will find encouragement in these films by Frederick Wiseman, which are comprehensive enough to embody not just our pain but also our courage, not just our callousness but our care.

BILL VEECK

STAN ISAACS

BILL VEECK'S MINOR-league team, the Milwaukee Brewers, trained in Ocala, Florida. One day, after working out with his team during a spring practice, Veeck went out to sit in the Jim Crow stands in the outfield where blacks were relegated to watch the game. Veeck decided to sit down with them and, as he said, "barber a little with them as was my custom as we watched the game."

Within a few moments, the sheriff came over to tell Veeck he couldn't sit there. When Veeck persisted, the sheriff called the mayor. He told Veeck he was violating a city ordinance. Veeck told him that if he were not allowed to sit there, he would move his team out of Ocala that night.

This was a threat to make the mayor's blood run cold, Veeck said. "We had taken over the town's hotel for six weeks; if we left, the town and the hotel would be hurt." The mayor left. Veeck sat there every day after that, "just to annoy them" he said, without being bothered again.

"It seems to me," Veeck said in his autobiography, *Veeck as in Wreck,* "that all my life I have been fighting against the status quo, against the tyranny of the fossilized majority rule. I would suppose that whatever impels me to battle the old fossils of baseball also draws me to the side of the underdog. I would prefer to think of it as essential decency."

Bill Veeck, the iconoclastic baseball owner, was a remarkable man—literate, pixieish, Falstaffian, a debunker of stuffiness, a curmudgeon, a rogue, always fun to be with. He was one of the most significant figures in baseball history and possibly the most beloved of owners because he catered to the fans. He made baseball fun and lit up franchises wherever he went.

There were three aspects to Veeck's genius:

He was a great entrepreneur, a spectacular showman.

He was a solid baseball man; his roguishness sometimes overshadowed the fact that when he had a fair shot at his opposition he had winning teams.

And he was a huge force for social good. He brought black players to the American League. He was an early supporter of players' moves to get out from under the reserve clause.

If Veeck had had his way, he would have broken the

color line in major-league baseball even before Branch Rickey signed Jackie Robinson for the Brooklyn Dodgers. During World War II, Veeck tried to buy the Philadelphia Phillies and stock them with Negro players for the 1944 season, but was foiled by baseball officials. He was too brash, not a member of the club, so they maneuvered to have the fast-sinking franchise go to an owner who got the Phillies for half the price that Veeck, backed by the CIO, was willing to pay.

Then, shortly after Jackie Robinson broke the color line in major-league baseball with the Dodgers in 1947, Veeck opened the American League to African-Americans when he signed Larry Doby with the Cleveland Indians in the middle of the 1947 season. Whereas Branch Rickey had plucked Robinson from a Negro League team for nothing, Veeck paid the owner of Doby's team, the Newark Eagles, $10,000 for his contract.

Daily Worker sports editor Lester Rodney, who had been one of the leaders goading the major leagues to break the color line, said, "You can't overestimate the importance of what Veeck did in signing Doby in '47. There was still a claque of owners who were working to confine the breakthrough to Brooklyn only, hoping it would die out with Robinson. Veeck gave them the finger by opening up the American League."

When he signed Doby, Veeck received 20,000 letters, most of them violent and sometimes obscene. A couple of his players made their objections known, and Veeck soon found faraway places to send them. The next year, he signed the legendary Satchel Paige and overcame critics who said he was committing a travesty on baseball by signing the irrepressible Paige when he was listed as forty-two years old. A year later, he enriched the Indians and baseball by signing the colorful slugger, Luke Easter out of the Negro Leagues.

After a poor start in 1947, Doby became a solid player, leading the league in home runs for the second time when the Indians won the pennant in 1954. Paige, signed in mid-season, went on to compile a record of six victories and one loss, and helped the Indians win the 1948 pennant. He played for Veeck later with the St. Louis Browns.

Veeck wrote a letter to then baseball commissioner, the dour Kenesaw Landis, suggesting that the reserve clause that bonded a player to the team that owned him was immoral and illegal and therefore should be abolished. Years later, when a suit by Curt Flood tested and over-turned the reserve clause, Veeck testified for Flood.

He is regarded as the ultimate showman of baseball, a laughing, irreverent, barrel-chested figure who dreamed up fan-friendly stunts that irritated the owners he loved to mock. He said, "The automatic turnstile was the last inno-vation greeted with approval by baseball moguls."

But he was also a shrewd baseball man. In the eighteen years between 1947 and 1964, the Yankees dominated the American League, winning the pennant fifteen times. Though he never operated with a huge bankroll, Veeck's teams were the only ones to break through the Yankee domination. His Cleveland Indians won the pennant in 1948, setting an American League attendance record. He won again in 1954 with the Indians, and then in 1959 shortly after he took over the Chicago White Sox. Win or lose, he enjoyed twitting the staid and lordly Yankees.

"The Yankees," he said, "always took the attitude that they were doing you a favor by permitting you to watch them."

I recall a trip I made to Chicago with the Yankees when I sought out Veeck at his downtown hotel the afternoon of a night game. I called from the lobby, was told to come right up, and I was welcomed to barge in and see him in the bathroom where he was soaking his leg. Veeck had been injured in the Marines in World War II. His right leg was shattered by a recoiling antiaircraft gun. He underwent some thirty operations, and eventually a part of his leg was amputated.

He chatted with his cigarette-husky laugh while lounging in the bathtub water with his good leg, holding the prosthesis of his other leg outside the tub. He unselfconsciously flicked the ashes of his cigarette into the socket of the prosthesis. Veeck, never embarrassed by his deformity, always said, "I am not handicapped, I am a cripple."

As we made our way through the South Side out to Comiskey Park, he was a pied piper of good cheer. When his driver stopped for lights, people recognized him and exhorted him and the White Sox to beat the Yankees. He cheerfully acknowledged their good tidings with a wave and a vow to do just that.

For more than thirty years, Veeck's innovations enlivened his franchises and baseball while other owners in the main rejected or ignored his constructive ideas, wincing when his promotional daring succeeded. He said, "If baseball owners ran Congress, Kansas and Nebraska would still be trying to get into the Union." He put the names of his players on the backs of their uniforms, forcing the other teams to do likewise. He staged ingenious promotional schemes and outrageous giveaways. He set up a nursery in his stadium, staffing it with professional nurses. He sat in the stands with fans. "I have discovered in twenty years of moving around ballparks," he said, "that the knowledge of the game is usually in inverse proportion to the price of the seats."

It was Veeck's contention that only one team could win a pennant, so it was incumbent upon owners to make sure that fans coming out to see his team had fun whether it won or lost. That ethic has come down to a new generation of owners who have adapted many of Veeck's ideas to make their ballparks and teams inviting.

Among the innovations copied by others is the exploding scoreboard he installed at Comiskey Park in Chicago. It flipped its lid when a White Sox player hit a home run, shooting off fireworks, exploding bombs with a coruscating display. Veeck once was one-upped on this one by none other than the hated Yankees on a visit to Comiskey Park. Bob Fishel, the Yankee publicity man who had worked for Veeck in Cleveland, had some sparklers smuggled into the Yankee dugout. When a Yankee hit a home run, the Yankee players in the dugout jumped up and paraded with lit sparklers, led by the gimpy-legged codger, manager Casey Stengel. Veeck, watching from the press box, chortled. Nobody more appreciated what he called "a brilliant satire" than he did.

He said of the canny Branch Rickey that he was the man who taught Machiavelli the strike zone. And he was surely a wise man. He said, "Always work at a job where your workplace is west of where you live. That way when you drive to work in the morning, you will not be looking into the sun and when you drive home in the evening, the sun will again be behind you."

Once he ordered a wooden rocking horse from a mail-order house for one of his sons. To Veeck's dismay the toy, which didn't arrive until the day before Christmas, had to be assembled. Veeck sweated at erecting the toy Christmas Eve and into the wee hours of the morning to be placed under the tree for his son. He then wrote out a check to the toy company, tore the check into pieces, put it into an envelope with the note: "I put your horse together, you put my check together." The canceled check came back from the bank soon afterward, all pasted together.

When illness forced him to sell the White Sox, he entered a period of retirement, living on Maryland's Eastern Shore because (a) the climate was temperate, (b) it was near an airport (in Easton), and (c) it was within less than an hour drive from a big city (Baltimore or Washington).

He had a flyer running the Suffolk Downs racetrack in Boston. The first thing he did was take down the barbed wire surrounding the plant. "A barbed-wire fence," he said," is not exactly a welcoming sight."

Pure Veeck was this: Getting the track ready for its first day, he frowned at the artificial flowers. As he ordered the artificial flowers removed for fresh ones, a sweet old lady came up to him and said how much she enjoyed the artificial flowers. Without batting an eye, Veeck picked up some of the to-be-discarded flowers and grandly handed them to the woman.

His most famous stunt, of course, was the signing of the midget, Eddie Gaedel, having him pinch-hit and draw a walk for the St. Louis Browns in 1951. Veeck, a prolific reader, revealed that he had gotten the idea from the James

Thurber short story, "You Could Look It Up," about the midget Pearl du Monville, who actually swings at a pitch and makes out. Veeck said he warned Gaedel about any such foolishness. One of the classic photos of baseball is of Gaedel at the bat with catcher Bob Swift on his haunches waiting to accept a pitch from Bob Cain.

Veeck was born on February 9, 1914. He died on January 2, 1986. He was voted into the Hall of Fame in 1991 for his innovations, for bringing black players into the American League, for being "a champion of the little guy," the jolliest character ever to occupy an owner's seat—even if his was often in the bleachers.

"My epitaph is inescapable," he said. "It will read, 'He sent a midget up to bat.' "

CURT FLOOD

WALLACE MATTHEWS

ON OCTOBER 7, 1969, Curtis Charles Flood declared, "Hell, no, I won't go."

In that regard, he was not unlike many Americans in the turbulent Vietnam War era.

But Curtis Charles Flood was not a peacenik or a draft dodger or a flower child or a conscientious objector. Curt Flood was a professional baseball player, and in 1969, such things simply were not done.

On that date, the St. Louis Cardinals traded Flood, their All-Star centerfielder, along with catcher Tim McCarver, pitcher Joe Hoerner, and outfielder Byron Browne to the

Philadelphia Phillies for slugger Richie (later, Dick) Allen, infielder Cookie Rojas, and pitcher Jerry Johnson.

More correctly, the Cardinals *tried* to trade Curt Flood. It wouldn't take.

Curt Flood had this strange notion that in spite of the fact that he was living many a boy's—and full-grown man's, for that matter—dream by playing America's Grand Old Game for pay, he was entitled to the same simple rights bestowed upon other American wage earners.

Curt Flood had played baseball in St. Louis for twelve years, played it exceptionally well. He was a .293 career hitter, a three-time All-Star and the winner of seven Gold Gloves for the excellence of his defensive play. No less a chronicler of baseball than *Sports Illustrated* named him the game's best centerfielder in a cover story, this in an era that boasted the likes of Willie Mays, Mickey Mantle, and Duke Snider.

He made $90,000 a year, a fortune by the standards of the average working man and, at thirty-two, still seemed to have several productive years ahead of him.

But Curt Flood was willing to walk away from it all because, plain and simple, he didn't want to leave St. Louis, uproot his family, and move to Pittsburgh.

"He had roots in the community," McCarver said. "His kids went to school there. His wife had a business there. He loved the city and he didn't want to leave. It was as simple as that."

And yet, Curt Flood also had a sense that what he was doing might have a greater significance than merely determining the future mailing address of his family.

"I told him that winning this case was a million-to-one shot, and getting any money out of it was probably even more unlikely," said Marvin Miller, the first president of the Major League Baseball Players Association. "He thought about it for a moment, and then he said, 'But if we win, it will help all the other players and the players yet to come? That's good enough for me.' This was a very principled man."

As an outfielder, Curt Flood never shied from the wall, and he didn't shy from this one. In fact, he ran head-on into a barrier a lot tougher than the twelve feet of concrete that ringed old Sportsman's Park in St. Louis.

And although he couldn't knock it over, Curt Flood shook that wall and left the first cracks in what would be the baseball equivalent of the fall of the Berlin Wall.

Nearly thirty years later, ask the average baseball fan, or even the average baseball player, about Curt Flood and you are likely to hear two things. The first is that he won a landmark case, and the second is that he did it for the money.

Neither is true. Flood lost a 5-3 decision in the Supreme Court, which was no surprise since it was the same Court, under the leadership of Oliver Wendell Holmes, that granted baseball its antitrust exemption in 1922. That decision, which stands to this day, essentially allows the owners of baseball teams to conduct business as they see fit, without regard for the rules of free-market competition.

And as for doing it for the money, the case wound up costing Flood not only a high-paying job, but whatever was left of what might have been a Hall of Fame career.

No matter. Curt Flood took one for the team. He was never adequately repaid.

Without Curt Flood, there would have been no Alex Rodriguez, professional sports' first Quarter-Billion Dollar Man. Without Flood, there would have been no Catfish

Hunter or Andy Messersmith, baseball's first true free agents, who by 1974 had knocked over the last remnants of the brick wall Flood had barreled into 1969. Without Flood, or another man like him, there would not have been a Major League Baseball Players Association as we know it.

By the time Flood died of cancer in 1997, the MLB players union was by far the most powerful in any sport, feared by the owners and in large part hated by the fans as a symbol of the greed and arrogance of the modern ballplayer. But in 1969, the union was in its infancy, and something so minor as having the minimum salary for a major-league ballplayer raised from $6,000 to $10,000 was considered a major victory. It was in that climate that Curt Flood undertook his fight.

Today, there are some who would blame Curt Flood for all of baseball's current ills—the grotesquely inflated salaries, the monstrously inflated egos of the players, the horrendous threat of a work stoppage every couple of years.

In truth, Curt Flood's heroic refusal to be pushed around by the tyranny of baseball's reserve clause paved the way for baseball players to get their fair share of a cash pie the owners had been hogging for themselves over the previous half-century. The bad stuff came later and had nothing to do with Curt Flood.

He was simply a man who believed that even baseball players should have some say in where and for whom they would work.

His case aroused strong emotions on both sides. After reading about Flood's case in the newspapers, twenty-two-year-old Donald Fehr, then a law student, was shocked to learn of how little say a ballplayer had in his own destiny.

"When I read that players were bound to their teams for life, I thought, 'That can't be right,' " Fehr recalled.

But it was. From 1922 on, baseball teams had the right to pay ballplayers anything they chose to, and to trade, sell, or fire them at will, as if they were cattle. A player as great as Mantle could win the Triple Crown—lead the league in batting average, home runs, and runs batted in—and have his salary cut because his average had dropped a few points from the previous season.

Still, even among his peers, there was a sense that Flood's fight was born either of greed, or race. It was an explosive time in U.S. history, barely a year after the assassinations of Bobby Kennedy and Martin Luther King, Jr., and just a few months after the race riots that tore up Watts and Detroit and Newark.

At a meeting of the Players Association in Puerto Rico that year, Flood was grilled intensively by the other player reps about his true motivation. "Are you doing this as a show of black power?" he was asked.

Flood laughed. "Actually, I see it more as a symbol of black weakness."

By the end of the day, the player reps had voted unanimously to support Flood's case, and to pay his substantial legal bills. As the legal fight went on, Flood sat out all of the 1970 season, but as spring training of 1971 approached, he got an offer to play for the Washington Senators.

But Flood's return to baseball was a disappointment. His skills eroded by the year off and his spirit sapped by the largely negative reaction from the fans, Flood retired after thirteen games. In his last season in the major leagues, Curt Flood batted .200, managing just seven hits and two RBIs.

"I have no doubt that all the legal wrangling took its toll on his abilities," McCarver said.

The next year, the Supreme Court handed down its decision. Flood wasn't around to hear it. By then, he and his family had moved to Paris, where he ran an art gallery. Marvin Miller broke the news to him by telephone.

"He was terribly disappointed, but he took it well," Miller said. "I asked him if he regretted doing it."

"Not a bit," Flood replied.

Over the years, Flood the ballplayer was largely forgotten. In his fifteen years of eligibility for the Hall of Fame, the most support he ever mustered was 71 votes, cast in 1996, his final year on the ballot, when he was already terminally ill. Most of the ballplayers who had benefited from his sacrifice—the $4 million shortstops and $6 million middle relievers—would not have been able to place his name, much less explain his case.

"Unfortunately, ballplayers are like any other people," said Don Fehr, who succeeded Miller as the president of the Players Association. "They tend to believe that the world began when they became aware of it."

But there was still one standing ovation left for Curt Flood, although it came not in a ballpark, but in a boardroom in Atlanta a few months before he died.

It happened at a meeting of the Players Association's executive committee, which Flood had been invited to by Fehr. The meeting was already in progress when Flood arrived, but when he walked through the door, everything stopped.

Recalled Miller: "Curt Flood got the longest, loudest ovation you have ever heard in your life."

Even after thirty years, it is never too late to say thank you.

HOWARD T. ODUM

CHARLES BOWDEN

THE SUN BEAT feebly against the January window, my
father lay dying in the back bedroom and in January 1974,
I first came to grips with the mind of Howard T. Odum.
The book was *Environment, Power, and Society* (1971), a
text crammed with strange schematic drawings chock-
ablock with gates, amplifiers, and other symbols that
bounced like esoteric messages off my head. Odum
claimed what I was seeing and reading in his pages was the
real world and that this world could be drawn, measured,
and understood as a whole. I never looked up from the
pages or looked back. I staggered though the dense text

without pause. My father died in the night, but by that time I had consumed Odum, and the book rocked my closely held ideas in a way few books ever have.

I'd bumped into Odum's name earlier when a paper he wrote on net energy gain, the notion that any power system (nuclear, coal, solar, et al.) should be judged by comparing energy production against energy cost, and this accounting was done with energy units, not dollars. In this tally, nuclear power, for example, cost more energy to produce than it created—in short, became a loser. The paper published by some obscure Swedish journal became a kind of Xeroxed samizdat throughout the scattered nooks and crannies of the academic wilderness where people tossed around something called systems science, the belief that there is an organization in world that transcends particular disciplines or subjects, an almost theological faith that has spawned such fields as cybernetics. I hailed from none of these areas, but I was hungry for some solid way to see the man-made world of industrialism and the natural world as a unit that could be examined by fact rather than metaphor. The implications of Odum's worldview seemed to offend everyone: The right was told that there really were limits to resources and to human-dominated power; the left learned that the managerial society with everything engineered and neatly distributed was a fantasy of centralized power and fatal; environmentalists learned that to sever the natural world as some kind of aesthetic playground separate from the human world was a delusion. For Odum it was if we all lived in a swamp together and had best get used to this idea.

I met him a year later when I finagled an invitation for

him to a conference in Tucson, Arizona. He came off the plane wearing a cheap suit, white socks and a cheerful countenance. We immediately retired to the airport bar for a beer and the good doctor, who lived in the bogs of Florida by choice, announced that he was, "happy to visit a new ecosystem," in this case the Sonoran desert. As we stared out on the booming Sun Belt city glowing with light and took in the blackness of the surrounding mountains, I mentioned that I wanted him to produce a drawing capturing what the surrounding wild terrain produced for the city. Instantly, a pen came out and the ranges, the Santa Catalina, Rinons, Tucsons, Santa Ritas, that I'd wandered since boyhood became schematic things as Odum grilled me for information and sketched out flows on bar napkin after bar napkin. I was bewitched both by his intensity and childlike delight. This torrent of ideas continued for five days. At one point, in the early light of morning, I found him crawling around a creosote flat absorbing desert botany and zoology like a ravenous beast.

I'd never met a genius before or thought much about the term save that it meant someone who was pretty damned bright. But in Odum's case I realized its true meaning, the ability to see the world afresh, without any filters and to hammer out a meaning and organization from this mishmash of impressions that bombard all of us. At one point, over another beer, Odum sketched out how much energy Leonardo Da Vinci's *Mona Lisa* had focused, all those human beings tramping to Paris to see this one rectangle, all the millions more studying prints of the same face, and so forth. It was more illuminating than my first acid trip.

A former student of Odum's once told me how in a lecture

he was trying to explain why water swirls down a drain clockwise in the northern hemisphere and counter clockwise in the southern and in the midst of this explanation filled the lab sink to demonstrate the obvious fact. And then became hypnotized by the phenomenon and for the rest of the hour kept refilling sink and simply watching the water swirl away. Naturally, Odum created a veritable army of masters and doctoral students who now dwell in the biological sciences like a fifth column warring against orthodoxy.

Odum died in September 2002 at age seventy-eight and left more fifteen books, more than 300 papers and an ongoing crusade to save the Everglades. His brother Eugene (who preceded him in death by a month) was a fellow titan in ecology and both of them won the Crafoord Prize, a kind of ecological Nobel. Their father, Howard Washington Odum, was a nationally known sociologist and folklorist (Negro work songs and the like) and became a pioneer in promoting regional planning. He also came out against segregation in any form in 1946 and did it from his academic post in North Carolina. Systems thinking seemed to run in the DNA of the Odum family. Along with a kind of primitive but bedrock concern for making the United States a decent and fair society with equal rights for all, in the case of the boys this desire extending to alligators, slime mold, and swamp cypress.

Odum gave us a systematic way to understand that natural and human systems must be managed for mutual benefit, or both will diminish and threaten human society as we know it. I remember questioning him back in the seventies about how we could devise a decent society in the face of diminishing cheap energy, particularly the shrinking supplies of fossil fuels we love to mainline. He looked at me and said with a smile, "It's as much fun to walk down the mountain as walk up the mountain." I thought, hey, that's glib. And then, toward the end of his life, he wrote, along with his wife Elizabeth, a book responding to my dismay. *A Prosperous Way Down* (2001) details how the soft merging of natural and human systems could work as the cheap oil slips from our grasp.

But mainly in our time together, Odum did not teach me to think outside the fabled box, he seemed ignorant of the existence of the box. For the first and last time in my life, I was with an academic who lived the life of the mind.

I remember telling him of my fascination with the big ruins in the Southwest, the giant buildings left by earlier Native Americans in Mesa Verde, Chaco Canyon and Canyon de Chelly. He looked at me quizzically and said, "I'd like to know what a Buddhist archaeologist would examine in this region."

People like Odum lack the flash to make it as celebrities in our brittle culture. And his ideas on measuring and managing this world were always too radical for normal forums. Instead of solving our simple problems, which always demand that *we* do not change but that whatever we crave become cheaper and easier to obtain, he trashed our problems by redefining reality for us. He didn't tell us how to magically get more oil, he told us of the tremendous work natural systems—those bogs, mountains, rain forests, deserts, and estuaries—produce for us and how our only livable future mandated working with and not against such systems. He failed miserably in staying within the tidy borders of any discipline and thus kept inventing new language and new structures that toppled our tidy academic departments. He was that amiable bull in our dull, safe china shop.

I've been unusually lucky in life. Twice I've seen a mountain lion in the wild at less than twenty feet. And three times I've met and wrangled with extraordinary people. Fannie Lou Hamer of the Freedom Democratic Party in Mississippi; Edward Abbey of monkey-wrenching ecological reengineering, and Howard T. Odum. They all taught me that there is no excuse for not grappling with the world and trying to both understand it and improve it. And they impressed equally on my mind that fame meant nothing compared to having consequence. I hope to God that someday no one needs to study the achievements of any of them, but rather that their ideas and examples become so embedded in our society that they become functioning commonplaces, just like those mysterious segments in our DNA.

Odum was that great rarity, the canary in the coal mine who not only sounded the alarm, but sketched out in detail how to move our society to safe and decent ground. God knows what Odum thought of his career. His father, after producing a wall of books, new schools and social programs, and three novels, cheerfully remarked that he figured his blooded Jersey cows were worth more than his books. I'm pretty sure his son Howard T. Odum felt that way about every bog that ever slopped over the top of his boots.

BILL HICKS

TOM GOGOLA

THEY NEVER TELL you just how funny the meetings can be.
Sure, there's a passing reference in the Big Book to AA-
style laffs, but not much detail, not much in the way of
expected punch lines. The humor is almost never light—
how can it be?—but rather the humor that induces one to
lowering one's head, rubbing one's eyebrows, and shaking
one's head as a fellow addict shares a story that all too often
sounds suspiciously like your own. In the immortal words
of Alfred E. Neuman, it's humor in a jugular vein. They
don't tell you this, possibly because to do so would violate
the spirit of anonymity in "the rooms," but the stand-up

aspect, at times, runs particularly strong. I've seen it happen again and again: The lights are dimmed and the "qualifier" is suddenly deadpanning his way through one tragicomic episode after another, preaching to a cramped room full of the fully converted and the counting-days alchs—and earning those grimace-grin nods of recognition and a few belly laughs along the way. Sometimes there's a well-timed but not-so-funny punch line that caps off a qualification and punctures the reverie, hammering the don't-drink message home. "Then I shanked my grandmother with a pair of scissors and did twelve years upstate." Silence. Chairs scrape. "Show of hands?"

But mostly you are left feeling relieved, franchised— "I'm not the only one who flushed $6,000 worth of pot down the toilet!" "I'm not the only one who seems to have misplaced the month of August 2002!" "I'm not the only one with an unrelenting, raging hatred for humanity!" These are the axioms that keep you coming back, the shock of recognition that makes the whole world go round, sans the room spinning—even in the face of the occasional dud qualifier who can't get off the subject of his poor cat with an eating disorder and then my mother died and I started wearing her wedding dress to work and got fired fuck them. Such are the perils of getting sober in Greenwich Village.

The AA-as-Caroline's Comedy Club routine puts catharsis first and clever last, generally eschews irony—except for the meatfist irony that this is the last place you'd thought you'd end up—and never laughs in the face of death, since, as we all know, death will always get the last laugh.

If there ever was a poignant reminder of this fact, it is to be found in the story of the late comedian Bill Hicks, an epically funny man who could leave you gasping for air at the observational power of his left-leaning invective, the brilliance of his avowedly un-PC misanthropy, and the sheer raging funny that poured out of his clever, sick, ecstatic mind.

Hicks died a classic drinker's death, succumbing in 1993 to the incurably unromantic pancreatic cancer at the ripe old age of thirty-two. From the department of Life's Unfair, Hicks had largely conquered his "demons" by the time he died—they apparently were legion and included just about every chemical agent found in a typical "garbagehead's" arsenal of oblivion. But he had purged his kit bag of just about everything by 1993, save psychedelic mushrooms and cigarettes. And, one is compelled to assume, pot. He is the only comedian that I know of ever to have cited 'shroom guru Terence McKenna in one of his bits, and not in that profoundly irritating Dennis Miller way of referencing for the purposes of deliberate obscurantism. (After taking a McKenna-prescribed, so-called heroic dose, five grams of mushrooms, Hicks reported, with great aural fanfare, that his third eye had been thoroughly squeegeed—he considered psychedelics to be evolution enhancers, and would also cite Jung to advance this argument.)

Hicks was Southern-born and raised, was never married, and was known for his relentless touring schedule; all those podunk nights on the road—sixteen years' worth—had the net benefit of leaving him totally at ease with his audiences. There is an unforced intimacy to a Bill Hicks performance, like you're at a party with a particularly funny guest who has something to say about everything, and everyone, and even though he's hogging up all the conversation, you're rapt in his presence, and put up with the occasional meandering anecdote because you know the funny is right around the corner. Hicks could be brutally self-deprecating one moment and shitting all over his audience the next, expressing open hatred for them, and then becoming aghast at the knee-jerk self-immolation he was engaging in—and the routine never failed to endear the room to him. His touchstones were Control and Complacency—he could be vicious in his jeremiads against distraction-addicted fat Americans and their equally despicable blubbery children. One of his most infamous, and therefore beloved bits involved telling the parents among his audience that their children, despite what they believed with all their hearts, weren't special at all. He knew this because after engaging in Onan-the-barbarian activities, he'd wiped "entire civilizations off of my chest. . . . with a gray gym sock."

There are many reasons Hicks was the best comedian of his generation, and the most-missed chronicler of the vulgar machinations and paradoxes that characterize American politics and culture. During a time when the dominant observational posture was one of ironic and maddeningly antiseptic detachment, an unfortunately long-lived modus operandi of the putatively engaged-and-literate set, Hicks was blunt, mortally engaged, and totally unshackled when it came to venting his rage. He had the strength and will to grapple mano-a-mano the absurdities and outrages of, say, Waco, or of the first Gulf War, without stooping to the smug-'n'-clever level—he was, in fact, as equally scornful of the sunken-chested fence-sitters of the irony era as he was of their over-the-horizon targets. Yes, that means you, Dennis Miller.

Plus, in true antihero fashion, he was big in England, and pretty much a cult sideshow in the States. Just like Noam Chomsky. In a way, Hicks was like the funny version of ol' Noam, except that unlike the linguist-provocateur, Hicks headed straight for the personal motives of the involved players to get a laugh, whereas Chomsky, to his ever-loving detriment, generally deems such motives to be irrelevant—ours is not to wonder why George Bush, Jr. invaded Iraq, ours is only to decry. Realizing full well that the aforementioned conjecture is perhaps a little too reductive for some, it nevertheless brings great pleasure, to imagine what Hicks might have been saying about the younger Bush. During the first Gulf War, Hicks had flipped the "Support the Troops" slogan on its head and repropagandized its gotcha message: "I support the war, but oppose the troops." No doubt, this time around he would have connected Saddam Hussein's 1991 claim that he would watch the senior Bush's head rolling down the equivalent of Main Street, Baghdad "like a soccer ball," with his eager-to-please draft-dodging former cokefiend of a son rolling the Abrams tanks, at long last, into said city to vindicate his prudent pappy. And we'd be laughing with him, bitterly and with no small measure of say-it-brother fellowship, all the way to the looted Bank of Baghdad. It's not ironic, it's RPG comedy, and as Hicks would also no doubt say, the joke is on you, America. Now go fuck off and get back to your *Webster* reruns.

Hicks's death is all the more embittering when you consider the torrents of media-generated gibberish, horrifying cultural trends, and plain old bad shit that have flowed down the pike in the decade since his passing. In 1993, he was railing against American Gladiators, Waco, and the pro-life movement. In retrospect, it all seems so . . . innocent. On the latter issue, it is worth noting that the Letterman show torpedoed a Hicks appearance some months before his death because the comedian had made the pretty uncontroversial, if not outright goofy suggestion that if those folks were so pro-life, they should stop picketing medical clinics and instead "link arms and block cemeteries." It's a little silly, but c'mon, the image is priceless. As it turned out, the *Late Show* on which Hicks was to appear happened to have as one of its sponsors . . . a pro-life organization.

Anyway . . . media-generated gibberish, horrifying cultural trends, and plain old bad shit. Of course, it seems that the past decade has had more than its fair share, that there has been an exponentialized acceleration of junk culture, jackass politics and endtimes mayhem in the U.S.A., but that may be only because it suits the writers' agenda to have it so. Still, it has been a doozy of an intervening decade—the O.J. trial, Monica Lewinsky, *Survivor,* cell phones, *Fox News, Fear Factor,* Princess Di, the Gingrich Revolution, Woodstocks II and III, Chadgate, JonBenet Ramsey, Columbine, OKC, SUVs, *The O'Reilly Factor,* Trent Lott, Senator Clinton, *Joe Millionaire,* Bush II, the WTC, the Genome—and had Hicks been around to chronicle it . . . hmmm. Dunno. The only certainty is that most Americans still wouldn't know who the hell he is.

CURTIS MAYFIELD

SCOTT SHERMAN

"HERE'S CURTIS MAYFIELD!" the emcee announced to thousands of concertgoers. It was August 13, 1990. Mayfield, looking professorial in his large glasses, strapped on his guitar and walked onstage for a free performance at Wingate Field in Brooklyn, at which point disaster struck. "Next thing I know," Mayfield told *Rolling Stone*, "I was on the floor with no guitar, no shoes on my feet, no glasses on, and I was totally paralyzed." A sudden gust of wind had brought down a lighting scaffold, which shattered several vertebrae in Mayfield's spine and left him a quadriplegic.

It was a cruel blow to one of soul music's most beloved figures, a man whose songs formed part of the musical soundtrack during the headiest phase of the civil rights movement. At the apex of Mayfield's influence in the 1960s, radio stations in Chicago banned his music, while Martin Luther King Jr. and thousands of his foot soldiers enthusiastically embraced it. Mayfield himself—who went on to produce some of the finest political anthems of the 1970s—was an unlikely rebel; his radicalism was rooted not in the socialist left but in the black church. In keeping with that background, his songs imparted a message of faith, courage, and self-reliance, the same values that guided him through the record business, where he was one of the very few black artists to own his own songs and record label, and where he worked to educate other musicians about their rights and responsibilities in the industry.

Mayfield was born in 1942, and grew up in the Cabrini Green housing projects in Chicago. At the age of eight, he began to perform in a family-based gospel quartet, many of whose performances took place in his grandmother's church. Mayfield dropped out of high school to form the Impressions. In 1964, shortly before the passage of the civil rights Act, the group released "Keep On Pushing." With its gospel harmonies, call-and-response singing, and twangy guitars, the song quickly became an anthem for the civil rights movement generally and for Martin Luther King Jr. in particular, who claimed it as one of his favorite songs: "Now maybe someday I'll reach that higher goal/I know I can make it with just a little bit of soul/'Cause I've got my strength and it don't make sense/Not to keep on pushing." The following year, the Impressions released what is probably Mayfield's greatest song—"People Get Ready," a stately gospel out-pouring that bore haunting witness to the movement's trials and travails: "People get ready, 'cause there's a train a-coming/And all you need is faith to hear the diesels hum-ming/. . . Don't need no ticket/You just thank the Lord." The tune singled out "the hopeless sinner who would hurt all mankind just to save his own" and affirmed solidarity with those "whose chances grow thinner." Activists distributed the song to black churches and neighborhood centers, and "People Get Ready" eventually became one of Mayfield's most recorded and best-loved compositions.

As the civil rights movement came up against white resist-ance in Chicago, Mayfield's songwriting took on a harder edge. "Too many have died and protected my pride, for me to go second class," he sang in "This Is My Country" (1968). "We've survived a hard blow, and I want you to know, you will face us at last." The Impressions—on whom Bob Marley modeled the Wailers—produced radiant songs about black pride and racial uplift, not revolution, but the cultural estab-lishment deemed their music subversive nevertheless. One Mayfield composition from 1967— "We're a Winner"—was banned by dozens of Chicago radio stations, who feared it would alienate white listeners. "It was a song with a message, it had an inspiring message," Mayfield later recalled. "And this wasn't really what radio was all about in those times."

From the earliest days of his career, Mayfield evinced a savvy understanding of the economic side of the music business. He started his first publishing company in 1960. "Somewhere I picked up that you had to copyright your songs," Mayfield later remarked. So he wrote to the Library of Congress, which informed him of his rights.

But his conflict with the Chicago radio stations in 1967—and the close-to-home example of Jesse Jackson's Operation PUSH— inspired him to create his own competitive, fully staffed record label, Curtom Records, a highly unusual move for a black musician in the late 1960s. But Mayfield, always his own man, felt it was an essential step in guaranteeing his own long-term independence. "I believed very early in life," Mayfield once said, "that it was important to own as much of yourself as possible." Decades later, Billboard would acknowledge Mayfield as one of a select group of black artists—Ray Charles and Sam Cooke among them—who "defied the odds by regaining possession of their master recordings."

Mayfield left the Impressions in 1971 and entered his most productive phase as an artist. The political climate had shifted: Dr. King was dead, the exuberant reveries of the civil rights struggle had diminished, and the Vietnam War dragged on senselessly. The gospel singer in Mayfield responded with songs like "We Got to Have Peace," which fused social commentary with infectious hooks and blaring horns: "We gotta have peace / To keep the world alive / And war to cease." The song continues in the next stanza with this triumphant, optimistic rhetoric: "We gotta have joy / True in our hearts / With strength we can't destroy." Finally Mayfield celebrates the democratic role that music can play in change: "People hear us / Through our voice / The world knows there's no choice."

When Mayfield performed the song on military bases around the globe, he emphasized the final verse: "And the soldiers who are dead and gone/If only we could bring back one/He'd say/'You gotta have peace.'"

Mayfield's solo records from the early 1970s—Curtis, Roots, Curtis/Live!—were intoxicating works of art that combined delicate ballads, funk-driven dance songs, and socially conscious anthems; the latter were darker and more explicitly political than anything Mayfield had done with the Impressions. Mayfield's songs now addressed themes like environmental degradation, the problems of the American Indian, and most significant, deteriorating conditions in his own community, beginning with ghetto nihilism, gun violence, and crime. (Mayfield's new political consciousness left a mark on his peers: Anthony DeCurtis has noted that Mayfield's first solo record, Curtis, pushed Marvin Gaye and Stevie Wonder in a more political direction.) In the melancholy, psychedelic "We The People Who Are Darker Than Blue," Mayfield cried out in his falsetto voice: "Are we gonna stand around this town and let what others say come true?/We're just good for nothing, they all figure/Our boys growing up shiftless jiggers/Now we can hardly stand for that/Or is that really where it's at?" The same song inquired darkly: "Shall we commit our own genocide?" But his essential message—black pride, courage, self-respect and equality—continued to drive songs like "Beautiful Brother of Mine" from 1971: "Beautiful sister of mine . . . Improving black pride is now true / At last we've outgrown Uncle Tom." The stanza ends with an assertion of optimism and pride: "Showing our own a new pride / That makes us feel all good inside."

Mayfield's views concerning black-on-black exploitation were put to the test the same year, when he produced the soundtrack to *Superfly*. He was repelled by the gaudiness and violence of the film—which looked to him like "a cocaine commercial." So he set out to subvert the images in the movie with unsentimental tunes like "Freddie's Dead" and "Pusherman." The lyrics of the soundtrack stood in stark contradiction to the gaudy fantasy on the screen. "If you want to be a junkie," Mayfield sang, "remember that Freddie's dead." He passed the test.

Mayfield's career faltered in the years after *Superfly*. In the late 1970s he wrote high-quality movie soundtracks for artists like Aretha Franklin, but his own records were poorly received. Curtom Records—in spite of its having signed numerous black artists—folded at the dawn of the Reagan era, and the 1980s were something of a lost decade for him, although he retained his popularity in Europe and Japan. Only after his accident did Mayfield reenter the public spotlight. He was the subject of two tribute albums in 1993, and in 1994 he garnered the Grammy Legend Award. Mayfield's work also found its way to a younger generation of black filmmakers and rappers. For his documentary on the Million Man March, Spike Lee used four songs by Mayfield—among them "People Get Ready" and "Keep on Pushing"—and dozens of leading rappers have subsequently sampled his work in their own music, a situation that enabled him to remain financially secure in the hard years following his accident. Mayfield passed away in 1999, and his death promoted an outpouring of praise from artists ranging from Aretha Franklin to Chuck D, who celebrated Mayfield as a "voice of reason and protest." But Mayfield himself always bristled at the phrase "protest singer." He was something else—a man whose work drew its inspiration not from political ideology, but from gospel music and the blues; a man who, when confronted with segregation in the 1960s and urban despair in the 1970s, responded with a luminous body of work affirming a consistent set of principles: courage, perseverance, self-reliance. He imparted those values in his songs, but—as a griot, troubadour, visionary, musical healer, and entrepreneur—he lived them as well. He flirted with despair—the cover of his 1975 album, *There's No Place Like America Today*, depicted a black unemployment line set alongside a cartoonish portrait of a giddy, all-American white family—but, as songs like "Beautiful Brother of Mine" demonstrate, he never succumbed to it: "With love, respect, and pride / Success will be on our side."

CLARENCE DARROW

DANNY GOLDBERG

DURING THE LATTER years of the Eisenhower administration, American liberals looking for inspiration in a stulti-
fying political environment rediscovered the legacy of
Clarence Darrow. In 1955, Paul Muni appeared as the legendary attorney in the Broadway hit play *Inherit the Wind*,
a work based on the famous Scopes "monkey trial" in
which Darrow defended a Tennessee schoolteacher
indicted for teaching the theory of evolution. In 1957,
Arthur Weinberg edited *Attorney for the Damned*, a stirring collection of Darrow's courtroom speeches. In 1959,
audiences saw Orson Welles as a character based on

Darrow in *Compulsion,* a film about the trial of rich-kid murderers Leopold and Loeb, both of whom were spared the death penalty by Darrow's eloquent moral indictment of public executions. The following year, Stanley Kramer directed Spencer Tracy as the Darrow character in the film, *Inherit the Wind.* Both film scripts borrowed heavily from Darrow's actual courtroom language. His emotionally powerful and intellectually supple arguments both against the death penalty and for academic freedom remain remarkably fresh, even now.

This lovingly retouched image of Darrow—a plain-spoken, idealistic curmudgeon who swayed average Americans on juries while holding his suspenders—was reinforced by portrayals of him in subsequent years by Jack Lemmon and Henry Fonda. And just as future rock stars forged their identity by miming Elvis Presley's pelvic thrusts, so did hundreds of future civil-liberties and civil rights lawyers imagine themselves as heirs to the idealized version of Darrow. He possessed an almost saintly common sense, courage in the face of ignorance and venality, and an unmatched ability to transform trials into political vehicles in which avant-garde ideas were translated into common language, rendering them accessible to juries and thus to huge portions of the American public.

Darrow's gift for oratory was indeed remarkable, equaled only by that of Martin Luther King in the annals of progressive movements. But the rest of Hollywood's well-intentioned version of Darrow falls far short of the truth. The real Clarence Darrow was both a far more radical progressive visionary, and deeply flawed and morally ambiguous character, than the myth allows.

Born in Ohio in 1857, Darrow moved to Chicago thirty years later. He began practicing law and participating in the progressive intellectual subculture that was thriving there, and soon became known as a riveting public speaker and writer on behalf of radical economic and political ideas. A widely reprinted speech he gave more than one hundred years ago to a Chicago prison makes the case for the link between poverty and crime more vividly than any current polemic. Yet, during the same period in his life, Darrow was also interested in conventional politics and in making large sums of money.

Darrow maneuvered himself into the position of Acting Corporation Counsel of the City of Chicago. Shortly thereafter he became an attorney for the Chicago and North Western Railroad—one of the giant American businesses whose agenda he had criticized in theory but whose interests he wound up defending. Yet, a few years later, when labor hero Eugene Debs of the American Railway Union was charged with conspiracy for his leadership in a strike against the Pullman Palace Car Company, Darrow remarkably switched sides and defended Debs. Crafting a strategy that would serve many subsequent generations of public-interest lawyers, Darrow rhetorically put the big corporation on trial and unexpectedly called several of their executives as witnesses. He succeeding in getting the charges against Debs dropped.

Following that success, Darrow became the number-one lawyer for labor unions at a time when unions were the vehicle for virtually all radical American political movements. Representing the coal miners' union in an arbitration ordered by President Theodore Roosevelt, Darrow condemned mining companies with an almost mystical sense of the arc of the battle ahead: "They are fighting for slavery while we are fighting for freedom. They are fighting for the rule of man over man, for despotism, for darkness, for the past. We are striving to build up man. We are working for democracy, for humanity, for the future, for the day that will come too late for us to see it or to know it or to receive its benefits." The Presidential Commission awarded back pay and a wage increase to the miners; Samuel Gompers, President of the American Federation of Labor, called it "the most important single incident in the labor movement in the United States." Darrow then wrote "Breaker Boy," a widely read short story about the abuses coal miners suffer which further popularized labor issues.

But Darrow was still torn by contradictory impulses, and he continued to represent giant corporations—for instance, the monopolistic private electric company Commonwealth Edison. In 1904, Darrow seconded the (unsuccessful) nomination of newspaper baron William Randolph Hearst as Vice-President at the Democratic National Convention.

In 1907, when he defended labor leader Big Bill Haywood and others for the murder of former Idaho Governor Frank Steunenberg, Darrow made his biggest national headlines to date. In his closing argument, Darrow evoked the larger issues of the trial saying, "If at the behest of the mob you should kill Bill Haywood, he is mortal, he will die, but I want to say a million men will grab up the banner of labor at the open grave where Haywood lays it down, and in spite of prisons or scaffolds or fire, in spite of prosecution or jury or courts, these men of willing hands will carry it on to victory in the end."

Despite his seeming passion in the courtroom, as the years had passed, Darrow had grown increasingly unhappy. Whether from frustration at the obstacles to social justice, or a tumultuous personal life, or a crisis of the spirit driven by his contradictions, Darrow was, according to one of his biographers, "bleak, cynical, and hopeless in his outlook." In the Haywood trial, this bitterness spilled into his summation: "I don't care how many crimes [are committed by] these weak, rough, rugged, unlettered men who often know of no other power but the brute force of their strong right arm, who find themselves bound and confined and impaired whichever way they turn—I don't care how often they fail, how many brutalities they are guilty of. I know their cause is just." This apparent endorsement of violence as a morally appropriate response to economic deprivation deeply offended many of his friends and even his co-counsel in the case. Nevertheless, Haywood and the others were all acquitted and Darrow became more famous than ever.

As with other great men, Darrow's peak of celebrity unleashed his worst demons. Geoff Cowan's brilliant book *The People v. Clarence Darrow* illustrates the turning point the famous lawyer hit in 1912. Two years earlier, Darrow had agreed to represent John and James McNamara of the International Association of Bridge and Structural Iron Workers on a murder charge deriving from a bombing of the *L.A. Times* in which twenty people were killed. Darrow received a $50,000 fee (roughly equivalent to $1 million today), raised predominantly in nickels and dimes from union meetings across the country. After encouraging labor leaders to believe that he would use the trial as a political platform on behalf of union issues as he had done in the past, Darrow abruptly changed course and pleaded the McNamaras guilty on the premise that this was the only way of saving them from execution. Not only was this a huge disappointment to union leaders around the country, Darrow himself was indicted for attempting to bribe a juror in that case; consequently, he spent the better part of a year in Los Angeles defending himself from those charges.

Literally defending his life at the age of fifty-five, Darrow had tears running down his face as he told the jury: "There are people who would destroy me. There are people who would lift up their hands to crush me down. If you should convict me, there should be people to applaud the act. But if in your judgment and your wisdom and your humanity, you believe me innocent and return a verdict of not guilty in this case, I know that from thousands and yea perhaps millions of the weak and the poor and the helpless throughout the world, will comes thanks to this jury for saving my liberty and my name." Newspapers reported that several jurors, and even the court stenographer, were weeping. Both Darrow's autobiography and Irving Stone's loving biography, *Clarence Darrow for the Defense*, portrayed the "not guilty" verdict as a victory for justice.

The truth was not so pretty. Cowan had access in researching his 1993 book to far more extensive files than had previous historians. Although he remains an ardent admirer of Darrow, Cowan concludes that he did, in fact, bribe two of the McNamara jurors. There is also evidence that during weak moments Darrow actually contemplated the kidnapping of a key prosecution witness. Cowan speculates that Darrow may have contemplated such behavior because he actually believed that such tactics were morally justified. Years later, Darrow wrote, "The high motive of the revolutionist is on one side, the strength of the government to protect itself is on the other." Even for many who were glad that Darrow beat the rap, rationalizations of immoral means to justify politically desirable ends remain troubling.

Despite his shortcomings, if Darrow had passed away at that time—even as he publicly defended the Wilson administration's pursuit of World War I while Eugene Debs and other of his old friends were under administration assault for opposing the war—he still would have left an enormous progressive legacy and been a profound influence on subsequent generations. Yet, only a few years later, in his sixties, Darrow performed a stunning and extended final act of his public life, and did the work for which he is best remembered. In 1920 he unsuccessfully but eloquently defended twenty members of the Communist Labor Party who were accused of conspiracy based on a draconian Illinois law that was interpreted to make mere party membership the equivalent of "advocating the overthrow of the government by force." Darrow argued the case on First Amendment grounds. As would occur in the Scopes trial, although he didn't win the desired verdict for his client, Darrow established arguments and ideas which ultimately would prevail.

The Leopold and Loeb case came in 1924. In early 1925, the newly formed American Civil Liberties Union recruited Darrow, by now sixty-eight years old, for Scopes. Later that year, the NAACP similarly enlisted Darrow for the murder trial of Dr. Ossie Sweet and ten other African-

Americans charged with murder after a mob that included Klansmen, protesting blacks moving into white neighborhoods, surrounded Dr. Sweet's home. Despite an all-white jury, Darrow succeeded in gaining acquittals for all defendants in what was a landmark civil rights case of the time.

In a self-aware moment at his own trial, the great man summarized his life: "My life has not been perfect. It has been human. Too human. I have felt the heartbeats of every man who lived. I have tried to be a friend of every man who lived. I have tried to help the world. I have not had malice in my heart. I have had the love of my fellow men. I have done the best I could."

Well, maybe Darrow was being a little self-aggrandizing. He almost certainly had moments of malice, and it seems likely that there were some heartbeats he did not feel. But not only did he do the best he could, he did as well as anyone in American history at using his mind and his force of will to expand and enforce the nation's stated goal of "liberty and justice for all."

PAUL WELLSTONE

JOE CONASON

WHEN PAUL WELLSTONE perished in a plane crash along with his wife, his daughter and three members of his staff in October 2002, the horror of his death nearly overshadowed the meaning of his life. His devoted supporters, including his two surviving sons, were understandably overwhelmed by the immediate pressures of trying to hold on to his Senate seat. His conservative adversaries, in Washington and elsewhere, were tempted by the opportunity to misuse his memory for their own purposes—to diminish his liberal colleagues, to emphasize liberalism's frustrations, to reiterate the complacent perspective he rejected.

In Wellstone's immediate secular canonization, through mass-media rituals that allowed us to transcend our grief about that terrible event, he became vulnerable to television's trivializing effects. This was a mixed benediction from a medium that had rarely paid him much attention before his death. He was presented as the quixotic radical, the gregarious populist, the lovable dissenter, the rare honest liberal, the minority of one. Wellstone was certainly all those things, and he was just as surely a great man. But what made him great seems to have escaped our understanding, even at the moment when the nation was transfixed by his image. He deserves much better than to be remembered as a cliché, whether condescending or flattering.

One clue to Wellstone's greatness is his rise to political prominence from utterly ordinary beginnings. He suffered through the kind of unpromising adolescence that, in America, sometimes precedes an extraordinary life. Growing up in suburban Washington during the 1950s, he was just a short, awkward kid with a learning disability, poor grades, and bad test scores. His middle-class Jewish parents both worked, struggling to earn enough money to cope with the crippling depression suffered by Paul's institutionalized older brother. For a while, the problems in school and at home drove him into delinquency, vandalizing buildings and stealing cars for "joyrides" that probably brought him little joy. He once called that period his "rebel without a cause" phase, as if Woody Allen had understudied James Dean.

Wellstone's chance to escape mediocrity arrived by the grace of that most American form of social and academic advancement, the athletic scholarship. He had discovered discipline and achievement as a high-school wrestler, a sport in which he excelled because of strength, tenacity and aggression that far exceeded his small size. The scholarship took him to the University of North Carolina in Chapel Hill, where he developed a passion for political science. He earned his undergraduate degree in three years, had his first child with his wife, Sheila, and won a regional wrestling championship.

He did well enough teaching political science at Carleton College, where he took the academic job that consumed the first two decades of his career. But Wellstone was hardly contented with scholarship. He was an indefatigable community organizer with rhetorical talents. At Carleton, he spent much of his time involved in a variety of left-wing and community-organizing efforts, like many other New Left veterans. Few of those endeavors, however worthy, achieved their objectives. To the horror of the college deans, he also had a habit of getting arrested, first at a Vietnam War protest at the federal building in Minneapolis, and later at a local bank where he was protesting farm foreclosures. In 1974 Carleton tried to dismiss him. He organized students and alumni to fight the decision and win him tenure.

By that point, as the New Left declined swiftly into violence and irrelevance, Wellstone had established himself as a certain familiar type: the leftist professor and campus gadfly who shows up at antiwar demonstrations, annoys the local veterans' organizations and occasionally publishes an op-ed article with a "radical" viewpoint. Obviously, he turned out to be something much more significant. The difference was his discovery that he was a politician, with the peculiar gift for charming and, more important, remembering each voter. It's a quality that wins elections nobody thinks can be won—and a skill that requires the ability to listen as well as talk. He also decided that he was a Democrat as well as a democrat.

That simple choice—to be politically where the people of his adopted state had been for so long—was the foundation of Wellstone's greatness.

Unlike other celebrated figures with origins on the New Left, he entertained no illusions about leading a revolution or even a third-party movement. Unlike some who were far better known during the 1960s, he was as much at ease in a union hall or a restaurant kitchen as he eventually became on the Senate floor. Though that quality was not necessarily a function of his populist views, it certainly complemented his outlook. Other politicians exude the common touch—real or counterfeit—and then betray the waitresses and the busboys by voting against the minimum wage. With Wellstone, there was neither fakery nor betrayal.

He had much to teach the left. His patriotism was the profound love of country that is expressed as deep, passionate concern for the people and the land. His lack of pretension and his dedication to healing the injuries of class belied the stereotype of the "limousine liberal." His own hero was Robert Kennedy, with whom Wellstone shared a tinge of cultural conservatism.

So there he was, a man of the people with an earnest desire to improve their lives and an unusual capacity to communicate. At the time, in the early 1980s, the populist heritage of Minnesota's Democratic-Farmer-Labor Party had been relegated to another era. The party's most celebrated figure was still Hubert Horatio Humphrey, an object of scorn on the New Left for his abject collaboration in Lyndon Johnson's escalation in Vietnam. The party that would soon nominate for President another Minnesotan named Walter Mondale hardly welcomed Wellstone's energy and style, let alone his radical perspective.

Yet however serious his differences with the party's more centrist leadership, in Minnesota and nationally, Wellstone never hesitated to call himself a Democrat. He liked to say that he belonged to "the democratic wing of the Democratic Party." When others of his generation veered off toward apocalyptic insanity or spiritual tangents, or dropped out of electoral politics altogether, he consistently understood that real politics and real power were located in the struggle between the major parties.

After an abortive and slightly silly race for state auditor, Wellstone persevered to seek a seat on the Democratic National Committee. If not a party hack, he was undoubtedly a party functionary, albeit of a particularly rambunctious stripe. He could not be deflected from that fundamental insight, even when the state party establishment tried to kick him off the DNC in 1988. Two years later, his perseverance was rewarded with the Senate nomination. The political and press establishment gave him little chance of defeating a popular, entrenched incumbent Republican. But he crafted a "blue-green" coalition of unionized workers, urban and suburban liberals and environmentalists, along with a slice of independent populists, that won an amazing victory.

Much has been made of the fact that as a senator, he often found himself at the short end of a 99-to-1 roll call. He took pride in that principled obstinacy. But whenever he talked about his own record, Wellstone put equal emphasis on the things he had accomplished with more conventional Democrats and on occasion with conservative Republicans. Those Senate conservatives, who had regarded him from the beginning as a rather dubious radical, came to know a quintessential American, the son of immigrants, who loved sports and married his high-school sweetheart.

He was in many ways an exemplary senator, not merely a maverick show horse. When nine miners trapped in a Pennsylvania pit became a national news story, politicians and pundits suddenly started to ask a few questions about mine safety. They found Wellstone already there, demanding better funding and exposing the deficiencies in the federal mine-safety bureaucracy. Until that moment, mine safety wasn't "hot," and the issue quickly lost its momentary cachet after the Quecreek miners were saved. That didn't matter to Wellstone, who pursued the issues he cared about—universal health care, minimum-wage increases, the lobbyist gift ban, campaign finance reform—not the fads and fashions that attract TV cameras.

What may stand as his single greatest achievement—the federal law mandating insurance parity for mental health care—came about through his unlikely but close alliance with New Mexico Senator Pete Domenici (a tough old conservative Republican who wept openly on television the day the Wellstones died). During his final campaign, Greens and various ultraleft poseurs increasingly denounced his pragmatism, as if the sole legitimate purpose of a principled senator is to irritate colleagues and achieve nothing.

Wellstone could speak as the conscience of his party and his country because he had earned the right to demand a hearing. He had long since left behind the theatrics of tantrum and posturing for the grinding, frustrating, joyful discipline of campaign and governance. What he had learned—and what he taught us by example—was the vast difference between illusions and dreams.

CLIFFORD AND VIRGINIA DURR

GEOFF COWAN

IN THE MOST dangerous period of the civil rights movement in Alabama, the era when parts of the South had far too much in common with South Africa, the years when fire hoses were trained on peaceful young demonstrators on the streets of Birmingham, when an angry mob threatened to kill the Freedom Riders and all of their allies crowded inside a church in Montgomery, and when Viola Liuzzo, a housewife from Detroit, was murdered after the march across Selma's Edmund Pettus Bridge; the decades when George Wallace blocked the doorway at the University of Alabama, when a black seamstress was arrested for refusing to sit in the back of a municipal bus, when Martin Luther King, Jr. was jailed in Birmingham and four schoolgirls were murdered in a Birmingham church; during those years Clifford and Virginia Durr were treated by the leaders of Alabama's political, social and commercial community as dangerous heretics, as white and, in the argot of the era, probably "Red" outcasts. (Virginia called her memoir *Outside the Magic Circle*.) But for many who loved freedom, and for those labeled "outside agitators," the Durrs were celebrated as the keepers and champions of a dream and as the proprietors of a home in Montgomery that served as small progressive island, an oasis and salon for civil rights workers, international visitors and working journalists, a world they had created out of conscience, conviction, and circumstance. For many who were privileged to know them then and later, the Durrs were much more than heroes of a momentary aberration in American history: They were, rather, exemplars of ideals to be remembered and emulated in every era.

Indeed, during my years heading the Voice of America in the middle 1990s, I displayed one nonfamily photo in my office overlooking the Capitol; a picture of Clifford Durr sitting on a chair near his weekend cabin in the woods, his arm embracing his black Labrador, seemingly contented with the choices he had made. Sadly, they were not choices that most members of his or any generation would make.

I had come to know and admire the Durrs in the of summer of 1965. For two months, I boarded in an apartment above their home along with several other young reporters, editors, and photographers working for a new weekly civil rights newspaper called *The Southern Courier.* Every morning I would wake up at daybreak and follow the scent of coffee downstairs to the Durrs' living room, where they were already reading the paper, smoking cigarettes, and discussing local and world affairs. During those early-morning visits, they reminisced (or, in Virginia's case, gossiped deliciously) about the world when they were young in FDR's New Deal Washington; about the heroes and victims (though they would never have used such words to describe themselves) of the McCarthy era; about the Vietnam War (it pained and infuriated them that it had by then become, after all, their friend Lyndon's war); and about the civil rights movement, including their lives as threadbare survivors in the still-segregated and segregationist South. Their stories and attitudes were more complementary than identical. Virginia was more of a political activist, more politically progressive; Cliff attacked issues as a lawyer and a Jeffersonian, primarily concerned with free speech, fairness, and due process. There was nothing he would not do to protect Virginia's right—and the right of others—to hold unpopular views.

Those early-morning visits were, for me, a lifelong education in the virtues of political integrity. I hoped that the picture of Cliff, and the memories that it brought to life, would guide, inspire, and empower me if I were ever forced to confront similar moral dilemmas.

Cliff and Virginia were, in fact, born inside the magic circle, children of privilege. When they met in the late 1920s, Cliff seemed headed for blue-blooded establishment success, a former Rhodes Scholar working for the Alabama Power Company's favorite law firm. Virginia, raised with the prejudices of her peers in Birmingham ("I thought of the Klan as something noble and grand and patriotic that had saved the white women of the South," she wrote in her memoir), had started to challenge her assumptions as a student at Wellesley College; but she had only begun to flirt with modernist views on what now might be called issues of race and gender. Their real transformation was prompted by the blinding poverty of the Great Depression, which led them to become even more concerned about class than about race. "It was the first time I had seen the other side of the tracks," she told Studs Terkel. "The rickets, the pellagra—it shook me up. I saw the world as it really was."

Both Durrs were quickly swept up in the New Deal, thanks, in part, to connections made through Senator (and later Supreme Court Justice) Hugo Black, who had married Virginia's sister. They moved to Washington, D.C., where Cliff became a member of the legal team at the Reconstruction Finance Corporation, joined the social and political world of southern activist contemporaries, including Lyndon and Lady Bird Johnson, and became major figures in 1941, when President Roosevelt asked Cliff to become a member of the Federal Communications Commission.

Today, with the public-interest obligations of broadcasters receding—or yielding to market forces—Cliff deserves to be widely celebrated and remembered for his legacy as a champion of the rights of listeners and of those without the resources or power to build a station of their own. With radio still in its infancy, Cliff led a small group of intellectuals who believed that the new medium could and should be used for the public good. They took seriously the concept that the airwaves belonged to the people, a concept that might be ridiculed today on talk radio and television stations that no longer live by his legacy, and he led the charge in persuading his fellow commissioners to adopt a series of policies including "the Blue Book" (more formally called the "Public Interest Responsibility of Broadcast Licensees") which set forth the clearest public-interest standards ever adopted. Never fully enforced at the time, it remains a quaint reminder of an idealistic—if perhaps unrealistic—view of the media and government regulations. In another and more lasting contribution to programming diversity, a move that might well be decried as foolishly left-wing if proposed in today's political climate, Durr, along with FCC Commission Frieda Hennock, who took his seat on the commission, deserves substantial credit for the FCC's decision to reserve broadcasting frequencies for educational and noncommercial stations.

But much as he loved his role at the FCC, Durr, perhaps prodded by Virginia, loved civil liberties even more. In March 1947, as the fear of Communism in the U.S. government began to mount, President Harry Truman adopted an executive order establishing a federal loyalty program which called on department and agency heads to conduct an investigation of all civilian employees, including those in nonsensitive posts, asking about past and present affiliations and political views. Since the program's broad range of inquiry violated his sense of civil liberties and due process, Durr felt that he could not, in good conscience, either enforce it or be renominated by a government that would expect it to be enforced. So, at the end of his impressive term, Durr refused to be reappointed to the commission.

In a letter sent to the *The Nation* decades later, Hugo Black described what happened next. "President Truman did his best to persuade Cliff to accept reappointment to the Federal Communication Commission," Mr. Justice Black recalled.

> He did this with full knowledge that Cliff was opposed to the loyalty program. The President talked to me in an effort to get Cliff to accept the reappointment. When I told the President that Cliff felt that he should not accept the reappointment because he was opposed to the loyalty program, the President said that that made no difference. When told that Cliff's views were so strong against the program that he might not even vote the Democratic ticket, the President again told me that made no difference in this appointment. He said that whatever his views, he knew that Cliff was a man of sturdy honesty and courage and, for that reason alone, he wanted him to continue serving as a member of the Federal Communications Commission. The President not only said that he would reappoint Cliff despite his beliefs but added that he would fight to the last ditch for his confirmation by the Senate.

I don't know how Cliff Durr voted in that election, but it is a fair guess that Virginia did not vote for Truman since she ran for the U.S. Senate in Virginia that year on Henry Wallace's Progressive Party ticket, championing the cause of equal rights, opposing the poll tax, and arguing that tax money should be used for social programs, rather than for armaments and militarization.

In our early-morning discussions back in 1965, smoking an endless chain of cigarettes which, over the years, had added a slight rasp to his warm Southern drawl, now stooped from back problems but no less outspoken or courteous than ever, Cliff mused about the offers that came his way from former New Deal colleagues, men who soon became the pillar of the Washington legal community and remained there for the next two decades, who asked him to join firms where he could make piles of money and assuage his conscience by representing government officials called before government committees to testify to their loyalty—the kind of proceeding that Durr abhorred and that had led him to leave the FCC. But when Cliff learned that his old friends would represent only clients who were being *falsely* accused of having once had Communist affiliations, he decided not to join them. He felt that the civil-liberties principles that he was defending must also apply to those who had actually once been supporters of the Communist Party and that if a firm only represented people who were falsely accused there would be a negative presumption associated with those whom it refused to represent.

So Durr hung out his own legal shingle (where his client list included Frank Oppenheimer, brother of J. Robert, who had, in fact, been a member of the Communist Party from 1937 to 1940). He taught part time at Princeton, and wrote a series of biblical parables about civil liberties including "Jesus a Free Speech Victim: Trial by Terror 2000 Years Ago."

Before long, Cliff signed on as General Counsel of the progressive National Farmers Union and the Durrs moved to Denver—but Virginia's outspoken opinions quickly made her a lightning rod for anti-Communist crusaders. At the request of Linus Pauling, the Nobel Laureate, she signed a postcard indicating her support for a group called the American Peace Crusade. A story in the *Denver Post* carried the headline: "Wife of General Counsel of Farmer's Union Insurance Corporation Signs Red Petition." When Virginia, with Cliff at her side, refused to sign a document publicly repudiating the Peace Crusade and its leaders, Durr was forced to leave the union.

They had resisted returning to Alabama, where they knew that their views on race would put them out of the mainstream. Now they felt compelled to move to Montgomery, but their concerns quickly proved well placed. In two dramatic episodes, Cliff's devotion to principle eliminated his final chance to have a lucrative law practice. Appropriately, one involved civil liberties and the other civil rights.

During a highly publicized hearing in New Orleans, a former Communist Party organizer named Paul Crouch told Senator James Eastland's Subcommittee on Internal Security that, during their years on Washington, Virginia had been a leading Communist, using the Durr home "as a frequent meeting place for the people connected with top Soviet espionage" and using their connections with Hugo Black to introduce top Communists into FDR's inner circle. Both Cliff and Virginia denied all of the charges under oath, but that wasn't enough for Cliff. Furious at the attacks on Virginia, he jumped over the jury rail, attacked Crouch, and shouted, "You dirty dog. I'll kill you for lying under oath about my wife!" A photograph on the front page of the *New York Times* the next day showed court-house guards restraining the patrician lawyer who, in his own way, was defending the honor of his Southern bride.

Although Senator Eastland held a press conference saying that he tended to believe the Durrs and not Paul Crouch, business quickly slipped away. But the last straw for prospective clients in Alabama took place on December 1, 1955, when Rosa Parks was arrested for sitting down near the front of a city bus.

The Durrs had known Rosa Parks for some time. As a seamstress, Rosa Parks had made dresses for some of the Durrs' daughters. Indeed, Virginia, also knew Ms. Parks through her work as secretary of the local chapter of the NAACP and had recommended that she attend a weeklong interracial workshop at the famed and controversial Highlander Folk School in Tennessee. So when the head of the local NAACP called Cliff to ask for help, Cliff agreed to represent her, and Cliff and Virginia went down to the jail to help her make bail and to find out more about the charges. From that time forward, they were pariahs to most of their white neighbors—but heroes to people around the country who cared about civil rights and civil liberties.

Amazingly, the Durr saga had something of a fairy tale ending. After barely squeaking by financially for many years, they became self-sufficient in the early 1970s, when his brother's Durr Drug Company went public, providing what amounted to an unexpected, if modest windfall for Cliff and Virginia. By the time he died in 1975, Cliff had been celebrated by countless institutions—universities, public broadcasters, civil-liberties organizations—

including some in Alabama. After Cliff's death, Virginia spent summers in Martha's Vineyard, holding court and surrounded by friends, admirers, and grandchildren at the home of her daughter, Lucy Hackney, a lawyer and child advocate, whose husband, Sheldon, became President of the University of Pennsylvania and later Chair of the National Endowment for the Humanities. Virginia's other daughters flourished as well, and she became something of a national icon, celebrated for her courage and her views.

But none of that fairy-tale ending seemed remotely likely, much less assured, during the years when the Durrs were taking risks for principles they held dear.

In 1999, on the hundredth anniversary of Clifford Durr's birth, I was privileged to give the Annual Clifford Durr Lecture at Auburn University's Montgomery campus. My topic, celebrating one of his many virtues, was "Cliff Durr and the Importance of Principled Resignations." For one of the character traits that set Cliff apart, that made him a particular hero for me, and that led me to keep his photograph in my office at the Voice of America, was his Spartan willingness to forgo power and financial success in the interest of ethical beliefs. I ended by suggesting that, at crucial moments of our lives, we all ask ourselves WWCD. What would Cliff do? If more of us asked that question more often, and were prepared to live with the consequences, the world would be a better place.

NOAM CHOMSKY

JAY PARINI

IN THE ICY winter of 2003, only weeks before the U.S. invasion of Iraq, two thousand listeners crowded St. Paul's cathedral in London to hear Noam Chomsky speak about the obsession of George W. Bush and Tony Blair with Saddam Hussein and his Weapons of Mass Destruction. As usual, he laid out the history of the region, the political dynamics of late capitalism, and the cynical, subservient behavior of the western press in unadorned, lucid sentences that, more often than not, were delivered with his characteristic twang of irony. The audience was, as usual, eager for his words, even desperate. His radical brand of thinking, couched in a wry cynicism that has always infuriated as many as it has inspired, stood in marked contrast to the usual fare of public discourse.

Because of his unrelenting critique of American foreign policy and his fiercely analytical style, Chomsky has been in demand as a public speaker since the early days of the Vietnam War, when he became a well-known figure in the protest movement. Over four decades as political agitator, foreign policy and media critic, he has given thousands of talks, attracting vast crowds from New York and Los Angeles to Istanbul and Cairo, Managua and Islamabad. His countless books have made their way in the world, attracting a wide audience. Chomsky has become one of the great dissenting voices of our time, a remarkably consistent analyst of American foreign policy and student of the propaganda system that underlies and sustains the status quo by "manufacturing consent" (a phrase of Walter Lippmann's that he has appropriated in interesting ways). He has been a political activist for nearly four decades as well, drawing thousands to his frequent public lectures, and a persistent presence on radio and television throughout the world.

That he has also been a major figure in the fields of linguistics, philosophy, and cognitive philosophy almost seems beside the point when writing about him as an American rebel, although the whole fits together nicely. His political and philosophical work have always been aimed at understanding the nature of human freedom, its limitations and possibilities. Like his great precursor, Bertrand Russell, he has never confined himself to one field, but has used his intellectual skills broadly and generously to comprehend, criticize, and effect changes in the larger world around him, motivated by a profound sense of social justice.

Born in 1928, he grew up during the Great Depression in Philadelphia, the son of Dr. William (Zev) Chomsky and Elsie Simonofsky. His father, a Russian immigrant, had fled the country of his birth to avoid conscription in the Tsarist army. William Chomsky worked for most of his life as an educator, eventually becoming principal of a Jewish school, and the author of a well-known book on Hebrew grammar. In a sense, Noam followed in his father's footsteps, taking up the family trade by becoming a professional linguist. From his mother, he seems to have inherited a strong interest in politics and a fierce social consciousness. The combination has been a powerful one.

Amazingly, Chomsky met his future wife, Carol, when he was "about five," as he puts it. Their families had been friends, and they became reacquainted as teenagers (Chomsky was at school with Carol's older brothers). Married young, they have remained close, raising three children in Lexington, a suburb of Boston. Carol taught education at Harvard until recently, while Chomsky himself remains on the faculty of M.I.T., where he has been a professor of linguistics and philosophy for nearly half a century, drawing students from around the world to his program in theoretical linguistics.

Early on, Chomsky developed a taste for radical literature, and sought out circles where he could listen to, and participate in, debates about socialism, anarchism, and libertarianism. He didn't have far to go, it so happens. One uncle in New York City ran a newsstand on Seventy-

Second Street, where he lived at the center of a lively circle. Chomsky made good use of this uncle and his friends to widen his reading and political thinking. "Jewish working-class culture in New York was very unusual," he later recalled. "It was highly intellectual, very poor; a lot of people had no jobs at all and others lived in slums. But it was a rich and lively intellectual culture." [*Chomsky Reader* 11] Chomsky would come into New York by train, and return with an armload of books by Marx and Freud, and by various anarchist figures such as Karl Liebknecht, Rosa Luxemburg, and Karl Korsch. He also read, with considerable passion, the work of Orwell, Dwight Macdonald, and Bertrand Russell—all lasting influences on his own writing.

The left world of early Zionists fascinated Chomsky, and he thought seriously of going to live in Israel on a kibbutz. It was the world of cooperative labor that attracted him, not so much the Stalinist or Trotskyist factions in the kubbutzim. Like many at the time, Chomsky strongly opposed the creation of a Jewish state in Palestine, aware of the larger problems of displacement that would follow. From the beginning, he has been a critic of Israel, although he didn't begin a systematic study of American foreign policy and Israel until the seventies, when he began to attract the harsh attention of Zionists and others who uncritically supported the Israeli occupation and U.S. support (military and financial) for this disastrous policy. Indeed, Chomsky has frequently been called "a self-hating Jew," even branded as anti-semitic because of his fierce opposition to Israeli tactics and political practices.

Chomsky might well have gone to Palestine to live had

he not encountered Zellig Harris, an influential Russian Jew who had become a major figure in structural linguistics at midcentury. Harris taught at the University of Pennsylvania, where Chomsky was an undergraduate. It seems clear that Harris, with his interest in linguistics and politics, provided an early model for Chomsky, who began his research in linguistics by extending and modifying, and ultimately transforming, certain ideas that originated with Harris. His teacher's anarchist, anti-Bolshevik Marxism also had a profound effect on Chomsky, who has remained in the anarcho-syndicalist tradition, supporting the idea of factory cooperatives and local governance.

The spectacular rise of Noam Chomsky as a theoretical linguist is legendary and, as with everything about Chomsky, controversial. He was seen by some as a bully, by others as the messiah. His search for a universal grammar, embodied in several groundbreaking monographs, including *Syntactic Structures* (1957), instigated what is now called the Chomskyan Revolution. As an early reviewer explained, "Chomsky's book on syntactic structures is one of the first serious attempts on the part of a linguist to construct within the tradition of scientific theory-construction a comprehensive theory of language which may be understood in the same sense that a chemical, biological theory is ordinarily understood in those fields." [Barsky, 89] Chomsky's work in the area of generative grammar, which made heavy use of mathematical notions, looked so different from the kind of work traditional linguists were doing that it seemed to create a whole new field; but Chomsky took great pains to establish connections between his thinking and work that occurred during the Enlightenment, centuries before him. Interestingly, Chomsky has continuously revised, modified, refuted, and reworked his ideas in linguistics.

Chomsky's work as a political activist began in the mid-sixties, with his opposition to the war in Vietnam, when he became a familiar speaker at rallies, sit-ins, and on the media. His first book in the area of politics and foreign policy was *American Power and the New Mandarins* (1969), a collection of essays that laid out "the responsibility of the intellectual" in vivid terms, condemning the U.S. invasion of South Vietnam. He explained in that book that "the process of creating and entrenching highly selective, reshaped or completely fabricated memories of the past is what we call 'indoctrination' or 'propaganda' when it is conducted by official enemies, and 'education,' 'moral instruction,' or 'character building' when we do it to ourselves." [*Chomsky Reader*, 124] The hypocrisy involved here is galling, and Chomsky has never hesitated to point this out; in fact, his main technique as a critic is to point out hypocritical differences resulting from shifting moral standards. Chomsky quite simply refuses to bend to the will of ideological pressures. He boldly lays out the ideological patterns and underpinnings that might easily be missed by lazy citizens. He calls the question, again and again, telling the truth where doing so, for the government, is often embarrassing.

A virtual raft of books, usually composed of published articles, followed *American Power and the New Mandarins*. Hardly a year has gone by in over three decades without one or two books by Chomsky, a few of them co-authored with his friend Edward S. Herman. He has studied the workings of the propaganda system in great detail, most comprehensively with Herman in *Manufacturing Consent: The Political Economy of the Mass Media* (1988). The Cold War and its aftermath have been a consistent focus of his attention, and in several books he has surveyed the Middle East conflict, especially in *The Fateful Triangle: The United States, Israel, and the Palestinians* (1983). In *Turning the Tide: U.S. Intervention in Central America and the Struggle for Peace* (1985) and other books, he has turned his attention to countries like Nicaragua, Guatemala, Honduras, and El Salvador. His eye always scanning the horizon, he has discussed U.S. influence in Indonesia (including East Timor, a particular focus of his anger), the Philippines, Bosnia, Kosevo, and elsewhere. In other works, he has analyzed the concept of terrorism, always refusing to distinguish between "state terrorism," such as that inflicted on weak countries by powerful ones, and the usual brand of terror, committed by so-called rogue states or free-floating factions such as Al Qaeda.

This massive body of writing is known for its matter-of-fact style, the vast number of detailed footnotes used to bolster argument and provide further examples, and the deadly irony of the author's tone, which some have faulted as being too cynical, even abrasive. Not surprisingly, given the nature of his subjects, Chomsky has attracted many critics. Indeed, he has been called unpatriotic, even anti-American, by some, especially in the wake of September 11 and his bestselling book of interviews related to this event, called *9/11*, which appeared shortly after the attack on the World Trade Center and provided a take on this tragedy and its context that has continued to challenge official views. The notion that Chomsky is anti-American is, in fact, nonsense, fueled by a refusal to listen closely to what he says. His critiques of American power in the world are, I think, simply designed to inform citizens of what their government has done, often without informing them.

What really drives Chomsky is a deep compassion for those who suffer, often invisibly, because of American power. "If we had the honesty and the moral courage," he says, "we would not let a day pass without hearing the cries of the victims." [*Chomsky Reader*, xviii] He refers here to victims of torture, poverty, war, and disease—all situations made worse by our own action or, in the case of citizens, our failure to act. Noam Chomsky has acted, supplying a radical counter-history of our times, presenting a challenge to our government and our media, and challenging readers as well. His work demands a response, insisting as it does that U.S. citizens accept responsibility for what their government does in their name. His work represents a call to justice, and inspires readers (myself included) to wake up and accept responsibility for what happens around us, often invisibly or distorted by the media, which commonly assists the government in getting its lies across in the guise of truth.

RACHEL CARSON

TERRY TEMPEST WILLIAMS

RACHEL CARSON. I first heard her name from my grand-mother. I must have been seven or eight years old. We were feeding birds—song sparrows, goldfinches, and towhees—in my grandparents' yard in Salt Lake City, Utah.

"Imagine a world without birds," my grandmother said as she scattered seed and filled the feeders. "Imagine waking up to no birdsong."

I couldn't.

"Rachel Carson," I remember them saying.

Later, around the dinner table, she and my grandfather were engaged in an intense discussion of the book they

were reading, *Silent Spring* as my mind tried to grasp what
my grandmother had just said about a muted world.

Decades later, I found myself in a used bookstore in Salt
Lake City. The green spine of *Silent Spring* caught my eye. I
pulled the classic off the shelf and opened it. First edition,
1962. As I read various passages, I was struck by how little had
changed. Each page was still a shock and a revelation:

> One of the most tragic examples of our unthinking bludgeoning of
> the landscape is to be seen in the sagebrush lands of the West,
> where a vast campaign is on to destroy the sage and to substitute
> grasslands. If ever an enterprise needed to be illuminated with a
> sense of history and meaning of the landscape, it is this. It is
> spread before us like the pages of an open book in which we can
> read why the land is what it is, and why we should preserve its
> integrity. But the pages lie unread.

The pages of abuse on the American landscape still lie unread.

Rachel Carson is a hero, a towering example within
American democracy of how one person's voice can make
an extraordinary difference both in public policy and in the
minds of the populace. Her name and her vision of a world
intact and interrelated has entered mainstream culture. We
can all rattle off a glib two-sentence summation of its text:
"All life is connected. Pesticides enter the food chain and
not only threaten the environment but destroy it." And yet,
I fear that *Silent Spring*'s status as "an American classic"
allows us to nod to its power, but to miss the subtleties and
richness of the book as both a scientific treatise and a piece
of distinguished literary nonfiction.

Rachel Carson presents her discoveries of destruction in

the form of storytelling. In example after example, grounded in the natural world, she weaves together facts and fictions into an environmental tale of life, love, and loss. Her voice is graceful and dignified, but sentence by sentence she delivers right hand blows and counter punches to the status quo ruled by chemical companies within the Kingdom of Agriculture:

> The 'control of nature' is a phrase conceived in arrogance, born of the Neanderthal age of biology and philosophy, when it was supposed that nature exists for the convenience of man It is our alarming misfortune that so primitive a science has armed itself with the most modern and terrible weapons, and that in turning them against the insects it has also turned them against the earth.

The facts she presents create the case against "biocide": We are killing the very fabric of nature in our attempt to rid the world of pests through these "elixirs of death." She indicts the insecticides by name: DDT, chlordane, heptachlor, dieldrin, aldrin, and endrin. And then adds to the toxic hydrocarbons, the alkyl or organic phosphates, among the most poisonous chemicals in the world: parathion and malathion.

The fictions she exposes are the myths we have chosen to adopt to our obsession to control nature. She reminds us of the story of Medea, the Greek sorceress who, overwrought with jealously over her husband's love of another woman, presents the new bride with a gift, a robe that will immediately kill whoever wears it. It becomes a garment of death. Carson calls our use of pesticides "death by indirection." We are killing insects and in turn, killing ourselves, as these toxins slowly and violently enter the waters and eventually our own bloodstreams. Rachel Carson did not turn her back from the ongoing chronicle of the natural history of the dead. She bore witness. "It was time," Carson said, "that human beings admit their kinship with other forms of life. If we cannot accept this moral ethic, then we too are complicit in the killing."

With each chapter, she adds to our understanding of the horrors of herbicides and hydrocarbons, the web of life unraveling. It is impossible for us not to be mindful of Rachel Carson's emotional and intellectual stamina, of her ability to endure the pain of the story she was telling.

But Miss Carson had a vision.

"Sometimes, I lose sight of my goal," she wrote in an essay in her first year of college. "Then again it flashes into view, filling me with a new determination to keep the vision before my eyes." Hers was a conscientious and directed soul who believed in the eloquence of facts. She loved both language and landscape. "I can remember no time when I wasn't interested in the out-of-doors and the whole world or nature," Carson said.

Writing became the expression of her passion toward nature. She published her first story when she was ten years old, winning the Silver Badge from the prestigious children's magazine, *St. Nicholas*. "Perhaps the early experience of seeing my work in print played its part in fostering my childhood dream of becoming a writer."

Here was young woman already on her path. In 1928, she graduated magna cum laude from Pennsylvania College for Women, now Chatham College, with a major in zoology. The strength of her course work in both science and literature provides evidence of her dual nature as both a scientist and a poet. "I thought I had to be one of the other," she said. "It never occurred to me that I could combine two careers."

Rachel Carson's editor Paul Brooks writes, "The merging of these two powerful currents—the imagination and insight of a creative writer with a scientist's passion for fact—goes far to explain the blend of beauty and authority that was to make her books unique."

Perhaps this is Rachel Carson's greatest gift to us, seeing the world whole.

Carson continued her education as a biologist, receiving a master's degree in zoology at John Hopkins University, where she studied genetics. Her thesis, "The Development of the Pronephros During the Embryonic and Early Larval Life of the Catfish (*Ictalurus punctatus*)," should quell the ongoing criticism that Rachel Carson was merely an "amateur naturalist."

In 1936, she accepted a position with the United States Bureau of Fisheries, which later became the U.S. Fish and Wildlife Services, as an aquatic biologist. Here she was able to forcefully fuse her talents as a scientist and a writer, eventually becoming chief of publications for the bureau. Early in her tenure at Fish & Wildlife, she continued teaching at the University of Maryland and John Hopkins.

Under the Sea-Wind was published in 1941. *The Sea Around Us* was published in 1951 to great popular and critical acclaim, receiving the National Book Award in nonfiction. It remained on the *New York Times* bestsellers list for months. "If there is poetry in my book about the sea," she said, "it is not because I deliberately put it there, but because no one could truthfully write about the sea and leave out the poetry."

In 1955, four years after the success of *The Sea Around Us*, Carson published *The Edge of the Sea*, extending her readers' knowledge of the ocean to the ocean's interface with land. She brought her naturalist's eye down to the intricacies of tidepools and illuminated the habitats of the sandy beach and rocky shore.

And then came *Silent Spring*.

Rachel Carson received a burning letter from her friend Olga Owens Huckins, a journalist, who asked her for help in finding people who could elucidate and speak to the dangers of pesticides. The Huckinses had a small place in Duxbury, Massachusetts, just north of Cape Cod, which they had made into a bird sanctuary. Without any thought of the effects on birds and wildlife, the state had sprayed the entire area for mosquito control.

Huckins sent a letter of outrage to the *Boston Herald* in January, 1958. Here is an excerpt:

The mosquito control plane flew over our small town last summer. Since we live close to the marshes, we were treated to several lethal doses as the pilot crisscrossed our place. And we consider the spraying of active poison over private land to be a serious aerial intrusion.

The 'harmless' shower bath killed seven of our lovely songbirds outright. We picked up three dead bodies the next morning right by the nests in our trees year after year. The next day three were scattered around the bird bath. (I had emptied it and scrubbed it after the spraying but YOU CAN NEVER KILL DDT).

. . . All of these birds died horribly and in the same way. Their bills were gaping open, and their splayed claws were drawn up to their breasts in agony.

Olga Owens Huckins bore witness. Rachel Carson responded. Four and a half years later in 1962, *Silent Spring* was published. Carson wrote to Huckins that it was her letter that had "started it all" and had led her to realize that "I must write the book."

Rachel Carson told the truth as she understood it. The natural world was dying, poisoned by the hands of power tied to corporate greed. Her words became a catalyst for change. A debate had begun: a reverence for life versus a reverence for industry. Through the strength and vitality of her voice, Carson altered the political landscape of America.

Loren Eisely wrote that *Silent Spring* "is a devastating, heavily documented, relentless attack upon human carelessness, greed, and responsibility."

Not everyone saw it that way.

The Monsanto Chemical Company, anticipating the publishing of *Silent Spring*, urgently commissioned a parody entitled "The Desolate Year" to counteract Carson's attack on the industry. Its intent was to show the pestilence and famine that the company claimed would occur in a world without pesticides.

Robert White-Stevens, the chemical industry's chief spokesman, made over twenty eight speeches against *Silent Spring*, charging that Carson was "a fanatic defender of the cult of the balance of nature."

In its weekly newsletter, the *American Medical Association* told the public how to obtain an "information kit," compiled by the National Agriculture Chemicals Association, to answer questions provoked by *Silent Spring*.

Time magazine called *Silent Spring* "unfair, one-sided, and hysterically over-emphatic," accused Carson of frightening the public with "emotion-fanning words," and claimed her text was filled with "oversimplifications and downright errors."

Former Secretary of Agriculture Ezra Taft Benson wrote to Dwight D. Eisenhower regarding Rachel Carson, asking simply, "Why a spinster with no children was so concerned about genetics?" His own conjecture was that she was "probably a Communist."

Spinster. Communist. A member of a nature cult. An amateur naturalist who should stick to poetry not politics. These were just some of the labels used to discredit her. Rachel Carson had in fact, lit a fire on America's chemical landscape.

In speeches before the Garden Club of America and the New England Wildflower Preservation Society, Miss Carson fought back against her detractors and addressed her audiences with great passion, "I ask you to ask yourself—Who speaks?—And Why?" And then again, "Are we being sentimental when we care whether the robin returns to our dooryard and the veery sings in the twilight woods? A world that is no longer fit for wild plants, that is no longer graced by the flight of birds, a world whose streams and forests are empty and lifeless is not likely to be a fit habitat for man himself, for these things are symptoms of an ailing world."

President John F. Kennedy became aware of *Silent Spring* when it was first serialized in the pages of *The New Yorker*. At a press conference on August 29, 1962, a reporter asked Kennedy about the growing concern among scientists regarding dangerous long-term side effects from he use of DDT and other pesticides and whether or not the U.S. Department of Agriculture of the U.S. Public Health Service was planning to launch an investigation into the matter.

"Yes," the President replied. "I think particularly, of course, since Miss Carson's book."

The Life Sciences Panel of the President's Science Advisory Committee was charged with reviewing pesticide use. In 1962, the committee issued a call for legislative measures to safeguard the health of the land and its people against pesticides and industrial toxins. The President's report had vindicated Carson. Her poetics were transformed into public policy.

Rachel Carson testified for over forty minutes during the Hearings before the United States Senate Subcommittee on Reorganization and International Organizations of the Committee on Government Operations, "Interagency Coordination in Environmental Hazards (Pesticides)," on June 4, 1964.

According to Carson's biographer, Linda Lear, "Those who heard Rachel Carson that morning did not see a reserved or reticent woman in the witness chair but an accomplished scientist, an expert on chemical pesticides, a brilliant writer, and a woman of conscience who made the most of an opportunity few citizens of any rank can have to make their opinions known. Her witness had been equal to her vision."

Senator Gruening from Alaska called *Silent Spring* equal to *Uncle Tom's Cabin* in its impact, and predicted it would change the course of history.

In 1967, five years after *Silent Spring* was published, the Environmental Defense Fund was born, with a mandate, in the words of one its founders, "to build a body of case law to establish a citizen's right to a clean environment." Three years after that, in 1970, the Environmental Protection Agency was established.

Rachel Carson died of breast cancer on April 14, 1964, at the age of 56. The irony is a painful one. Diagnosed in

1960, she wrote *Silent Spring* through her illness and faced her powerful detractors with limited physical strength, often having to be hospitalized after strenuous professional obligations. But the public never knew. She proceeded with great presence and resolve, even completing a rigorous television interview on CBS months before her death, where she was paired with a spokesperson from the chemical industry. Miss Carson's "grace under fire" with compelling facts to back her sentiments finally won public opinion over to her side. Brooks Atkinson in his column in the *New York Times* proclaimed her the winner. He wrote, "Evidence continues to accumulate that she is right and that *Silent Spring* is the 'rights of man' of this generation."

In spite of her cancer, Rachel Carson never lost "the vision splendid" before her eyes. Her love of the natural world, especially all she held dear in the coastal landscape of Maine, sustained her, giving her uncommon strength and peace.

Before her death, she wrote to her friend, E.B. White, "It is good to know that I shall live on even in the minds of many who do not know me and largely through association with things that are beautiful and lovely."

And she does.

Consider these examples: Rachel's Daughters, a film about the environmental causes of breast cancer; Rachel's Network, a political organization committed to seeing women in positions of power and leadership within the conservation community; And consider the thousands of references to Rachel Carson within American culture, including one by a puzzled Richard A. Posner, who wondered in his book, *Public Intellectuals,* why Rachel Carson had more citations in Lexus Nexus than the French Deconstructionist

Jacque Derrida. What a perfect metaphor for Rachel Carson's impact. After all, didn't she deconstruct the entire chemical industry until we were able to see, collectively, the essence of what it does—destruction of natural systems— where the dark toxic roots of pesticides were exposed?

And she continues to guide us.

Recently, an open letter was signed and sent to the U.S. Senate to ban reproductive cloning and to place a moratorium on therapeutic cloning by a broad coalition of scientists, environmentalists, feminists, healthcare workers, religious leaders, political leaders, philosophers, and writers. If Rachel Carson were alive, her name would have appeared on that list.

Similar political actions have been taken to elucidate the dangers of genetic engineering, from the possibility of infecting wild salmon populations to the perils of genetically modified foods. Rachel Carson understood that tampering with nature is tampering with health in the broadest, ecological sense.

In 2003, I want to recall and remember Rachel Carson's spirit. I want to be both fierce and passionate at once. I want to remember that our character has been shaped by the diversity of America's landscape and it is precisely that character that will protect it. I want to carry a sense of indignation inside me to shatter the complacency that has seeped into our society in the name of all we have lost. Call it sacred rage, a rage that is grounded in the knowledge that all life is intertwined. I want to know and continue to learn from the grace of wild things that hold a power that sustains hope.

Can we find the moral courage within us to step forward and openly question every law, person, and practice that denies justice toward nature?

Can we continue in this American tradition of bearing witness to beauty and terror which is its own form of advocacy?

And do we have the imagination to rediscover an authentic patriotism that inspires empathy and reflection over pride and naturalism?

Rachel Carson's name is synonymous with courage. She dared to expose the underbelly of the chemical industry and how it was disrupting the balance of nature. In *Silent Spring* we see her signature strength on the page where a confluence of poetry and politics and sound science can create an ethic of place.

But perhaps Rachel Carson's true courage lies in her willingness to align science with the sacred, to admit that her bond toward nature is a spiritual one.

I am not afraid of being thought a sentimentalist when I say that I believe natural beauty has a necessary place in the spiritual development of any individual or any society. I believe that when ever we destroy beauty, or whatever we substitute something man-made and artificial for a natural feature of the earth, we have retarded some part of man's spiritual growths.

WILL ROGERS

RAY ROBINSON

IN HIS DAY—the Roaring Twenties and the Depression thirties—the gum-chewing cowboy philosopher Will Rogers was quoted more often than baseball's sage, Yogi Berra. In almost every respect Will was ahead of his time—a "poet lariat" of many causes—but he always tried his darndest to pretend that he wasn't all that smart. That characteristic-perhaps you might call it playing humble—stood him in good stead with the public, until he died in a tragic plane crash in a remote outpost of Alaska in 1935, while flying with Wiley Post, then regarded as America's top pilot.

Will Rogers probably would have ducked his head bashfully if you had accused him of being a rebel, yet, in looking back at the crinkly-faced guy, he managed to fit well into that category. As a one-man wrecking crew against arrogance and pretense, he measured up as a sly combination of Mark Twain, H. L. Mencken and the Gashouse Gang pitcher, Dizzy Dean. Never as mean as the acerbic Mencken, Will scalded the hypocrites, and punctured the pompous, most of whom were Republicans. "I'd rather be right than Republican," he said. All the while he expressed his high regard for poor working men and women who had fallen victims to The Great Depression. One Washington admirer of Will insisted that "the United States 'would never go to war unless Will was for it . . . he'd destroy the plans of the jingoes in a week . . . the people would believe him and laugh the politicians into defeat." Will would have been a good fellow to have had around in the year 2003.

True, there were some who regarded Will as little more than a village explainer. To those detractors he was just a non-stop blatherer and bull-shitter, who got paid entirely too much for talking. However, he would always reply to those people that he never claimed that he possessed ultimate wisdom.

In fact Will was a successful cowpuncher, rancher, actor, author, humorist, show business personality, newspaper columnist, flying enthusiast, and polo player, who could bring smiles to the faces of millions, most of whom didn't have much in the bank or in their iceboxes. His specialty was in taking on everybody who was anybody. It didn't make a difference who they were. He needled the stuffed shirts, celebrities, gangsters, Presidents (Warren Harding, Cal Coolidge, Herbert Hoover, even Franklin D. Roosevelt, on occasion) and took potshots at economic royalists like Henry Ford and John D. Rockefeller. And he gave it pretty good to dictators like Hitler and demagogues like Huey Long and the Jew-hating Father Charles Coughlin. He could sniff out the acrid smell of the mucker and charlatan a mile away, while leaving untouched life's eternal underdogs. James Whitmore, who has played Will in one-man shows, since 1969, that were startling in their verisimilitude, tried to sum up Rogers. "He was one hell of a guy for any time," he said, "a prescient fellow with all of the right gut instincts. Like heliotrope, he always wanted to face the sun."

How did Will Rogers get this way?

William Penn Adair Rogers was born in 1879 in the Cooweescoowee District of the Cherokee Nation, Indian Territory, four miles northeast of Oolagah, in an area that later became part of the state of Oklahoma. It was in the midst of cattle country, and not far from what would become the city of Tulsa. There wasn't even a birth certificate to attest to the fact that Will had been born. But that was simply because in those days people living in the Territory didn't have such things. In later years Will couldn't resist telling reporters that his Cherokee ancestors "met the folks on the Mayflower in 1620."

Will's story was *not* one of rags to riches. He was neither deprived nor impoverished, as so many others in the area were. His father, Clem, was a tough, hard-driving fellow who had amassed a good deal of ranch land and was the third richest man in the Territory when Will was born. Clem also became engaged in local politics once his coffers were full. The harsh frontier of John Ford's Hollywood movies bore no resemblance to Will's growing-up environment. He was indulged by both his father and his mother and practically grew up on a horse's back. "There's plenty of mule in that boy," Clem once remarked about his son, anticipating Will's rebelliousness as a young adult.

Will was always closer to his mother, Mary, than he was to Clem. Having lost three of her children, Mary couldn't do enough for Will and invariably took Will's side in all disputes he had with his father.

There was a mix of white, Negro and Indian kids in and around Oologah, thus providing Will with a daily exercise in democracy. When he uttered his famous phrase, "I never met a man I didn't like," he probably had his own neighborhood in mind.

Uncle Dan, a black cowboy, employed by Clem to perform various chores around the house, taught Will to do all sorts of tricks with ropes. In a while Will could "cut curlicues" with the best of them. There didn't seem to be anything he couldn't lasso, whether it was a cow, or a snake or even one of his friends.

Disturbed by Will's lack of discipline, Clem sent his son off to Kemper Military Academy in Missouri. He arrived there in flamboyant cowboy style, with a vest that practically talked for itself. From the start Will hated the place, although he did excel in history and talking. In no time at all Will could rattle off Lincoln's Gettysburg address, Brutus' speech about Caesar and Patrick Henry's ode to liberty. Other than that, Will spent most of his days in the guardhouse.

At the turn of the century Will developed "happy feet." He longed to travel, rejecting Clem's advice that he stay at home and run the ranch. So Will went forth in the world, without Clem's money or support. Armed only with his rope and his wanderlust, Will went to Argentina, New York and England, supporting himself wherever he went by taking odd jobs. Once he signed on as a night watchman on a ship. At other times he made a few dollars by getting into roping contests.

On a trip to South Africa, Will put in at Capetown. There, in a rowdy saloon he met a juggler by the name of William Claude Dukinfield, who came from Philadelphia. They talked of their respective talents. Will spoke of his dazzling rope trick and Dukinfield, between belts of whiskey, spoke about his juggling. They would meet again later on the vaudeville stage, when Dukinfield had evolved into W. C. Fields.

By roaming around the world, Will had learned a thing or two about other people—and also about himself. In time he would reach the New York stage, where producer Florenz Ziegfeld, who usually glorified pretty young women in ostrich feathers, made him into a star and a favorite of Gotham audiences. As Will spun his rope, he talked and told jokes, and as he talked the money rolled in. By the late twenties he was in Hollywood making movies, and when talkies came in he was in constant demand, with his homespun, unabashedly American style. Only Shirley Temple, the child star, was in greater demand.

In the glamorous motion picture colony of Doug Fairbanks, Mary Pickford, Charlie Chaplin, Rudolph Valentino, Tom Mix, Harold Lloyd, John Gilbert and others, Will played it low key. "I guess I'm a failure," he said. "I hold two distinctions in this business. I'm the ugliest fella around and I still have the same wife I started with."

Even his social life was different from the other millionaires. He retained his reputation as Hollywood's certified populist by giving away large wads of money to needy people (he paid for Florenz Ziegfeld's funeral), and by striking up a friendship with writer Anzia Yezierska, a hotheaded Polish Jew who embraced many long forgotten social causes. Long before Jack Lemmon and Walter Mathau arrived on the scene they were an odd couple.

Everywhere you looked in those days Will was a presence, with his Oklahoma voice whining like a lake wind. He swapped stories with all of the major sports headliners of the period, people like Babe Ruth, Jack Dempsey, Red Grange, Lou Gehrig, Knute Rockne and Bobby Jones. He admired the Lone Eagle, Charles Lindbergh, and even while dining and playing golf with Presidents like Harding and Coolidge, he wasn't afrad to needle them, or criticize them. On the other hand, Will, to his embarrassment, said some nice things about Italy's dictator Benito Mussolini, and also dropped in some plugs for "those rascals in Russia who may have some very good ideas."

Will was an outspoken backer of Franklin D. Roosevelt at the Democratic Presidential Convention in 1932, even though his own Oklahoma delegation chose to award Will its 22 votes. During the campaign Will joyfully skewered President Hoover and his running mate, Charles Curtis, by calling them "nothing but a vaudeville team."

Occasionally there was some mumbling about Will's beliefs. These objections came mainly from the female side. Maureen O'Sullivan, who played Will's daughter in a 1930s movie, thought he was a prude and he didn't like women wearing long pants around him. "He may never have met a man he didn't like," she said, scornfully, "but he sure didn't care much for women!"

But after Will died in the plane crash, the testimonials rolled in. Perhaps the best of them came from the young actor, Joel McCrea, who had been befriended by Will. He summed up Will in a way that Will might have chosen for his own epitaph. "He didn't preach one syllable, but attitudes towards foreigners, black people, Jews and America were always better with him around," said McCrea. "He led by example."

Here are a few of Will's many one liners:

"We are the first nation in the history of the world to go to the poorhouse in an automobile."

* * *

"There's no more independence in politics than there is in jail."

* * *

"Do you think the pilgrims would have let Indians land the way the Indians let the pilgrims land?"

* * *

"The question of the world today is not how to eat soup, but how to get soup to eat."

* * *

"My epitaph: Here lies Will Rogers. Politicians turned honest and he starved to death."

* * *

"My idea of an honest man is a fellow who declares income tax on money he has sold his vote for."

* * *

"Nicholas Murray Butler (President of Columbia University) would never be satisfied with Columbia's expansion until he had annexed Grant's Tomb."

* * *

"I never buy anything that I don't understand."

* * *

"Congress is going to start tinkering with the Ten Commandments just as soon as they can find somebody in Washington who has read them."

* * *

"Coolidge didn't do anything, but that's what the people wanted done."

* * *

"I'd rather be the one to pay too much than the man to charge too much."

ABOUT THE CONTRIBUTORS

PETE HAMILL is the former editor of both the *Daily News* and *New York Post*, and author of *Memoir of the Drinking Life*, the novel *Snow in August*, and nine other books.

STEVE EARLE a singer/songwriter, is the author of *Doghouse Roses*, a collection of short stories.

TOM HAYDEN has served 18 years in the California Legislative, is the author of ten books and a member of *The Nation*'s editorial board.

MARK JACOBSON's most recent book, *12,000 Miles in the Nick of Time*, is a teenage parenting manual disguised as an account of a family trip around the world.

GENE SANTORO, music columnist for *The Nation*, is author of *Myself When I Am Real: The Life and Music of Charles Mingus and Highway 61 Revisited: Alternative Visions of Jazz, Blues, Folk, Rock and Comedy*.

MAURICE ISSERMAN is the William R. Kenan Jr. Professor of History at Hamilton College, and author of *The Other American: The Life of Michael Harrington* (Public Affairs, 2000), from which this piece is adapted.

TERRY BISSON is the author of several books including *The Pickup Artist* and *On A Move: The Story of Mumia Abu-Jamal.*

JACK NEWFIELD is the author of nine books, the winner of an Emmy Award for his documentary on Don King, and a protégé of Mr. Kempton.

ADAM SHATZ is the literary editor of *The Nation.*

JIM CALLAGHAN has been an investigative reporter in New York since 1978 and is a regular contributor to the *New York Observer.*

PETER EDELMAN served as a legislative assistant to Senator Robert F. Kennedy, and is now a professor of law at Georgetown University Law Center.

BUDD SCHULBERG's novels include *What Makes Sammy Run?* and *The Harder They Fall*; his screenplay *On The Waterfront* won an Academy Award.

GERRI HERSHEY is the author of *Nowhere to Run: The Story of Soul Music.*

ROBERTA BRANDES GRATZ is an urban critic and author of *City's Back from the Edge: New Life for Downtown* and *The Living City: Thinking Small in a Big Way.*

ELLEN CHESLER, Ph.D., is a senior fellow at the Open Society Institute in New York and author of *Woman of Valor: Margaret Sanger and the Birth Control Movement in America.*

JUDITH COBURN has been a columnist for the *Village Voice* and written for many magazines, newspapers, Internet sites and films. Her memoir of her years as a war reporter in Indochina, Central America and the Middle East will be published in 2004.

J. HOBERMAN is the senior film critic for *The Village Voice*; his most recent book is *The Dream Life: Media and the Mythology of the Sixties.*

LUCIUS SHEPARD is a prizewinning science-fiction writer. His novel *A Handbook of American Prayer* will be published in the winter of 2003-2004.

STANLEY CROUCH is a jazz historian and *Daily News* columnist.

RICHARD LINGEMAN a senior editor of *The Nation*, is the author of *Don't You Know There's a War On?* and biographies of Theodore Dreiser and Sinclair Lewis.

ROBERT W. SNYDER is the director of the journalism and media studies program at Rutgers-Newark; his books include *Transit Talk: New York's Bus and Subway Workers Tell their Stories.* He is at work on a book about New York City since 1945.

NICHOLAS PILEGGI is a journalist, mob historian, and co-author of the screenplays *Casino* and *Goodfellas.*

CHRIS BARRETT is a freelance journalist who lives in New York City.

WAYNE BARRETT is a freelance journalist who writes frequently for the *Village Voice* and is the author of *Rudy!: An Investigative Biography of Rudolph Guiliani.*

ROGER WILKINS is Clarence J. Robinson Professor of History and American Culture at George Mason University.

PATRICIA BOSWORTH is a contributing editor to *Vanity Fair.* She is completing a biography of the actress / activist Jane Fonda.

TERRY GOLWAY is the author of *So Others Might Live*, a history of the fire department of New York.

NAT HENTOFF writes for *The Village Voice*, Editor and Publisher and the United Media Newspaper Syndicate. He is the author, most recently, of *The War on the Bill of Rights.*

VICTOR NAVASKY is Publisher and Editorial Director of *The Nation.*

SIDNEY ZION is a columnist for the New York Daily News, an author of five books including the novel *Markers.*

MICKEY KNOX is a blacklisted screenwriter and actor who has appeared in such films as *Knock on Any Door* and *Any Number Can Play.* He is the author of the forthcoming *The Good, the Bad and the Dolce Vita.*

DAN WAKEFIELD's memoir *New York in the Fifties* is the basis of a documentary film of the same name. He also wrote *Island in the City*, the acclaimed book about East Harlem.

RICHARD GAMBINO is the author of *Camerado*, a play about Walt Whitman. He is a professor Emeritus at Queens College.

STUART KLAWANS is the film critic of *The Nation*. He is author of *Film Follies* and *Left in The Dark*.

STAN ISAACS is a former Newsday columnist who writes for the website thecolumnists.com.

WALLACE MATTHEWS is a veteran sports columnist who now writes for the *New York Sun*.

CHARLES BOWDEN is a journalist and author of many books including *Down By the River: Drugs, Money, Murder and Family*.

TOM GOGOLA is a freelance writer in Montauk, New York.

SCOTT SHERMAN is a contributing editor at *The Columbia Journalism Review*.

DANNY GOLDBERG is the chairman of Artemis Records and the author of *Dispatches From the Culture Wars: How the Left Lost Teen Spirit*.

JOE CONASON is national correspondent for *New York Observer* and writes a daily journal for salon.com. He is the co-author of *The Hunting of the President* and author of *Big Lies*.

GEOFF COWAN is the dean of the Annenberg School of Communications at the University of Southern California.

JAY PARINI a poet and novelist teaches at Middlebury College. His books include *The Last Station, Benjamin's Crossing, House of Days, Robert Frost: A Life* and *The Apprentice Lover.*

TERRY TEMPEST WILLIAMS is a writer of creative non-fiction whose work focuses on landscape and culture. Her books include *Refuge: An Unnatural History of Family and Place, An Unspoken Hunger, Leap,* and most recently Red: *Passion and Patience in the Desert.* A recipient of a Guggenheim and Lannan Literary Fellowship, she lives in Castle Valley, Utah.

RAY ROBINSON is a former magazine editor and author of many books, including *Iron Horse: Lou Gehrig in his Time,* and his current, *Famous Last Words.*